Managing Water Resources in a Time of Global Change

Global change poses serious challenges for water managers and scientists. In mountain areas, where water supplies for half of the world population originate, climate and hydrologic models are still subject to considerable uncertainty. And yet, critical decisions have to be taken to ensure adequate and safe water supplies to billions of people, millions of farmers and industries, without further deterioration of rivers and water bodies. While global warming is known to cause glaciers' retreat and reduced snow packs around the world, it is not clear that mountain discharge will be lower. What is widely recognised is that water management must be adapted to accommodate significant regime changes. However, this inevitably involves managing transboundary rivers, adding further complexity to putting principles into practice.

This book takes global warming and the importance of mountain areas in world water resources as its starting point. First, it provides detailed reviews of the processes going on in several river systems and world regions in Europe (Rhône and Ebro), North America (Canadian Rockies, Western US and Mexico), the Middle East (Jordan), and Africa (Tunisia, Kenya and South Africa). These contexts provide case studies and examples that show the difficulties and the potential for adaptation to global change. Land use, economics, and numerous modeling approaches are some of the cross-cutting issues covered in the chapters. The volume also includes the views of water practitioners, with two chapters authored by members of the US-Canada International Joint Commission, an industrialist from Western Canada and an environmental leader in Spain.

By combining a rich set of contexts and approaches, the volume succeeds in offering a view of the global challenges faced by water agencies, international donors and researchers around the world. A case is made in some chapters to seek adaptive strategies rather than trying to reduce or control resources' variability. This requires factoring in land use, social and economic aspects, especially in developing countries. Another conclusion is that complex problems can and must be posed and negotiated with the help of models, mapping techniques and science-based facts. However complex these may be, there are ways to translate them to easily interpretable visualisations of alternative scenarios and courses of action. This book provides numerous examples of the potential of such approaches to draft environmental programmes able to solve transboundary disputes and to reduce the economic consequences of droughts and climate instability.

Alberto Garrido is Associate Professor in the Economics department at the Technical University of Madrid. **Ariel Dinar** is Professor of Environmental Economics and Policy, and Director, Water Science and Policy Center, University of California, Riverside, USA.

Contributions from the Rosenberg International Forum on Water Policy
Edited by Henry J. Vaux Jr.

Managing Water Resources in a Time of Global Change
Mountains, valleys and flood plains
Edited by Alberto Garrido and Ariel Dinar

Managing Water Resources in a Time of Global Change

Mountains, valleys and flood plains

Edited by Alberto Garrido and Ariel Dinar

Contributions from the Rosenberg International Forum on Water Policy

LONDON AND NEW YORK

First published 2009
by Routledge
2 Park Square, Milton Park, Abingdon, Oxon, OX14 4RN

Simultaneously published in the USA and Canada
by Routledge
270 Madison Avenue, New York, NY 10016

Routledge is an imprint of the Taylor & Francis Group, an informa business

First issued in paperback 2011

Typeset in Times New Roman by Pindar NZ, Auckland, New Zealand

British Library Cataloguing in Publication Data
A catalogue record for this book is available from the British Library

Library of Congress Cataloging-in-Publication Data
Managing water resources in a time of global change: mountains, valleys
and flood plains / edited by Alberto Garrido and Ariel Dinar.
    p. cm.
    Includes bibliographical references and index.
    1. Water-supply—Management. 2. Integrated water development. 3.
Watershed management. I. Garrido, Alberto, 1964- II. Dinar, Ariel, 1947–
    TC409.M27 2008
    363.6'1—dc22   2008027937

ISBN10: 0-415-77778-X (hbk)
ISBN10: 0-415-61977-7 (pbk)
ISBN10: 0-203-88438-8 (ebk)

ISBN13: 978-0-415-77778-0 (hbk)
ISBN13: 978-0-415-61977-6 (pbk)
ISBN13: 978-0-203-88438-6 (ebk)

Contents

Figures and tables

Figures

Tables

Contributors

Richard M. Adams is Professor Emeritus of Resource Economics at Oregon State University, Corvallis, Oregon. His research interests include resource and environmental issues, with emphasis on water management. He has published more than 100 peer-reviewed articles, and more than 20 books and book chapters, and also serves on numerous federal and international advisory boards dealing with water and environmental issues.

Pedro Arrojo-Agudo is an Economics Professor in the Department of Economic Analysis, University of Zaragoza (Spain). He founded and was the Managing Director of the New Culture of Water Foundation (FNCA) during its beginning years. In 2003 he was awarded the Goldman Prize. He has authored tens of books and journal articles on many issues related to the economics of water projects and water allocation.

Eng. Yousef Hasan Ayadi is currently the Planning Director at the Ministry of Water and Irrigation/Jordan Valley Authority in Jordan. He has worked since 1980 in many projects and programmes dealing with the integrated development of the Jordan Valley as field engineer and director of the Technology Transfer and Special Projects Directorate, and presented a number of papers in water management in local and international workshops and conferences.

Sihem Benabdallah is an Associate Professor and Researcher at the Tunisian Center for Water Research and Technologies. Her research interests include watershed modeling, water management and impact assessment of hydraulic structures. She also worked as a professional engineer and headed a number of water management projects in West and North Africa. She is a member of several water project steering committees in Tunisia.

Ger Bergkamp is Head of the IUCN Water Programme and has a background in hydrology, irrigation and drainage, and soil and water conservation. He has a wide experience in both field level projects and water and environment policy work throughout Latin America, the Mediterranean, Africa and Asia. He has experience in water resource management with a particular emphasis on environment-related issues. He was the Water Resources Specialist for IUCN, 1997–2000 and Coordinator of the Water and Nature Initiative.

Jack P. Blaney is a Commissioner with the International Joint Commission. He co-created and was founding director of Action Canada, a unique Government of Canada–private sector partnership whose mission is to build leadership for Canada's future. Dr. Blaney was appointed chair of the Citizens' Assembly on Electoral Reform in May 2003 by the British Columbia Legislature. He is president emeritus, Simon Fraser University.

Jean-Paul Bravard is Professor of Geography in University Lumière-Lyon 2 at the Institut Universitaire de France. He is Head of the Rhone Watershed Workshop Zone (ZABR), which federates research laboratories to help decision makers in managing large rivers of the Rhône watershed. He has published several books on the Rhône and many papers on large French and world rivers.

Katharine Cross works in IUCN's Water Programme on issues relating to groundwater and river basin management. She completed an MSc in Environment and Development at the London School of Economics. Previously she worked as an environmental scientist for Komex International, undertaking environmental site assessments and management. She has a Master's in Environmental Engineering from the University of Alberta. She has also worked on technical projects in Bolivia and Ghana with Engineers Without Borders.

Michael Demuth is a glaciology research scientist with the Geological Survey of Canada, and has broad research interests in cold regions hydrology. He leads studies of glacier mass balance in relation to climate change and water-reliant sectors in western and northern Canada. Mr. Demuth leads Canada's National Glacier-Climate Observing System and is the chair of the Glaciology Committee-Canadian Geophysical Union-Hydrology Section.

Ariel Dinar is a Professor of Environmental Economics and Policy, and Director of the Water Science and Policy Center, University of California, Riverside, USA. This book was prepared while he was Lead Economist of the Development Research Group at the World Bank, USA. His research focuses on international water and cooperation, approaches to stable water allocation agreements, water and climate change, economics of water quantity/quality, and economic aspects of policy interventions and institutional reforms. His most recent understaking is the RFF book series 'Issues in Water Resource Policy' that aims to produce publications on contemporary water policy issues in various countries and states.

Alberto Garrido is an Associate Professor at the Technical University of Madrid (Spain). His work focuses on water economics; water use in agriculture; climate risks; and water, agricultural and natural resources policies.

Holger Hoff is Research Fellow at the Stockholm Environment Institute (SEI), coordinating the Green-Blue Water Initiative and the Green Water Credits project at SEI; and is research fellow at the Potsdam Institute for Climate Impact Research (PIK), co-chairing the ecosystems work package of the CIRCE EU project on climate adaptation in the Mediterranean, coordinating the GLOWA

Jordan River project and advising the German Development Cooperation (GTZ) on mainstreaming of climate adaptation.

Donald J. Lowry is President and Chief Executive Officer of EPCOR Utilities Inc. Headquartered in Edmonton, Alberta, Canada, EPCOR builds, owns and/ or operates power plants, electrical transmission and distribution networks, water and wastewater treatment facilities and infrastructure in Canada and the United States. The company's water and wastewater operations serve more than one million people in 50 communities across Western Canada. Mr. Lowry holds Bachelor of Commerce (Honours) and Master in Business Administration (MBA) degrees. He also serves as Chairman of the EPCOR Power L.P. Board of Directors, Chair of the Canadian Electricity Association, and as a Director of Canadian Oil Sands Trust, Alberta Economic Development Authority, and The Banff Centre. He is also a member of the Alberta Carbon Capture and Storage Development Council.

Bruno Messerli completed studies in geography and geology. He became a full Professor in 1968, Director of the Institute of Geography in 1979, Rector of the University of Berne in 1986, and Professor Emeritus in 1996. He has undertaken field work on problems of glaciation, environmental change and natural resources in the Alps, mountains of Africa, Himalayas and Andes. He chaired the UNESCO MAB programme in the Swiss Alps, was Co-coordinator of the UNU mountain programme and President of the International Geographical Union.

John Nevin is Senior Advisor in the United States Section of the International Joint Commission.

Claudia Pahl-Wostl, Professor of Resource Management at University of Osnabrueck, is an internationally leading expert on adaptive water management, water governance and participatory integrated assessment. Her research focuses on developing innovative concepts for managing transformation processes towards sustainability with an emphasis on an improved understanding of dynamics and management of actor networks and the implications of complexity and uncertainty. She is the coordinator of the EU project NEWATER.

Dannele E. Peck is Assistant Professor of Agricultural and Applied Economics at the University of Wyoming, Laramie, Wyoming. Her research interests include production and natural resource economics, with emphasis on water resources, decision making under uncertainty, and issues at the interface of agriculture and the environment, such as wildlife and livestock interactions.

Alain Pietroniro is Research Scientist with the Aquatic Ecosystem Impacts Research Branch of Canada's National Hydrology Research Centre. His expertise is in water resources engineering, hydrological modeling, GIS and remote sensing. Dr. Pietroniro is secretary, International Association of Hydrological Sciences Committee on Remote Sensing and secretary-treasurer, Canadian Geophysical Union-Hydrology Section.

Alon Rimmer has been a Senior Scientist in the Kinneret Limnological Laboratory (KLL), Israel, since 2001. He specializes in modeling natural water sources such as groundwater, surface water and lakes. He is the author of more than 25 peer-reviewed articles on various types of modeling approaches in hydrology, soil physics, and physical limnology.

Dave Sauchyn is Professor and Research Coordinator, Prairie Adaptation Research Collaborative, University of Regina. His main research interests are the climate of the past millennium in Canada's western interior and how this knowledge contributes to modeling of future climate impacts and change. Dr Sauchyn is a lead author of Canada's National Assessment of Climate Change released in 2008.

Dennis L. Schornack is Chair of the United States Section of the International Joint Commission.

Henry Vaux Jr. is the Chair of the Rosenberg International Forum on Water Policy and the series editor.

Daniel Viviroli has undertaken studies in geography and geology. He gained his PhD in 2007 at the University of Bern and the Swiss Federal Institute of Technology in Zürich with a thesis on process-based flood estimation. Currently he is research associate in the Hydrology Group at the Institute of Geography. His research interests are mountain hydrology, water resources, hydrological modeling and flood estimation.

Rolf Weingartner has undertaken studies in geography and geology. He has been head of the Resarch Group on Hydrology and editor-in-chief of the Hydrological Atlas of Switzerland since 1989, and Professsor in the Institute of Geography at the University of Bern since 2003. He has conducted research projects in the Alps, in the Southern Alps of New Zealand and in the Himalayas. His research interests are regional and mountain hydrology, floods, and processes of runoff generation.

Series editor's preface

The Rosenberg International Forum on Water Policy was created with an endowment gift from the Bank of America to the University of California to honor Bank Chairman Richard Rosenberg on the occasion of his retirement. Chairman Rosenberg had rallied the California business community to address the drought of 1987–92 and had an abiding interest in the development of good water management practices. The Forum itself is held every two years at different locales around the world, principally in arid and semi-arid regions. To date, Forums have been held in San Francisco, USA; Barcelona, Spain; Canberra. Australia; Ankara, Turkey and Banff, Canada. The purpose of the Forum is to share research results and management experiences from around the globe. The objective is to improve global water management practices and reduce conflict in the management of water resources.

Participation in each Forum is limited to fifty water scholars and senior water managers. Participants in a typical Forum will come from 25–30 countries. They are asked to read papers commissioned by the Forum prior to the actual meeting and thus come prepared to engage in the interactive discussions which are at the heart of the Forums themselves. The theme of each Forum is identified by the Rosenberg Forum Advisory Committee. Currently, Advisory Committee members hail from Australia, Canada, Côte d'Ivoire, Israel, Palestine, Spain, Turkey and the United States.

The present volume, the first in a projected series to be published by Routledge, contains the commissioned papers which formed the basis for discussion at the 2006 Forum, which was held in Banff, Canada. The theme of that conference was *Managing Upland Watersheds in an Era of Global Change*. Participants examined some of the evidence of global warming and considered a wide array of resulting impacts. The implications for water and watersheds, as well as for human activity and welfare, received particular emphasis. Some of the impacts have already become manifest, while others are anticipated to occur in the short term. The importance of effective water management institutions in adapting to environmental change was also underscored. The papers in this volume are authored by some of the most distinguished authorities on global warming and water resources in the world. The editors of the volume, drawn from the Advisory Committee, were Alberto Garrido from the Technical University of Madrid and Ariel Dinar of the World Bank. The lessons that emerge from these papers constitute an important contribution to the growing literature on managing global warming and global environmental change.

Henry Vaux, Jr.
Chair, Rosenberg International Forum on Water Policy
Series Editor

1 High water, low water, no water

Upland water resource management in times of global change

Ariel Dinar and Alberto Garrido

Mountains are the main world water suppliers. Their counterparts – valleys and flood plains – have been experiencing human interventions that jeopardize the integrity of the entire ecological system by mismanagement of land and water resources. The nature of this problem is global for two reasons. First, many of the upland water resources feed transboundary water systems (systems that span more than one country); and second, climate change directly and indirectly affects the performance of the mountains-flood plains system. The various chapters in this book cover management options to address the sustainability of upland water resources, using approaches that rely on hydrological, ecological, institutional, and economic disciplines. The book also integrates experiences from many developed and developing countries around the world, covering examples of arid and wet regions, and low and high latitudes.

1.1 Introduction

Mountains, valleys, and flood plains comprise an interlinked system, which depends upon each individual component. We know very well that water flows from high elevation to low elevation. This is simple physics. Some cynics say that water can flow up slope, towards the source of money. This is simple politics. But most important, we also realize that water can stop flowing from both high to low elevations and from low-value uses to high-value uses. This is simple mismanagement.

Mountains are considered by many experts (e.g., Merz 2004; Viviroli *et al.* 2004; Messerli and Ives 1997) to be the water reservoirs of the world. Mountains are the world's major water supplier by several criteria. Seventy-five per cent of the world's freshwater is contained in glacial ice in mountain areas (IUCN 2004); these areas provide water resources for drinking, irrigation, ecosystem use, and hydropower. One half of the world's population drinks water from mountain areas (McDonald and Jehl 2003). Messerli *et al.* provide a detailed account in Chapter 1 of this volume of the share of the mountains in total discharge, ranging from 20 to 50 per cent of total discharge in humid-temperate regions, to 50 to 90 per cent in arid and semi-arid regions.

By storing water as ice and snow during winter months, when water is in relatively low demand, and releasing it during spring and summer months, when demand for water increases, mountain regions are a significant contributor to the stability of water supply and river flows.

Not only are mountains important to the water cycle, they are also very sensitive to mismanagement of water resources and are affected by human interventions such as increased demand for water for drinking, food production (particularly irrigation), industrial production, and sanitation; and by water pollution. These interventions lead to impacts on quality and quantity of the resource both upstream and downstream. For example, the Himalayan Mountains provide water and other related resources for populations in many basins in many countries. Among the basins benefiting from the Himalayans' water tower are the Indus, the Ganges, the Mekong, the Salween, the Yangtze, and the Yellow River basins (Rodda 2001).

The risk to future water supply from the diminution of world water reservoirs is further exacerbated by yet another man-made externality – climate change – which may add further pressures on an already vulnerable system. Climate change adds another dimension to the already complicated and delicate relationship of human-natural systems' co-existence. Questions regarding cause and effect and the proper way to address mismanagement of the mountain ecosystems do not always have a right answer. However, experience accumulated in the past decade or so could provide a good basis for mountain water management.

This book was prepared with the purpose of filling a gap in the literature, which does not address mountain water in a holistic way. To our best knowledge, the important links between upland and lowland water and the impact of climate change and development on the quantity and quality of those links have not been included in one analysis that also addresses management options for their sustainability. Furthermore, the inclusion in the book of a multidisciplinary set of approaches, including hydrology, ecosystem analysis, economics and geography, accompanied by a rich set of case studies covering a wide range of climates, water scarcity levels, socioeconomic situations and other parameters, constitutes a timely novelty in the literature.

With this in mind, the purpose of this book is to provide both scientific background and a policy context to the understanding of the complicated system of integrated water resource management that includes mountains, valleys, and flood plains. Following this introductory chapter, the book is composed of 14 chapters, organized into three parts, and a concluding chapter. The introductory chapter provides the plan of the book and the main objectives of each part and chapter. One message from this book is well fitted with the trend of Integrated Water Resource Management that was initiated at the 1992 Rio Conference. As we start to think about global, multiple jurisdictions, it is quite clear from the evidence presented in this book that not only should we consider water systems in their entirety, but also we should adopt a more comprehensive approach when considering a multi-system of mountains and water ways. With this message, we turn now to the description of the three parts of the book and the approach and objectives of the individual chapters.

1.2 Mountains and upland areas – the scientific background

In part I of the book, Messerli, Viviroli and Weingartner; Sauchyn, Demuth and Pietroniro; Rimmer; and Bravard provide evidence that allows realization of the scale of the issues involved, and the risks faced by policy makers and societies in general.

In Chapter 2, Messerli *et al.* provide a detailed account of the role of mountain water in regional water cycles. With a focus on the Alpine and many other mountain regions, they demonstrate the interaction of impacts of climate change and human activities on mountain ecosystem services, including water resources. Being aware of the transboundary nature of many of the river systems as well as the mountain systems that feed them, the authors highlight the governance structure in Alpine and Carpathian conventions as a useful example for other mountain-river systems around the world. Other matters discussed in the chapter include the physical nature of the mountain-water nexus, such as ice and snow storage; the relationship between climate change, precipitation and flow; and the human intervention impacts on the water cycle of mountains. Gaps in knowledge that need to be addressed include interaction between recharge and groundwater levels. This chapter highlights the great uncertainties involved in the causality of global change and the mountain rivers' discharge regimes around the globe.

Sauchyn *et al.* discuss in Chapter 3 how water policy and management, which were developed during periods of stable and abundant water supply, would need to be adjusted to address a long-term drought and lower average flows than experienced in the twentieth century. Using long-term data for the North and South Saskatchewan River basins, loss of glacier extent was estimated for 1975 and 1998 to show a significant reduction in flow to South and North basins. The authors demonstrate the importance of glacier runoff contributions to the water catchment and its diminishing influence downstream and over time (both intra- and inter-annual), due to change in climate. They further identify a knowledge gap stemming from the need to adjust water management practices to a variable and uncertain future water regime.

Rimmer focuses in Chapter 4 on a semi-arid region of the world – the Middle East. Rimmer argues that changes in rainfall distribution and increase of evaporation throughout the rainy season are expected to affect both water availability in the upper catchments of the Jordan River, and the salinity of Lake Kinneret in Israel. Rimmer also mentions a development intervention – the National Water Carrier that transfers water to the southern part of the country – but he does not evaluate its likely role on the water regime in the watershed. Rimmer uses applications of system modeling to allow informed management in assessing the impacts of a changing water supply regime on the upper catchments of the Jordan River and the Lake Kinneret watershed.

Bravard focuses in Chapter 5 on a truly upland river, originating from the Alps, that has inspired a great deal of scientific work for decades – the Rhône River. He acknowledges, as do Messerli *et al.*, the role of the Alps as the water reservoir of the Rhône. In addition to the impact of climate change on the snow and glacier melt and, hence, water flow, as discussed in the other chapters in Part I of the book,

Bravard introduces the role of economic development in the entire watershed in triggering complex impacts on river and lake hydro systems. The estimates of the impacts on future sector performance in the Rhône basin include hydro and thermal power production, tourism, and agriculture. Negative impacts are estimated also for human health, and floods. Bravard candidly accepts that many changing processes in the Rhône observed in the course of decades cannot be directly attributed to global warming, because intense man-made interventions in the Rhône have had profound impacts in the entire watershed during the second part of the twentieth century. The case of the Rhône is also analyzed in Part II of the book.

1.3 Management opportunities – issues and approaches

In Part II of the book, Pahl-Wostl, Berkamp and Cross; Adams and Peck; Ayadi; Benabdallah; and Hoff review and analyze issues and approaches to better manage upland water in the light of global changes. Issues and experiences from developed as well as developing countries are presented and discussed.

In Chapter 6, Pahl-Wostl *et al.* refer to extreme weather events likely to be caused by climate and global change, in the context of the Rhône. The chapter identifies the new challenges upland rivers face now and in the future. It then identifies several conditions for change, and offers some robust, flexible, and adaptive strategies that are available for implementation. With a more specific look, the case of the Rhône River is analyzed in some detail from the perspective of hydro-geomorphological alterations, most of them meant to ensure continuous cooling capacity to nuclear plants and even more importantly to prevent flooding in highly urbanized and intervened river beds. Drivers for and barriers to the implementation of new management approaches and the importance of processes of social learning are illustrated and discussed in the context of the Rhône.

Adams and Peck in Chapter 7 review the current understanding of climate change on water resources, with emphasis on the frequency and intensity of droughts. They use two examples: (a) effects of more frequent and severe droughts on irrigated agriculture in Oregon, and (b) opportunities to use ENSO predictions to improve the productivity of crop rotations and land allocation in five southwestern states of Mexico. In both case studies, they examine the efficiency of alternative mitigation strategies and find that use of long-term weather forecasts, coupled with improved management practices, may offset some of the adverse consequences of more frequent and/or more intense droughts.

In Chapter 8, Benabdallah reviews issues and experiences in developing countries, with a focus on Tunisia. She identifies crucial problems facing semi-arid regions and relevant management opportunities. Benabdallah identifies and discusses the complexity of managing upland watersheds in developing countries. Issues addressed include soil conservation and natural resource preservation, water management policies, land use planning, development of legal and institutional frameworks, regional economic development, and the livelihood of rural communities. With a focus on Tunisian soil and water conservation policies, the chapter illustrates the strengths and weaknesses of watershed management programs in Tunisia and the ability of these programs to address simultaneously the local socioeconomic and environmental challenges in light of likely climate change. Benabdallah's chapter is an example of downscaling to the local, regional and global processes, with a practical focus on policies that permit adaptation and socioeconomic resilience.

The experience of a downstream riparian to the Jordan River basin is provided by Ayadi in Chapter 9 and, together with other watersheds, by Hoff in Chapter 10 (see Chapter 4 by Rimmer for issues affecting an upstream riparian). The Hashemite Kingdom of Jordan is one of the most water-stressed countries in the world. Therefore, issues and experience in managing its Jordan basin watershed are of extreme value elsewhere. The Jordan Valley, which is the focus of this chapter, contains most of Jordan's scarce water resources, including those shared with other riparian states. The chapter describes three components of a management policy, namely good governance, effective and innovative management and determined political will. These three components are intermingled in policies that address several issues in resource development that include water shared with other riparian states, resource management, on-farm management, stakeholder participation, appropriate water tariff, and drought management. The chapter addresses both the difficulties faced with each issue and how solutions have been implemented by the Jordan Valley Authority.

Innovative concepts for management of upland water that have not been addressed so far in the volume are offered by Hoff in Chapter 10. The departing point is that increased water scarcity requires a more holistic Integrated Water Resource Management (IWRM) approach, to include both "green water" (ecosystem-used water) and "blue water" (in rivers, lakes, and groundwater), and requires them to be jointly managed. The author argues that, if ecosystem services are incorporated into various sectoral adaptation policies and cost-benefit calculations, the overall benefits would surpass those associated with the conventional infrastructure-based blue water management solution. When the entire system is captured in a holistic manner, including physical, socioeconomic and institutional aspects, the solutions would be more relevant and acceptable. The chapter then focuses on the principle of payments for environmental service (PES) in the green water credits project, and demonstrates its potential role in light of future climate change in the Tana River basin in Kenya, and the Jordan River basin. Hoff also reviews schemes that permit mutually beneficial connection of upland-lowland land and water users in upstate New York and in South Africa, showing that the same policy principles can be applied to developed and developing countries.

1.4 Views of practitioners and stakeholders

In part III, Lowry; Schornack and Nevin; Blaney; and Arrojo-Agudo provide the view and assessment of issues and management approaches needed by the policy makers and non-governmental organizations (NGOs) who are in the front line of coping with global changes and addressing them.

The view of the utility that supplies water for hydropower, and water supply and sanitation is provided by Lowry in Chapter 11. With a focus on Western Canada, the chapter addresses the challenges that Canada faces with regard to its water resources, including growing populations, declining infrastructure capacity, and inadequate watershed protection practices. The author calls for a significant shift in both public attitudes and policy towards upland water management. While the chapter focuses on Canada's issues and experiences, the principles proposed are relevant to other countries as well. The approach consists of three pillars: empowering communities, recovering the full cost of water supply and delivery, and multi-stakeholder involvement, such as public-private partnerships.

The role of the Boundary Waters Treaty of 1909 to address transboundary issues between Canada and the United States is discussed and analyzed in chapters 12 and 13. Interpretation of the issues facing Canada and the United States on their shared water bodies, and the extent of success in addressing them, is provided by Schornack and Nevin in Chapter 12. The chapter focuses on the Boundary Waters Treaty of 1909, and the institution created to provide nonbinding and independent advice to both countries – the International Joint Commission (IJC). Issues addressed over the years, and in various parts of the shared water bodies, include navigation and power generation, pollution, and apportionment of water. The authors claim that the IJC's success stems from it having a dual role as regulator of projects that affect levels and flows on both sides of the boundary and as a nonbinding advisor to the governments on controversial issues relating to both water quantity and quality. Several examples of the IJC's work and initiatives are provided. The authors list and explain several reasons for the Commission's success, including the provisions for equality in the Treaty; the geography; social, economic and cultural ties; the IJC's commitment to consensus; the bi-nationally balanced joint fact-finding process; and the focus on public engagement.

An overview of the IJC and its role in the shared water bodies between Canada and the United States is provided by Blaney in Chapter 13. As suggested, the Treaty of 1909 created a comprehensive, rules-based regime with an effective dispute avoidance and settlement mechanism that has been effective in resolving and preventing transboundary water disputes between Canada and the United States for almost 100 years. The author raises an interesting point that could be useful in understanding success in this case, and perhaps in some others as well. Unlike many other international organizations, commissioners (who manage the implementation of the Treaty) do not formally represent their countries, but rather, feel obliged to act in the best interests of both countries (and thus, their shared water bodies). The author provides several examples of success and of still existing problems. He discusses some of the issues that are relevant to the holistic management of the watershed. These include: (a) restoring the lakes since the first Great Lakes Water Quality Agreement was signed in 1972 (serious problems remain, and new threats continue to emerge, such as new chemicals and pharmaceuticals, invasive species, and the effects of intensive agriculture and ongoing urbanization); and (b) the highly contentious issue of bulk water removals from the Great Lakes basin, and whether the waters of the Great Lakes could sustain bulk removals of water to locations beyond their basin, particularly to the United States.

Finally, a comparison between the experience with large dams and water management in mountain regions in California and Spain is provided by Arrojo-Agudo in Chapter 14. The author criticizes water management approaches, based on water supply issues and public subsidy policies. The author argues that this approach promoted the development of large dams, mainly in mountain areas, leading to the flooding of inhabited valleys, negatively affecting the livelihood of communities in mountains and valleys, and degrading the aquatic biodiversity. Arrojo-Agudo promotes the ecosystem approach, which addresses principles of sustainability, inter-territorial equity, and participative governance. The chapter uses various examples, mainly from California and Spain, to make an argument for holistic management. Among the more specific issues considered are: mountain ecosystem and landscape values; the resource value associated with water quality; opportunity cost of man-made interventions and developments such as dams; recreational and emotional values of upstream water; the resource value of downstream irrigation; the value of downstream social-environmental service; and values of inter-regional socioeconomic development.

1.5 Summary

Global change affects many ecological and economic systems either directly via human interventions, or indirectly via impacts of global climate change. Impacts on upland water resources are very significant, leading to economic and ecological losses. The chapters in this book touch upon gaps in knowledge that need to be filled and possible ways to address associated problems. The overarching message from the book is the importance of using integrated water resources management approaches. Specifically, the chapters demonstrate the interdependencies of land use and surface water regimes as well as the linkages between green and blue waters; inter-basin water transfer; use of sophisticated system modeling to inform policy makers; inclusion of social aspects, such as human health, and floods; allowing for social learning; including basin riparian states and local stakeholders in addressing basin planning and management, side payments, and comprehensive treaties. Once the values assigned by the various riparians to the benefits and costs of each of them are recognized, proper assessment can be made of the cost of man-made interventions and developments of upstream water. In addition, evaluating the resource value of downstream activities will lead to a more balanced approach that may eliminate the externalities the entire system faces. This book attests to the serious impediments surrounding this daunting task, but it also provides frontier knowledge and numerous examples and experiences from around the world that may help overcome the direst difficulties.

References

(IUCN) The World Conservation Union (2004) *Guidelines for planning and managing mountain protected areas*. Synthesized and edited by Lawrence Hamilton and Linda McMillan. Gland, Switzerland and Cambridge, UK: IUCN.

McDonald, B. and Jehl, D. (eds) (2003) *Whose water is it?: the unquenchable thirst of a water-hungry world.* Washington, D.C.: National Geographic Society.

Merz, J. (2004) 'Water balances, floods and sediment transport in the Hindu-Kush Himalayas: data analyses, modeling and comparison of meso-scale catchments.' *Geographica Bernensia*, G72, Berne, Switzerland: University of Berne.

Messerli, B. and Ives, J.D. (eds) (1997) *Mountains of the world: a global priority*. New York and London: Parthenon.

Rodda, J.C. (2001) Water under pressure. *Hydrological Science Journal*, 46(6): 841–853.

Viviroli, D., Weingartner, R. and Messerli, B. (2004) Assessing the hydrological significance of the world's mountains. *Mountain Research and Development*, 23: 32–40.

Part I
Mountain and upland areas

2 Mountains of the world

Water towers for the twenty-first century?

Bruno Messerli, Daniel Viviroli, Rolf Weingartner

The mountain chapter in the Agenda 21, accepted in the United Nations Conference on Environment and Development (also known as the Rio Summit or Earth Summit), held in Rio de Janeiro in June 1992, marked the beginning of a mountain water policy at regional to global scales. Mountains account for 20 to 50 percent of total discharge in humid-temperate regions and 50 to 90 percent in arid and semi-arid regions. Increasing impacts of climate change and of human activities on mountain ecosystems – especially on mountain water resources and their significance to the adjacent lowlands – are serious and challenging problems for future mountain research and development. Transboundary river systems, beginning mostly in mountain regions, cover nearly half of the Earth's land surface and concern about half of the world's population. Therefore the Alpine and the Carpathian conventions have played a key role in stimulating other mountain regions' governments to develop similar agreements for a better transboundary and peaceful management, preservation, and development of common natural and cultural resources.

2.1 Mountain water resources – the development of a global policy

The strong orientation of the Earth Summit in Rio de Janeiro in 1992 towards the environment and development provided the setting for an intervention in the preparatory commission of 1991 in Geneva and that of early 1992 in New York to ensure the inclusion of a mountain chapter in Agenda 21. This was enthusiastically supported by delegates from the Himalayas, the Andes and East Africa, who had experienced international co-operation through the International Centre for Integrated Mountain Development (ICIMOD, founded 1983 in Kathmandu, Nepal, for the eight Hindu Kush and Himalayan countries), the African Mountain Association (founded 1986 in Addis Ababa, Ethiopia), and the Andean Mountain Association (founded 1991 in Santiago, Chile). The new chapter was unanimously accepted at the 1992 Rio conference. However, its importance was not properly understood by many political delegations. Rather, it was assumed that natural hazards, land use problems, agriculture and forestry, and all aspects of development and conservation were part of national policies and national competences that could hardly be classified as having international or even global importance.

This perception changed for the better at the special session of the United Nations General Assembly for the evaluation of Agenda 21 in New York in 1997, five years after the Rio conference. The Food and Agriculture Organization (FAO) of the United Nations was officially designated task manager for implementation of the mountain chapter of Agenda 21. In addition, UNESCO and the United Nations University (UNU) with their mountain research and development programs, the foundation of the Mountain Forum 1995, and many local to regional non-governmental activities were fundamental in providing greater awareness of the mountains of the world. But most important was the rethinking of the global significance of mountains between 1992 and 1997. As a result, the book *Mountains of the World – A Global Priority* (Messerli and Ives 1997), and an attractive brochure titled *Mountains of the World – Challenges for the 21st Century* (Mountain Agenda 1997) were presented at the special UN General Assembly in New York in 1997. It was at this point that the political delegates began to understand the global significance of mountains. The expression "water towers" was used as a catchword for the first time, and attention was focused on mountains as providing biological and cultural diversity, vital recreation areas for a more urbanized world population, sacred places for different cultures and religions, privileged regions for protection and, especially, for water resources. These aspects not only have a local or national importance but, more important, an international regional-to-global significance.

One year later, in 1998, water problems were the main topic on the Agenda of the United Nations Commission for Sustainable Development (UNCSD) in New York. For this commission meeting, another brochure was created, titled *Mountains of the World – Water Towers for the 21st Century* (Figure 2.1), and presented to the national representatives of the United Nations member countries (Mountain Agenda 1998). Presenting a global overview of mountain water resources was very difficult, due to missing data and methodical approaches. But case studies from Europe, Africa, Asia and the Americas showed very clearly that most major rivers of the world form their headwaters in mountains, and probably more than half of humanity relies directly or indirectly on the freshwater that accumulates in the mountains. This message was well understood in the global political arena: the mountains of the world were no longer merely local and national problems, they gained global significance, especially for the twenty-first century. Based on this new understanding, the decision to designate an "International Year of Mountains 2002" was established shortly after this UNCSD meeting. In addition, the General Assembly decided in the year 2000 to declare 2003 as the "International Year of Freshwater." These two joint international years on mountains and on freshwater offered possibilities for co-operation and improved information for the political community, and encouragement for the scientific community to take new initiatives and new responsibilities for basic and applied research projects on mountain watersheds and mountain water resources.

Besides the official United Nations policy decisions, numerous international

Figure 2.1 Front cover of the publication about the hydrological significance of the world's mountains for the spring session 1998 of the United Nations Commission on Sustainable Development (UNCSD) with the cross-cutting topic: Strategic Approaches to Freshwater Management. The picture shows the High Atlas, Morocco, Toubkal, 4,165 m, with the snow cover in springtime: A water tower for the intensively irrigated land use systems in the valley bottoms and adjacent lowlands (Mountain Agenda 1998).

institutions and initiatives focusing on mountain water resources were established, and more are expected to follow. For instance, major international conferences on Headwater Control have taken place since 1989, focusing on field-oriented grassroots movements. UNU, together with the International Association of Soil and Water Conservation, published the so-called Nairobi "Headwater Declaration for the International Year of Freshwater 2003" (UNU 2002), but without any quantification of mountain water resources. Another example is the United

Nation's "World Water Assessment Program". However, the preliminary program of the third World Water Forum in Kyoto 2003 did not include mountain water resources. Thanks to a last-minute intervention by UNESCO (2003), mountain water resources became one of many symposia in a huge conference.

In summary, the five years from Rio 1992 to New York 1997 was the time required to upgrade the significance of mountains and their resources from the national to the international and global level. The years following New York 1997 brought the "World Summit on Sustainable Development" (WSSD) in Johannesburg in 2002, which launched the "International Mountain Partnership." The "International Year of Mountains" (2002) and the "International Year of Freshwater" (2003) were followed by the United Nation's "Decade for Water for Life" (2005–2015). Finally, the United Nations General Assembly accepted on 12 December 2007, a resolution with 42 paragraphs, titled, "Sustainable Mountain Development." Paragraph three begins with the following words: "Recognizes the global importance of mountains as the source of most of the Earth's freshwater ..." (UN General Assembly 2007). These milestones on a global level were and still are stimuli to rethink the matter of missing co-operation on the regional level from the Alps to the Carpathians, Caucasus, Central Asia, East Africa, Himalayas, Andes, Rocky Mountains, and others. Mountain rivers cross borders and create problems and conflicts about quantity and quality of water resources between neighbors and between countries in the highlands and lowlands. Legally binding agreements among all the different countries of a mountain system exist for only the Alps, the Carpathians, and the Rocky Mountains, and not yet for all the other much more critical mountain regions, especially those in the developing countries. Therefore, we need not only political goodwill and good scientific data, but also a better co-operation between policy and science. We must discuss not only the development of a global mountain water policy as a support for the urgently needed regional agreements, but also the development of hydrological mountain knowledge as a basis for just and peaceful solutions.

2.2 Mountain water resources – the development of scientific knowledge

Mountains and highlands play a fundamental role in the availability of freshwater in the surrounding lowlands. However, as far as quantification of the significance of this role is concerned, there is a good deal of uncertainty in the scientific world (Rodda 1994). A recently published study estimated the proportion of mountain discharge to global total discharge at 32 percent (Meybeck *et al.* 2001), while other studies indicate figures of between 40 and 60 percent (Bandyopadhyay *et al.* 1997). From a regional point of view and especially for the arid zones, mountain discharge can represent 90 percent or more of the total discharge of a catchment (Mountain Agenda 1998). But in the developing world, in the tropics and subtropics, few assessments exist for discharge in mountainous regions, and the periods they cover are extremely limited. This restricted data base does not adequately measure the high degree of spatial and temporal heterogeneity of discharge conditions in mountain areas. To assess the hydrological importance of mountains, we must take into consideration the increasing uncertainty and generalization from the local to the global level. Additionally, in water-scarce regions discharge data have a high strategic value and are frequently kept confidential. This makes basic scientific studies more difficult and mitigation of conflicts over water resources quite impossible.

2.2.1 Basic knowledge gained in the European Alps

The European Alps may serve as a model for studies in mountain hydrology because of its reliable and detailed data. In the case of the River Rhine, a clear contrast in the discharge pattern can be detected between the mountainous upper section and the lower reaches of the river as a result of the change in the feeder supply from snow in the mountains to rain in the downstream areas. In an average year, discharge in the mountainous Swiss section of the Rhine, above Lake Constance, contributes 34 percent of total discharge at Lobith, near the mouth in the Netherlands, although the mountain catchment area within Swiss territory represents only 15 percent of the total watershed. In summer months, the discharge contribution of this Alpine Swiss section, when the melting of snow and glacier ice produces high and reliable discharge volumes, clearly surpasses 50 percent (Viviroli and Weingartner 2004a). Besides high precipitation, the central Alps show also low evaporation values. Consequently, a large part of precipitation is available for runoff as well as seasonal and long-term storage. Shifting the focus to the European Alps in their entirety, Table 2.1. examines the four major streams which drain the Alpine arc. As observed in the Rhine River, runoff formation is disproportionately high in relation to relative catchment areas. The Alps, situated in a humid temperate climatic zone, play a remarkably important role for western Europe, with a mean contribution of 26 to 53 percent of total discharge and 36 to 80 percent of summer discharge. This raises two questions. How would Europe look without the Alps? And, more important, if the mountains have such an

Table 2.1 The hydrological significance of the four main rivers of the Alps for western Europe

	Mean alpine contribution to total discharge (%)	Summer alpine contribution to total discharge (%)	Alpine share in surface area (%)	Disproportional influence of the Alps
Rhine	34	52	15	2.3
Rhone	41	69	23	1.8
Po	53	80	35	1.5
Danube	26	36	10	2.6

Source: Viviroli and Weingartner 2004b.

importance in the humid–temperate zone, what is their hydrological significance in the most critical and vulnerable arid and semi-arid regions (covering more than 40 percent of the land surface), which experience a rapidly growing population, and are a meaningful part of the developing world?

2.2.2 General knowledge gained in the world's mountains

In sharp contrast to the large temporal and spatial variability of hydrological processes in mountain areas, the availability of long-term data for higher altitudes is very limited, especially in the mountains of the tropics and subtropics. Public access to data is further hindered in regions of frequent water-scarcity for political reasons, especially in South Asia. On the basis of knowledge gained from studying the hydrology of the Alps, a data-based approach to assess the hydrological significance of mountains was taken using discharge data provided by the Global Runoff Data Centre in Koblenz, Germany (GRDC 1999). The pattern of mean monthly discharge, changes in specific discharge with increasing catchment size and the coefficient of variation in mean monthly discharge proved to be particularly suitable parameters for assessing the hydrological significance of mountainous regions. More than 20 river basins in various parts of the world were selected for case studies (Figure 2.2) on the basis of climatic and topographical criteria and availability of data (Viviroli *et al.* 2003). The case studies were chosen to cover a wide range of climatic zones and the most important mountain ranges. The inner tropical area with the two major rivers – Amazon and Congo – was omitted because high tropical rains in the lowlands clearly dominate the hydrograph and override mountain influences. Polar, and part of the subpolar, regions were also

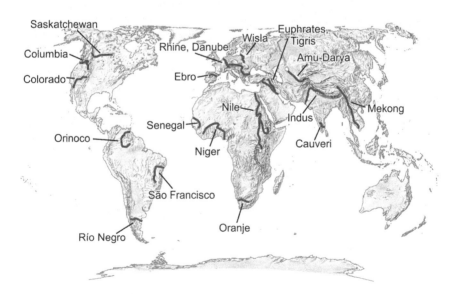

Figure 2.2 Selected case studies, based on gauge record data, shown in figure 2.3.

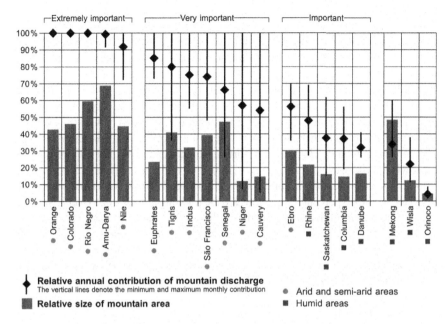

Figure 2.3 Mean annual mountain contribution to total discharge of freshwater
and proportion of mountain areas (represented by a gauging station in a
mountainous area in the vicinity of 1000m altitude or higher) relative to the
entire catchment for the selected river basin. The vertical lines denote the
maximum and minimum amount of discharge (Viviroli *et al.* 2003).

omitted because they do not depend solely on mountain water resources, because
the melting snow in the big plains of the northern continents have a strong impact
on the total discharge.

In choosing suitable case studies, the most restricting criteria proved to be the
presence of accessible, reliable and representative data, with gauging stations
suitably distributed across the river course. The interrelation between mountain
and lowland discharge for each case study was examined through a gauging
station above an altitude of 1000 meters, which served as a "mountain station,"
and a second one in the vicinity of the river mouth, which served as a "lowland
station." Each "mountain station" was carefully checked to ensure it was in an
area with mountain relief, in order to exclude plains in higher altitudes. Rivers
influenced by major dam storage also were excluded. To assess specific discharge
patterns along the rivers, all available stations were used. Regions without suitably
located stations were excluded from the study. In addition, regional precipitation
and temperature conditions were taken into account in order to incorporate the
discharge regime into the climatic context of the region.

The particular hydrological characteristics of mountain areas are manifested by
disproportionately large discharge, typically about twice the amount that could be
expected from the areal proportion of the mountainous section. Mountain discharge

proportions of 20–50 percent of total discharge are observed in humid areas, as could be shown for the Alps; while in semi-arid and arid areas, the contribution of mountains to total discharge amounts to 50–90 percent, with extremes of over 95 percent (Figure 2.3). The Orange (South Africa) and Colorado Rivers (USA), the Rio Negro (Patagonia), the Amu-Darya (Aral basin) and the Nile are by far the most dependent on mountain discharge. In the Euphrates and Tigris, Indus, São Francisco (Brazil) Senegal, Niger (West Africa) and Cauvery (South India) river basins, the rate of mean mountain contribution is lower, but still exceeds 50 percent. In addition, there are months when mountain discharge represents almost 100 percent of total discharge. Therefore seasonal data are of vital importance for the lowland areas downstream. For most of the remaining catchments (Ebro, Rhine, Rhône, Saskatchewan, Columbia, and Danube), the mountain contribution remains between 30 and 60 percent. Exceptions are the Mekong and Orinoco river basins, in which runoff contributions from the mountains are less than expected. These results are corroborated and refined by a recent study from Viviroli *et al.* (2007), which has established an exhaustive global typology of the hydrological significance of mountains in a $0.5° \times 0.5°$ raster. The study substantiates that more than 50 percent of mountain areas have an essential or supportive role for downstream regions.

The compensatory effect of mountain discharge on total discharge was estimated through comparison of year-to-year variability of monthly flows at the selected mountain and lowland stations. The difference signifies the reduction in total discharge variability through the influence of the more reliable mountain runoff. This effect generally corresponds with disproportionate mountain runoff contributions; its magnitude is vast for the Colorado and Indus rivers and is clearly discernible in basins under significant mountain influence. Even for the Orinoco and Mekong rivers, which do not benefit so much from disproportionate volumes of mountain runoff, a clear reduction in runoff variability can be observed thanks to mountain influence (Viviroli and Weingartner 2004a).

2.2.3 The retarding effect of snow and ice storage

Knowledge of snow cover dynamics is a prerequisite for all studies of hydrology, climatology, and biology in mountain areas. As an example, the spatial variability of snow cover in the European Alps is very high, due to the orientation of the west winds, the different climatic situation on the north and south side and the change from the more oceanic western to the more continental eastern side. Such differences are probably much more pronounced in huge mountain systems like the Himalayas and the Andes, but only point measurements of snow height and water equivalent have been investigated. Longer time series of the highly sensitive and dynamic snow cover in most mountain regions do not yet exist. In respect of the Alps, there are archives with daily NOAA-AVHRR data since 1981 without any interruption, covering the entire Alps area. Since 2001, an operational status has been reached, and data with a resolution of 1.1 km^2 for the whole Alps are available immediately after receipt by the ground station (Wunderle *et al.* 2002).

This example shows that the same methods and techniques could be used for the Himalayas, Andes, or Central Asian mountains.

The Aral basin is a very instructive example of such a snow regime (Spreafico 1997). In the high mountains of Tien Shan and Pamir, the annual precipitation ranges from 600 to 2000mm, with 30 percent falling as snow. The lowland deserts cover most of the basin and are characterized by less than 100mm/yr rainfall and high evaporation. Because of snow and glacier melt, the flows of the two rivers – Amu Darya and Syr Daria – are highest in summer and are characterized by a low interannual variability, which is very important for the management of water resources in a densely irrigated land use system. If we take into consideration that the mountains provide more than 90 percent of the basin's freshwater, then we understand the high significance of the snow cover in the mountains for the calculation of the water resources in the desert lowlands. This means for the near future that research projects focusing on the potential impact of climate change on the snow cover in the Pamir and Tien Shan and its consequences for the Aral basin are urgently needed.

2.2.4 Missing knowledge – uncertain assessment of vulnerability

The runoff-generation in mountain areas is characterized by an extraordinary heterogeneity of topography, vegetation and soils, by a spatially and temporally differentiated snow cover and, especially, by extreme events and high seasonal and annual climate variability. Long-range data series are missing in the mountains of the developing world and especially – as we mentioned above – in the critical zones of the tropics and subtropics. All this means that our knowledge about runoff generation in different altitudes and under different natural conditions and land use systems is very limited (Gurtz *et al.* 2003). It is important, especially for semi-arid and arid zones, to know how far the recharge of the groundwater in the alluvial plains is directly connected to the runoff from mountain areas, as can be seen and measured in the valley bottoms around the Alps. Taking into account the increasing water scarcity in semi-arid and arid regions, especially for irrigation and food production, today's state of knowledge about mountain hydrology is insufficient and makes sustainable water management quite impossible.

2.3 Natural driving forces and their impacts on mountain water resources

2.3.1 The complex relationship between global warming, precipitation and runoff

Ascertaining how differentiated temperature change will affect the local to regional precipitation regime in the mountains of the world is a daunting task. Temperature and precipitation changes must always be regarded as coupled variables. "On a global scale, the term climate change is often equated with the term climate warming. However, the energy cycle of the climate system is intrinsically linked with the hydrological cycle. To a first approximation, it would indeed be more appropriate to equate climate change with climate moistening. The total moisture content of the atmosphere will increase by about 6 percent per degree warming" (Schär and Frei 2005: 258–259). This statement may show the significance of the hydrological cycle, but also indicates the difficulty in evaluating potential changes. Precipitation will not occur uniformly, but changes will be associated with specific geographical and topographical patterns and will vary with seasons. More specifically, the mid and high latitudes are expected to experience a higher relative increase in total precipitation, particularly during winter, while there is evidence that sub-tropical and semi-arid regions might experience an increased risk of summer droughts (Weatherald and Manabe 1995). Moreover, heavy precipitation events, which are most important for the hydrological processes, are not directly linked to mean precipitation amounts. Without going into more details of this relevant discussion, we must state that investigation of the consequences of global "warming" and the global "moistening" are still a very complex and partly contradictory research process. The Intergovernmental Panel on Climate Change (IPCC, 2001) published a report with the projected changes of the mean annual runoff data for 2050, compared with the values 1961–1990. Two different general Ocean-Atmosphere-Circulation Models of the Hadley Center, with a 1 percent annual increase of CO_2, were used to draw two instructive world maps. A comparison shows the very different results, especially for mountain regions like the southern Rocky Mountains, the Andes, parts of East Africa, Central Asia, the Himalayas, and the Indian plains. Moreover, new studies in the Andes show that there is no clear pattern of increasing or decreasing precipitation trends. On a regional scale, there is a weak increasing trend in northern Peru and a decreasing trend in southern Peru. The temperatures indicate the greatest warming in lower elevations on the Pacific side, while the trend on the eastern side is rather moderate. Surprisingly, the warmer trend is slightly decreasing with elevation above 3500 metres, which is different compared to the observations in Tibet, the Himalayas, and the Alps (Vuille *et al.* 2003, Chalise *et al.* 2005, Nogués-Bravo *et al.* 2007). All this means very clearly that we are confronted with serious uncertainties, especially for the developing world, in which the mountain water resources play a fundamental role in supplying the adjacent lowlands. Moreover, we should not forget that even slight changes in the temperature and precipitation regime can have strong impacts on the snow cover and glacier storage, but also on extreme events and droughts, which influence or even change the runoff regime.

2.3.2 Global warming and water resources in snow dominated regions

Without discussing in detail the worldwide retreat of glaciers and its impact on the water cycle, we focus on the more rapidly reacting snow cover, which plays an important role in water supply of the so-called middle mountains at lower altitudes. In a warmer world, less winter precipitation falls as snow, and the melting of winter snow occurs earlier in spring. Even without any changes in precipitation intensity, both of these effects lead to a shift in peak river runoff in winter and early spring, away from summer and autumn when demand is highest. Where storage capacities are not sufficient, much of the winter runoff will immediately be lost to the oceans. With more than one-sixth of the Earth's population relying on glaciers and seasonal snow packs for their water supply, the consequences of these hydrological changes for future water availability – predicted with high confidence and already diagnosed in some regions – are likely to be severe (Barnett *et al.* 2005). On a global scale the largest changes in the hydrological cycle, due to warming, are predicted for the snow-dominated basins of mid to high latitudes, but they also will play an important role in the mountains of the other climatic zones. As an example, if it is true that approximately 80 percent of the water used for agricultural, industrial and domestic purposes in the western USA originates from the high-elevation winter-spring snowpacks (Price and Barry 1997), then the consequences of any climate change could be very serious. If warming is accompanied by little or no change in precipitation, then this could lead to a large reduction in mountain snow pack and a substantial shift in stream-flow seasonality. Therefore, by 2050 the spring stream-flow maximum will come about one month earlier in the year. These hydrological changes will have considerable impacts on water availability (Barnett *et al.* 2005). In Canada's western prairie provinces, Schindler and Donahue (2006) have shown that climate warming and human modifications to catchments have already significantly reduced the flows of major rivers during the summer months, when human demand and in-stream flow needs are greatest (see also Sauchyn *et al.* in Chapter 3). All the major rivers crossing the western prairies originate in the Rocky Mountains, where deep snowpacks and melting glaciers maintain river and groundwater supplies. There are signs that these mountain water supplies are diminishing. The authors predict that in the near future climate warming, via its effects on glaciers, snowpacks and evaporation, will combine with cyclic drought and rapidly increasing human activity in the western prairies. This could cause a crisis in water quantity and quality with far-reaching implications. For the Australian Alps, snow cover duration is highly sensitive to temperature changes. A 1°C warming could reduce snow cover duration by 50 percent or more at low to moderate elevations, while a 3°C increase would eliminate the snow cover at sites around 1800–2000m, which have a duration of about 100 days (Whetton *et al.* 1996).

Altogether, mountains with their high elevation snow and ice cover and highly sensitive ecosystems above and below the upper timberline will play a fundamental role in a changing climate in order to maintain the function of water towers for the more intensively used surrounding lowlands (Viviroli *et al.* 2007; see Bravard in Chapter 5 about the Rhône River).

2.3.3 Climate change and mountain observatories

Climate variability and climate change are important elements for the assessment of changing freshwater resources in the mountains of the different climatic zones (Messerli *et al.* 2004). In this sense, a network of high mountain observatories would be beneficial in establishing an early warning system and to observe continuously the water cycle and the water supply in regions with an uncertain precipitation regime. The Mountain Research Initiative (MRI), in co-operation with the Mountain Biosphere Program of UNESCO, has taken up this problem and initiated a planning process for a new and longer term observation and research program in the mountains of the world. Of special interest would be a transect Pole-Equator-Pole from Alaska to Tierra del Fuego. The highest ecosystem above the timberline is the only one that connects all the different climatic zones. It is situated at the edges of the land-atmosphere interface – which hosts glaciers, snow, permafrost and the uppermost limit of vegetation – and is one of the most sensitive and globally comparable indicators of climate change. Significant networks of mountain observatories would be of interest also in the Himalayas, Andes, Africa, Europe, and other mountain regions as a contribution to the ongoing Global Change Programs (Huber *et al.* 2005; Björnsen Gurung 2006).

2.4 Human driving forces and their impact on mountain water resources

In the world of the twenty-first century, it is quite a challenge to disentangle the natural and the human driving forces, because the so-called natural driving forces, discussed in the previous section, are also dominantly caused by human processes. Irrespective of this difficult assessment, natural and human driving forces have a strong impact on vulnerable mountain ecosystems, because the different altitudinal belts – over a short horizontal distance – represent a compression of different climatic zones along vertical gradients from agricultural land in the valley bottoms to glaciers and permafrost in the summit region. Therefore, mountains are highly sensitive indicators not only for climate change, but also for human-induced changes (deforestation, soil erosion, mass movements, land use and irrigation problems, food insecurity, and poverty). This means that natural- and human-driven forces have an impact on the following ecosystem services (Millennium Ecosystem Assessment 2005): provisioning (food, freshwater, wood and fiber, fuel); regulating (climate regulation, flood regulation, disease regulation, water purification); and cultural (aesthetic, spiritual, educational, recreational). In the context of our focus on mountain water resources, we select for a more detailed discussion two components: poverty and food insecurity. Both are highly integrative, represent the social and economic situation, and are influenced by different natural and human forces and impacts.

2.4.1 Poverty and food insecurity – vulnerability of mountain populations in the developing world (Figure 2.4)

The Food and Agriculture Organization (FAO) of the United Nations published, based on its own unique databank, a special GIS-based report about mountains and mountain populations (FAO 2003). As a result, FAO estimates the total number of people living in mountainous regions at 718 million for the year 2000. Of these, 625 million live in developing countries and the CIS (Commonwealth of

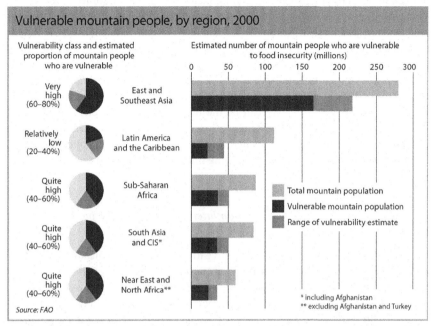

Figure 2.4 Food and Agriculture Organization (FAO) of the United Nations estimates
that 625 million people are living in the mountains of the developing
countries and Commonwealth of Independent States (former Soviet Union),
and probably more than half are living in a situation of food insecurity, see
text (FAO 2002).

Independent States, former Soviet Union). Although urbanization and the growth
of mountain cities is important in some regions like the Andes, more than three-
quarters of people living in the mountains in developing countries and the CIS are
still rural (FAO 2002). FAO estimates that about 40 percent of the mountain area in
developing countries and the CIS produces less than 100 kg of cereals per person,
per year. Rural people living in such locations face hardships in maintaining
adequate livelihood levels from agriculture. FAO has used estimates of their
number together with other constraints to arrive at a preliminary number of people
living in the mountains who are vulnerable to food insecurity. For the developing
and CIS countries it is in the range of 250–370 million people. This estimate of
vulnerability should not be confused with FAO's estimates of the undernourished
population. Typically, about half of those identified as vulnerable are actually
undernourished (FAO 2002). Of course, there are a lot of other natural and human
factors and constraints that could contribute directly or indirectly to uncertain food
supplies: for example, climatic conditions and extreme events, water availability
and poor soil quality, demographic pressure and social aspects, political constraints,
difficult accessibility and isolation, lack of education and health services, no
integration in a local market or a national economy, and others. It is not possible to
discuss all these factors in detail, but it is understandable that food insecurity is not

only an important, but also an integrating factor for the vulnerability of a society. The consequences of such a situation are serious, resulting in either emigration or an extension and intensification of the land use system. Extension means to use marginal land and cross some ecological thresholds, such as going to elevations that are too high, endangered by frost; or going to terrains that are too steep, endangered by erosion. Excessive intensification can lead to the impoverishment of the soils, to erosion, or, with the use of too much fertilizer, to pollution of the water sources. Food insecurity can be the beginning of destructive impacts on land use and land cover on mountain ecosystems and, especially, also on the most sensitive headwater system and its hydrological balance. Growing population and land use intensification can lead to growing impacts on ecosystems and ecosystem services.

2.4.2 Mountain watersheds and human interventions from the past to the future

Looking into the past, it is always instructive to pay attention to paleoenvironmental experiences. The Greek philosopher Plato wrote about 400 years BC: "… and it had much forest land in its mountains, what now remains compared with what then existed is like the skeleton of a sick man …" (Bury 1961). Looking at Greek history 2400 years ago, we are always fascinated by the cultural achievements, but we don't want to see the real-life conditions that must have existed in the mountainous rural areas. The following generations had to survive in a degraded environment and with an unbalanced hydrological system. The high price for that damage continues to be seen today as eroded hills and mountains, and accumulated soil material in the surrounding basins and valleys. What is happening today in some parts of the African mountains happened more than 2000 years ago in some parts of the Mediterranean mountains.

Looking at the present, climatically driven changes in water supplies need to be coupled with the surface infiltration and runoff processes, and these are heavily affected by today's land-use activities. It is necessary to focus not only on melting processes of snow and ice, extreme events and historic records, but also on the heavily modified surface conditions. Creating impervious surfaces, compacting soils through agricultural and forestry activities, removing wetlands, minimizing stream buffer zones and regulating streams have altered the hydrological processes in such a way that the runoff response will be different between historic and current climatic events of similar magnitude (The Royal Swedish Ac. 2002). In this sense, the FAO (2006) initiative, "Preparing the next generation of watershed management programs and projects for sustainable mountain development," must have a high priority for capacity building and for cooperation in transboundary water problems and conflicts.

Until recently dams and reservoirs were constructed in the mountains to store the water used for irrigation in the dry season. Today new technological and engineering possibilities allow not only the storage of water, but its diversion and transport over long distances. An instructive example is the recent report about the "River Link Mega Project" in India (Bandyopadhyay and Perveen 2003). Today 97 percent of the Brahmaputra water flows unused into the gulf of Bengal, while India is suffering from water scarcity. Therefore, India is likely to establish river linkages from north to south through 37 big river systems with 32 dams, 9600 kilometres of canals, pumps and power stations. The overall goal is to connect southern India to the Himalayas with the water from the Brahmaputra and Ganges. However, no one is questioning how much water in these two big rivers is coming from Nepal, Bhutan, and China. Another impressive example is China's huge project, called the "South–to–North Water Transfer," from the Yangtze River to the Yellow River on three levels from west to east: with an upper, a middle, and a lower canal system. The longest of these canals extends more than 1000 km (Changming and Zhen 2002, Li Guoying 2003, Stone and Jia 2006). Other examples are found in Lesotho, which is selling its mountain water to the agglomeration of Johannesburg, and Spain, whose project to transfer water from the Pyrenees to Andalucia in southern Spain became a politically acceptable alternative for decades until it was stopped in 2004. Are these giant projects the future trend for the coming 20 to 50 years? Will the critical mountain systems become a "battlefield" for the construction of reservoirs, dams, canals and hydropower stations not only for a rapidly growing population, but also for a rapidly growing urbanization, industrialization and irrigation in the adjacent lowlands, where the political–economic power centers are existing and expanding? Will the natural mountain landscape become a technical landscape?

2.4.3 Conflicts and cooperation in the mountains of the world

More projects and more conflicts will come, especially where water crosses international borders. A total of 145 countries have on their territory transboundary water flows and, worldwide, there are 263 river systems which belong to two or more riparian countries. Transboundary river systems cover nearly half of the Earth's land surface and concern about half of the world's population. The number of transboundary groundwater aquifers may be much greater and their non-measurable potential for conflicts may grow in a time of increasing water demand and decreasing water supply, especially also in connection with uncontrolled water pollution, due to fast-growing industrialization and urbanization (Liebscher 2004). In the 263 transboundary river systems developed between 1948 and 1999, there were 1831 water disputes. Of these, 1228 ended peacefully, 96 remained neutral, but 507 were conflict ridden. Of these, 21 led to hostile actions, and 16 resulted in only small and local hostile actions (Wolf *et al.* 2003). As a whole, based on an analysis with many different components, Liebscher (2004) concluded that rivers with a high conflict potential are Euphrates-Tigris, Jordan, Nile, Indus, and Ganges-Bramahputra.

Today we see a completely new trend in the formation of international mountain partnerships and in legally binding mountain conventions. The so-called "Alpine Convention" of 1995 convened all Alpine countries with the goal of working together on mountain development and protection, including water resources. In

2003, the seven Carpathian countries adopted the "Framework Convention on the Protection and Sustainable Development of the Carpathians." Now the United Nations Environmental Programme (UNEP), the Food and Agriculture Organization (FAO), the International Union for Conservation of Nature (IUCN) and other non-governmental organizations are working on transboundary mountain systems in south-east Europe, on the Caucasus region and on the mountains of Central Asia in order to follow the examples of the Alps and the Carpathians. An exchange of experiences is planned with the "Consortium for Sustainable Development of the Andean Region" (CONDESAN) in Lima and with the "International Centre for Integrated Mountain Development" (ICIMOD) in Kathmandu, which is responsible for the cooperation of the eight Hindu Kush-Himalayan countries. In this sense, it is fascinating to see that mountain regions, with their important natural and cultural resources and treasures, begin to play a special role for peaceful transboundary co-operation between neighboring states, although they still have a long way to go.

2.5 Outlook and conclusions

First of all, we have to look back on the twentieth century in order to understand the ongoing processes and their significance for the future. Figure 2.5 shows, with a selected range of data, the quite unbelievable change of driving forces and the consequences of that change for the twenty-first century (McNeill 2005). All these data must be interpreted in such a way that the dominant changes happened in the second half of the twentieth century. Moreover, much of these data provide an indication of the growing demand for water for life, and water for food – perhaps also sounding a warning about the limited resources for a continuously growing world population and world economy. Let us keep in mind the central message of the author regarding this data set: "Nothing like this ever happened in human history. The mere fact of such growth, and its unevenness among societies, made for profound disruptions in both environment and society" (McNeill 2005).

A new dialogue between scientists and policymakers is needed more than ever before. The cooperation between scientists and politicians in the IPCC is

Driving forces behind Environmental Change		Scale of Environmental Change		
Human Population	grew 4 fold	Freshwater Use		9 fold
		Marine Fish		35
Urban Population	13	Cropland		2
Global Economy	14	Irrigated Land		5
Industrial Production	40	Cattle Population		4
Energy Use	13	Life Expectancy at Birth Globally		
CO2 Emission	17	1800: 30	1935: 35	1950: 45	2000: 67

Figure 2.5 The Twentieth Century: Modern Global Environmental History. A turbulent and dramatic scenario (McNeill 2005).

Two models for connecting scientific knowledge to policy decision-making

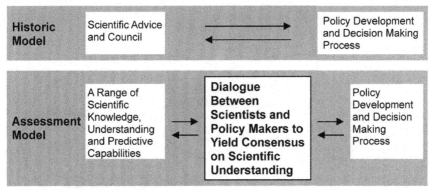

Figure 2.6 Two models for connecting scientific knowledge to policy decision making.
OECD: Workshop on Global Scale Issues, Stockholm (OECD 1998).

perhaps an interesting example for the future. In a workshop of OECD (1998) in Stockholm about "Global Scale Issues," the same dialogue began and led to the following agreement: the Historic Model in Figure 2.6. shows how it was handled until now. In this model the scientific expert presents his findings in a report to the politician or decision maker. Either it is read or not, but the scientist doesn't care, because he has done his job and it is not his responsibility to control the politician. Therefore, a lot of good work has been done without any results and without any implementation. The second approach, the Assessment Model in Figure 2.6, is very different. A group of scientists analyze a complex problem and present not only a simplified result, but show – besides the well proved knowledge – also the cluster of uncertainties and the difficulties in the predictive capabilities. Only then can we start a dialogue between a team of scientists and a group of politicians with the aims of understanding the complexity of the problem and of reaching a consensus. After that, the political process and the preparation of a decision follows. All this means that on one side, the scientists have to learn that a political decision must be taken in the full understanding of all the positive and negative effects. Moreover, scientific advice can be realized only in small steps (but in the right direction). The main aim could be reached, possibly, only beyond one four-year parliamentary period. On the other side, the politicians know that a scientific analysis of a complex problem and advice for a political decision can have positive and negative effects. It is their responsibility to assess the feasibility of the solution.

This complexity in mountain science and in mountain policy is shown in Figure 2.7. It is also expressed in the title of the mountain chapter number 13 of Agenda 21: "Managing Fragile Ecosystems – Mountain Sustainable Development." In mountain areas, fragile ecosystems and sustainable development must be strongly connected. Without an engaged cooperation between natural, socioeconomic, and technical sciences, we shall never reach satisfactory solutions for a development policy. Such a policy, in agreement with the local population, is needed to

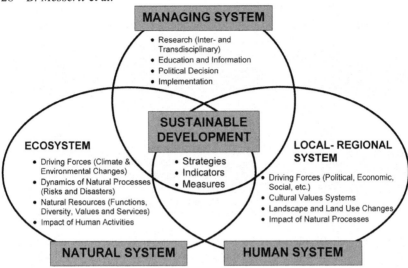

Figure 2.7 "Managing Fragile Ecosystems – Mountain Sustainable Development"
(Title of chapter 13 of the Agenda 21). An attempt to draft an integrated and
transdisciplinary approach for mountain research and development.

preserve intact ecosystems and to compensate for the disadvantages of living in
the mountains. Only an experienced mountain population has the competence to
preserve and develop the natural and cultural treasures, and especially the water
resources, for the highland and the lowland people.

Not only is the global climate changing: in addition, population growth in
critical lowland areas will accentuate the pressure on mountain water resources.
This may be shown more clearly by the large-scale projects in India and China
mentioned above. According to the World Development Indicators of the World
Bank (2001), 65 countries use more than 75 percent of their available freshwater
for agriculture and food production. Included in this list of 65 countries are Egypt,
India and China – all countries that rely on mountain discharge. Even if these
data are not very reliable, as the World Bank confirms, the order of magnitude
is impressive. If a country has to use more than 75 percent of its freshwater for
agriculture alone, how much is then available for rapidly growing urbanization
and industrialization? Of course there are possibilities to improve agricultural
production systems, but all the same, conflicts between water users are foreseeable
inside and outside national borders. The dependence on scarce water resources for
the whole development process is alarming, and feedback from mountain resources
and mountain ecosystems is inevitable. Perhaps we should keep in mind the
following quotation from Lonergan (2005): "If there is a political will for peace,
water will not be a hindrance. If you want reasons to fight, water will give you
ample opportunities."

References

Bandyopadhyay, J. *et al.* (1997) Highland waters – a resource of global significance. In: Messerli, B. and Ives, J. D. (eds) *Mountains of the world – a global priority.* New York and London: Parthenon, pp. 131–155.

Bandyopadhyay, J. and Perveen, S. (2003) *The interlinking rivers: some questions on the scientific, economic, and environmental dimensions of the proposal.* Occasional Paper No. 60, SOAS Water Issues Study Group. London: School of Oriental and African Studies/ King's College.

Barnett, T. P., Adam, J. C. and Lettenmaier, D. P. (2005) Potential impacts of a warming climate on water availability in snow-dominated regions. *Nature,* 438: 303–309.

Björnsen Gurung, A. (ed.) (2005) *GLOCHAMORE – Global change in mountain regions.* MRI, UNESCO-MaB and EU Framework Progr. 6. Bern: Institute of Geography, University of Bern.

Bury, R. G. (ed.) (1961) *Plato, the complete works.* Vol. VII, Plato, Critias, III a-c. Harvard: Loeb Classical Library.

Challise, S. R., Schresta, M. L., Thoki, K. P. B. and Shresta, M. S. (2005) Glacio-hydrological aspects of climate change in the Himalayas: mitigation of glacial lake outburst floods in Nepal. Proceedings, 7. *IAHS General Assembly,* Brazil.

Changming, L. and Zheng, H. (2002) South-to-north water transfer schemes for China. *Water Resources Development,* Vol. 18, No. 3: 453–471.

FAO (2002) *Environment, poverty and food insecurity. The vulnerability of mountain environments and people.* FAO special feature.

FAO (2003) *Towards GIS-based analysis of mountain environments and populations.* Environment and Natural Resources Service, Rome: FAO.

FAO (2006) Water resources for the future. Preparing the next generation of watershed management programmes and projects. *Watershed management and sustainable mountain development.* Working paper 9. Eds: Tennyson L. and Zingari C. (Conference proceedings, Sassari, 2003), Rome: FAO.

GRDC (1999) Global Runoff Data Centre. D–56068 Koblenz, Germany http://bafg.de/grdc.htm.

Gurtz, J. *et al.* (2003) A comparative study in modeling runoff and its components in two mountainous catchments. *Hydrological Processes,* 17: 297–311.

Huber, U. M., Bugmann, H. K. M. and Reasoner, M. (eds.) (2005) Global change and mountain regions. An overview of current knowledge. *Advances in Global Change Research,* Vol 23. Dordrecht, Netherlands: Springer.

IPCC (2001) *Climate change. Third assessment report of the Intergovernmental Panel on Climate Change.* WMO/UNEP. Cambridge: Cambridge University Press. Synthesis Report, Bonn 2002.

Li Guoying (2003) *Ponderation and practice of the Yellow River control.* Yellow River Conservancy Press.

Liebscher, H. J. (2004) Potenzielle und aktuelle Wasserkonflikte in grenzüberschreitenden Flussgebieten. *HW* 4, H.2: 71–79.

Lonergan, S. (2005) Water and war. *UNEP: Our Planet,* Vol. 15, No. 4, Nairobi: 27–29.

McNeill, J. R. (2005) Modern global environmental history. A turbulent and dramatic scenario. UPDATE, IHDP, 02: 1–3.

Messerli, B. and Ives, J. D. (eds) (1997) *Mountains of the world: a global priority.* New York and London: Parthenon.

Messerli, B., Viviroli, D. and Weingartner, R. (2004) *Mountains of the world: vulnerable water towers for the 21st century.* AMBIO. special report No. 13, Royal Swedish Academy of Sciences, Stockholm: 29–34.

Millennium Ecosystem Assessment (2005) *Ecosystems and human well-being, Synthesis.* Washington, DC: Island Press.

Meybeck, M., Green, P. and Vörösmarty, C. J. (2001) A new typology for mountains and other relief classes: an application to global continental water resources and population distribution. *Mountain Research and Development,* Vol. 21 (1): 34–45.

Mountain Agenda (1997) Mountains of the world: challenges for the 21st century. Contribution to chapter 21, Agenda 21. Institute of Geography. Bern: University of Bern.

Mountain Agenda (1998) *Mountains of the world: water towers for the 21st century. A Contribution to Global Freshwater Management.* Lead authors: Liniger, H. P., Weingartner, R. and Grosjean, M. Insitute of Geography. Bern: University of Bern.

Nogués-Bravo, D., Araujo, M. B., Errea, M. P. and Mawrtinez-Rica, J. P. (2007) Exposure of global mountain systems to climate warming during the 21st century. *Global Environmental Change,* 17: 420–428.

OECD (1998) *Workshop on global scale issue.* Stockholm 4–6 March. (unpublished report).

Price, M. F. and Barry, R. G. (1997) Climate change. In: Messerli, B. and Ives, J. D. (eds) *Mountains of the world: a global priority.* New York and London: Parthenon, pp. 409–445.

Rodda, J. C. (1994) Mountains – a hydrological paradox or paradise? In: *Hydrologie kleiner einzugsgebiete. Beiträge zur hydrologie der Schweiz,* Nr. 35. Bern: Swiss Hydrology and Limnology Society, pp. 41–51.

Schär, C. and Frei, C. (2005) Orographic precipitation and climate change. In: Huber, U. M., Bugmann, H. K. M. and Reasoner, M. A. *Global change and mountain regions. Advances in global change research* Vol. 23., Dordrecht, Netherlands: Springer, pp. 255–266.

Schindler, D. W. and Donahue, N. F. (2006) *An impending water crisis in Canada's western prairie provinces.* National Academy of Sciences (PNAS), Canada.

Spreafico, M. (1997) Without mountains there is no life in the Aral Basin. In: Messerli, B. and Ives, J. D. (eds). *Mountains of the world.* New York and London: Parthenon, p. 145.

Stone, R. and Jia, H. (2006) Going against the flow. News Focus. *Science,* 313, 25. Aug.: 1034–1037.

The Royal Swedish Academy of Sciences (2002) *The Abisko Agenda. Research for mountain area development: rethinking agenda 21, chapter 13.* Ambio Special Report Nr. 11.

UNESCO (2003) *Water for people, water for life.* World Water Programme. The United Nations World Water Development Report. Paris and Barcelona: UNESCO and Berghahn Books.

UN General Assembly (2007) *Sustainable mountain development.* Resolution 12 December 2007. (Sixty-second session, Agenda item 54 (h). (A/C.2/62/L.18/Rev.1).

UNU (2002) United Nations University. *Sustainable management of headwater resources.* (Brochure). Tokyo: UNU.

Viviroli, D. *et al.* (2007) Mountains of the world – water towers for humanity. Typology, mapping, and global significance. *Water Resources Research,.* 43, WO7447.

Viviroli, D. and Weingartner, R. (2004a) The hydrological significance of mountains: from regional to global scale. *Hydrology and Earth Sciences,* 8 (6): 1016–1029.

Viviroli, D. and Weingartner, R. (2004b) The hydrological significance of the European Alps. In Weingartner. R. and Spreafico. M. (eds.) *Hydrological atlas of Switzerland.* Plate 6.4. Bern: Federal Office for Water and Geology.

Viviroli, D., Weingartner, R. and Messerli, B. (2003) Assessing the hydrological significance of the world's mountains. *Mountain Research and Development,* 23: 32–40.

Vuille, M., Bradley, R. S., Werner, M. and Keimig, F. (2003) 20th climate change in the tropical Andes: observations and model results. *Climate Change,* 59: 75–99.

Weatherald, R. T. and Manabe, S. (1995) The mechanism of summer dryness induced by greenhouse warming. *Journal of Climate,* 8: 3096–3108.

Whetton, P. H., Haylock, M. R. and Galloway, R. (1996) Climate change and snow cover duration in the Australian Alps. *Climate Change,* 32: 447–479.

Wolf, A. T., Yoffe, S. B. and Giordano, M. (2003) International waters: identifying basins at risk. *Water Policy,* 5: 29–60.

World Bank (2001) World Development Indicators. Table 3.5 – Freshwater. Available online at http://www.worldbank.org. Accessed 12.2. 2002.

Wunderle, S., Droz, M. and Kleindienst, M. (2002) Spatial and temporal analysis of the snow line in the Alps, based on NOAA-AVHRR data. *Geographica Helvetica*, Jg. 57, H.3: 170–183.

3 Upland watershed management and global change

Canada's Rocky Mountains and western plains

Dave Sauchyn, Michael Demuth, and Alain Pietroniro

Myths of abundant and stationary water resources have influenced water policy and management in western Canada. Data presented in this chapter demonstrate that water use, policy and management were established during a period of fairly stable and reliable water supplies as compared to preceding and projected hydrological regimes. These data include tree-ring and historical evidence of prolonged drought, recent trends (glacier wastage, declining snowmelt runoff and summer flows), and global circulation models (GCM)-based scenarios of precipitation and runoff. We consider how water policy and management might be adjusted to compensate for a long-term view of the surface hydrology that includes more prolonged drought and lower average flows than observed and experienced in the twentieth century.

3.1 Introduction

> No country on Earth has such contrasts of drought and water plenty as Canada. None has so much water ready and available for use. But Canada is learning that national statistics do not begin to portray the complexity of its relationship with its most vital resource. … a new reality is emerging. It is a reality in which water is in increasingly short supply in some places at some times, where water suddenly has a real value rather than being an unlimited resource – and where rivers truly can run dry.
>
> (Pearce 2006)

A "myth of abundance" has historically influenced Canadian water policy and management (Mitchell and Shrubsol 1994; Sprague 2006). An explicit assumption also has been made that "the hydrological regime is stationary and will continue to be stationary in the future" (Whitfield *et al*. 2004: 89). While about 25 percent of the world's freshwater is stored within Canada, most of this is underground or in largely inaccessible glaciers and lakes. Sprague (2006) argued that Canada's water supply is the 2.5 percent of annual global precipitation that falls on our populated regions. Thus, there is "limited availability of freshwater in Canada at different times and places" (Quinn *et al*. 2004: 1). The place and time of the least amount of freshwater is the Western Plains during recurrent drought. The hydroclimate of this region (Figure 3.1) is the subject of this chapter. We examine the hydroclimatic

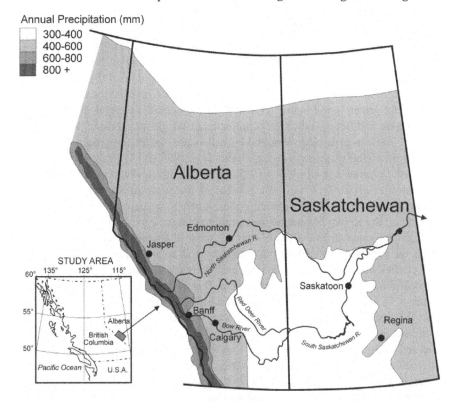

Annual Precipitation (mm)

300-400
400-600
600-800
800 +

Figure 3.1 The North and South Rivers shed runoff from the southern Rocky Mountains and across the subhumid to semi-arid Prairie Ecozone of southeastern Alberta and southwestern Saskatchewan.

variability from 1600–2100 as a context for the observations and experiences of the twentieth century, upon which water policy and management strategies have been based. We consider how water policy and management might be adjusted to compensate for a long-term view of the surface hydrology.

Western water policy and management practices reflect the dry climate of the continental interior. In contrast to the accessible surface water and riparian laws of eastern Canada and United States, the principles of first appropriation and apportionment evolved in the west to guarantee access to water for the first users (irrigators) and to allocate water among jurisdictions (Arnold 2005; Quinn *et al*. 2004). Apportionment agreements and guidelines for minimum flows ensure water supplies by jurisdiction and for instream flow needs. If natural flows reach unprecedented levels, the uncertainties and assumptions inherent in the calculation of flows for apportionment agreements and to maintain aquatic ecosystems become more significant. This implies the question: how likely is it that future low flows will result in conflicts between users and jurisdictions?

In Canada's southern prairies (Figure 3.1), apportionment and first appropriation of water supplies, and more recently water conservation objectives to protect aquatic systems, are policy responses to a subhumid to semi-arid climate. Mean annual water deficits are 35 percent to 50 percent, in terms of the shortfall of precipitation (P) relative to potential evapotranspiration (PET). The extent of this Canadian drybelt increases by approximately 50 percent when P/PET is mapped using output from the CGCM2B2 (Canadian Global Climate Model, version 2, greenhouse gas emission scenario B2) for the 2050s (Sauchyn *et al.* 2002). While more severe and frequent drought is projected under global warming (Kharin and Zwiers 2000), an expanded subhumid climate is not outside the geographic range of natural variability, since in drought years (e.g. 1937, 1961, 1988, 2001) a large part of the prairies has a P/PET < 0.65, although with devastating consequences (Wheaton *et al.* 2005). The management of water in the western interior is essentially a process of redistributing the runoff from source areas with excess water (i.e., the Rocky Mountains and prairie uplands; e.g., the Cypress Hills) to the adjacent water-deficient plains that are most of Canada's farmland. In most years, the supply of water from the mountains and uplands is high, relative to the water deficit on the plains. This gap becomes precariously small, however, during years of drought such as 2001, when there were serious economic consequences resulting in adjustments to water policy and management (Alberta Environment n.d.; Wheaton *et al.* 2005).

Immediately following two of the driest years on record, 2001–2, Alberta released its groundbreaking Water for Life Strategy (Alberta Environment 2003). The rationale for a provincial water strategy included the need for major shifts in the approach to managing a water supply that in recent years had been "fluctuating and unpredictable." A "clear set of principles" emerged from consultations to develop the provincial water strategy. They include:

- all Albertans must recognize there are limits to the available water supply.
- Alberta's water resources must be managed within the capacity of individual watersheds.
- knowledge of Alberta's water supply and quality is the foundation for effective decision-making.

Applying these principles to science-based decision making will require estimates of "the limits to the available water supply" and "capacity of individual watersheds". Knowledge of Alberta's water supply is incomplete until data on trends, variability and extremes, and thereby limits and capacities, are derived from the observation and modeling of hydroclimate over time frames that extend before and beyond our short experience with hydrologic systems.

This chapter provides evidence that current perceptions of water supplies and variability may be skewed by the observations and experience of the twentieth century and may be unrepresentative of both natural and future hydroclimate. The extensive wastage of glacier ice from the Rocky Mountains increased local streamflow above the net income of annual precipitation, but it is almost certain that this effect is in decline as the glaciers retreat rapidly towards their least extent in the past 10,000 years (Demuth and Pietroniro 2003). Furthermore climate change scenarios suggest that a significantly larger proportion of winter precipitation will fall as rain, as opposed to snow (Lapp *et al.* 2005). This hydrologic regime, with less natural storage, will tend towards greater extremes, including a higher probability of drought. According to records and models of pre- and post-twentieth century climate, as described in this chapter, the twenty-first century will almost certainly include droughts of greater severity and duration than those previously observed and experienced by western Canadians since European settlement. The results of our research on the hydroclimate and stream hydrology of the Rocky Mountains and western plains suggest that the myths of an abundant and stationary water supply are misconceptions but also based in physical reality.

3.2 Recent trends and future projections

A recent study for Alberta Environment (Pietroniro *et al.* 2006) comprises three major investigations of recent and potential future trends in water resources within the North and South Saskatchewan River basins (NSRB and SSRB). These studies catalogue glacial extents; examine streamflow records for evidence of trends and variability related to changes in glacial extent; and model changes in flow regime under future climate/glacier configurations. Combined, these analyses provide an assessment of the impacts that climate change may impose on the "water towers" of the Canadian prairies. In this chapter, we summarize the results of these investigations. For a description of the methods of analysis, the reader should consult Demuth (1996), Demuth and Pietroniro (2003) and Pietroniro *et al.* (2006). The headwater study basins contain historic records of streamflow and climate obtained from Environment Canada Archives, and glacier information from the Geological Survey of Canada.

3.2.1 A changing glacier landscape

Documenting land ice influences on the water resources of the NSRB and SSRB requires periodic mapping of snow and ice extents. These extents can then be incorporated into hydrological modeling- and remote sensing-based glacier-climate scaling frameworks. Landsat satellite images since the 1970s enable repetitive, synoptic, and high-resolution multispectral mapping. Glacier extent in the Nelson headwaters was estimated for 1975 and 1998, and changes in area extent were documented. An example of the delineated glacier extent is shown in Figure 3.2. Total glacier area change as a ratio of 1975 glacier extent was approximately 50 percent in the South Saskatchewan River basin and 23 percent in the North basin.

3.2.2 Streamflow trends in headwater catchments

The influence of changing glacier cover was examined using parametric and non-parametric statistical trend analysis of streamflow and basin yield for several

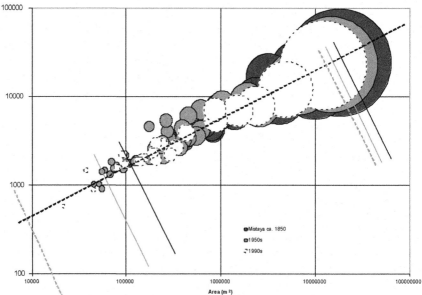

Figure 3.2 Example of recent and past-century glacier cover extent changes for the
Saskatchewan River Basin. Mistaya sub-basin depicted as log Perimeter
vs. log Area for three epochs. Note the rate of change (fiducial lines) for
the largest and smallest glaciers in the sample (after Demuth and Pietroniro
2003).

reference headwater catchments. During periods of precipitation deficit, basin water
yield declines and inter-annual flow variability tends to increase with continued
glacier shrinkage (Young 1991). The extent to which this situation is evolving
in the study area was investigated by analysing longer sequences of historical
streamflow data in relation to secular glacier-climate variability (1950–1998) in
selected catchments.

The parametric analysis was concentrated on the Mistaya River record (initiated
in 1950) and the annual Transition to Base Flow (TBF) period from August to
October, when there is maximum contribution from glacier ice melt. Figure 3.3
illustrates the yield from the Mistaya catchment for the period of study. The trend
line depicts declining yields for the TBF period, despite evidence that precipitation
in the montane is increasing for the same period (August 1–October 31). The
coefficient of variation (standard deviation/mean) for the streamflow (Figure 3.3)
is increasing over the available record, suggesting that the influence of glacier on
streamflow may have been in decline since the mid 1900s.

The streamflow regime was also examined using the minimum, mean and
maximum daily discharge data available from the Water Survey of Canada
(Environment Canada 2003). The TBF change for the Mistaya basin (1950–98) is
quantified using a simple linear regression analysis depicted in Figure 3.4. There

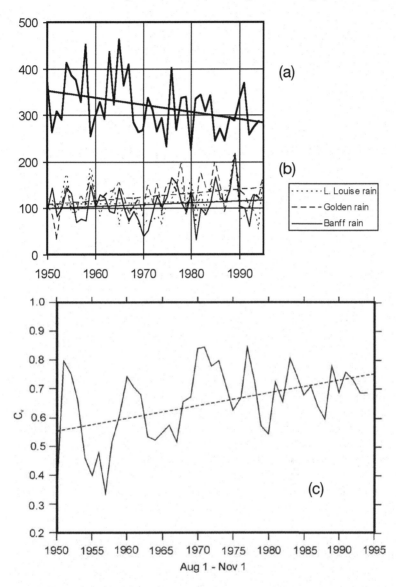

Figure 3.3 Yield (a), precipitation (b) and streamflow (c) coefficient of variation (Cv) for the Mistaya River catchment at gauge 05DA007 over the TBF period (after Demuth and Pietroniro 2003).

is a significant decreasing trend in the mean (R^2=0.33) and minimum (R^2=0.43) TBF time series, and a weaker increasing trend in the maximum (R^2=0.02) TBF time series (Figure 3.4). The initial inference from this analysis is that significant reductions in the mean and minimum flow regimes and increasing flow variability are the result of extensive glacier contraction to the degree that glacier melt

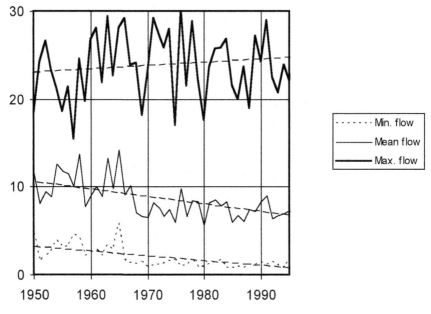

Figure 3.4 Regression analysis for TBF flow period showing trends in minimum, mean and maximum flows for the Mistaya Basin (after Demuth and Pietroniro 2003).

contributions during dry periods, notwithstanding high antecedent snow cover conditions, have been in decline over the period of observation.

All historic records available for the headwater region were examined for use in a non-parametric trend analysis of glaciated and non-glaciated headwaters (Table 3.1). Selection criteria centered primarily on the length and completeness of discharge records obtained from the HYDAT 2003 CD (Environment Canada 2003). Analyses of annual trends were further limited to those stations with discharge data for all months; for a lesser number of months (e.g. April–October) gauge records were used only for analyses of the TBF and/or spring periods and for some observations about changes in monthly trends over the period of record. Spring was defined as March to May, and the TBF period is August to October. Station selection proved exceedingly difficult, since common periods of record of significant duration were never collected. This highlights the importance of systematic and consistent hydrometric data collection. Nonetheless, a total of 18 discharge stations (5 in the NSRB and 13 in the SSRB) were chosen for Mann Kendall (MK) analysis of streamflow trends.

The results for the 14 stations (Table 3.1) show that the majority of trends detected are negative, indicating decreasing streamflow. In particular, for the North Ram, Siffleur and Mistaya sub-basins of the NSRB, whose percent glacier covers increase from 0 percent to 2.5 percent to 8.5 percent, respectively, there is a decreasing trend in TBF as the percentage of glacierization increases. Unfortunately, there is no equivalent comparison for basins with differing glacier

Table 3.1 Results Mann Kendall (MK) analysis of streamflow trends in the NSRB

Station Name	Station ID	Drainage Area	Cumula-tive Area	% Glacier Cover	Period of Record	Total Years	Tr/No Tr (Direction)
NSRB							
Siffleur River Near The Mouth	05DA002	514.74	514.74	2.5	1975–1996 (May–Oct)	22	Jun **Tr** (↑)
Mistaya River Near Saskatchewan Crossing	05DA007	204.31	248.02	8.5	1950–2001 (May–Oct)	52	TBF mean **Tr** (↓) TBF min **Tr** (↓) Jul, Oct **Tr** (↓)
Clearwater River Above Limestone Creek	05DB003	1342.75	1342.75	0.4	1960–1992 (May–Oct)	33	No Tr
North Ram River At Forestry Road	05DC011	347.31	347.31	0	1976–2001 (May–Oct)	26	No Tr
SSRB							
Johnston Creek Near The Mouth	05BA006	122.95	122.95	0	1974–1996 (May–Oct)	22	No Tr
Brewster Creek Near Banff	05BB004	110.15	110.15	0	1971–1996 (May–Oct)	26	No Tr
Redearth Creek Near The Mouth	05BB005	150.61	150.61	1.3	1974–1996 (May–Oct)	23	TBF min **Tr** (↓)
Cascade River Above Lake Minnewanka	05BD005	452.09	452.09	0	1973–1996 (May–Oct)	24	No Tr
Mud Lake Diversion Canal	05BF013	29.00	29.00	4.4	1949–1992 (May–June)	44	TBF mean **Tr** (↑) TBF max **Tr** (↑) Jun, Aug, Sep, Oct **Tr** (↑)
Ghost River Near Black Rock Mountain	05BG002	209.77	209.77	0	1942–1993 (Apr–Nov)	52	No Tr
Jumpingpound Creek Near Cox Hill	05BH013	36.91	36.91	0	1976–2001 (May–Oct)	26	No Tr
Fish Creek Near Priddis	05BK001	260.51	260.51	0	1968–2001 (Mar–Oct)	34	No Tr
Red Deer River Above Panther River	05CA004	941.30	941.30	2.0	1967–2001 (Apr–Oct)	35	Jun **Tr** (↓)

Source: revised from Pietroniro *et al.* 2006.

extent in the SSRB, and thus the pattern with respect to glacier extent and change in streamflow is less clear than for the NSRB. Overall, 50 percent of the stations analyzed exhibited no trends in discharge over the periods of record. Interestingly, and perhaps predictably, of those 50 percent in which no trend was detected, 78 percent were for non-glacierized basins.

3.2.3 Modelling headwater catchments

The methods of hydrological modeling described by Pietroniro *et al.* (2006) were used to assess both the impacts of projected future climate on flows in the Nelson headwaters and the feasibility of estimating the glacier contributions through simple sensitivity analysis. The WATFLOOD (Kouwen *et al.* 1993) model was used; and calibrated well to conditions in the North and South Saskatchewan River basins. The model was run with a continuous time series for 1961–1990 and 2040–69, standard time slices for constructing climate scenarios (IPCC 2001).

Sensitivity analysis showed the important contribution of glacier runoff to the headwater catchments and its diminishing influence further downstream. This analysis of the impacts of glacier melt on total flow used the 1975 and 1998 glacier extents from the Landsat analysis described earlier. In Figure 3.5, the Mistaya River displays gradually decreasing volumes and variability during the TBF period when moving from the 1975 to 1998 extent. The hydrographs also show the estimated flows with no glacier extent. This analysis demonstrates that basins such as the Siffleur have already been de-glaciated to the point at which future changes in glacier mass will have very little impact on the runoff regime.

Climate change scenarios derived from GCM output for this region were used to assess possible future changes to the streamflow regime. The ECHAM4 (European Centre Hamburg Model) and NCAR-PCM (National Center for Atmospheric Research – Parallel Climate Model) GCMs achieved the lowest errors, highest correlation coefficients and could best model the magnitude of annual and seasonal precipitation and timing of the monthly precipitation in the region (Toyra *et al.* 2005). The potential changes in temperature were applied as offsets, and precipitation was normalized. Spatial gridding of these data produced the anticipated future temperature and precipitation forcing for WATFLOOD. The Hadley Centre and ECHAM models both provided reasonable simulations of the seasonal and annual observed climatology. The WATFLOOD model was re-run using this modified forcing so that current and future streamflow could be compared. This analysis was done using the 1998 glacier extent, and no projections of future extent were added to the model. The results indicate lower overall mean annual flows. Mean monthly flow for the Bow River at Banff shows the influence of changing glacier extent. The 1975, 1998 and "none" hydrographs represent the modelled 10-year monthly flow values using the fixed glacier extents for those years. "None" refers to complete removal of the glaciers from the basin. There is a clear reduction in overall flow volume, and a small reduction in peak magnitude in all three glacier scenarios. The 1998 glacier extent, and climate change forcing from the ECHAM and Hadley Centre models, results in similar patterns with a slight change in peak (increase for Hadley and decrease for ECHAM) and a shift in monthly flows to a higher spring runoff. The TBF period shows very little change resulting from climate change alone, and is more influenced by the glacier extent than by the climate warming. This is simply because the glacier extents are fixed for each grid element in the model at a pre-determined level. Clearly changes in precipitation and temperature will have an influence on the dynamic response of the glacier, and it is likely that glacier recession will continue. The resulting flow

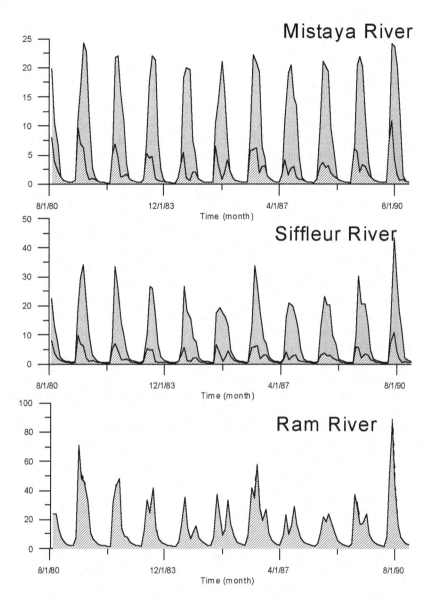

Figure 3.5 Analysis of glacier contributions to flow using the WATFLOOD model. The
stippled area represents the model simulation with the 1975 glacier extent.
The hatched area represents the runoff in the basin in the absence of glacier
contributions (after Pietroniro *et al.* 2006).

regime for the Bow River headwaters will likely include early and increased spring melt and decreased late summer flows as shown in Figure 3.6.

3.2.4 Hydroclimatic variability

The recent and projected streamflow trends described above in part reflect the impact of global warming on a snow-dominated hydrologic regime, but also include a significant component of natural hydroclimatic variability: "many hydro-climate datasets exhibit inter-decadal variability, where some inter-decadal periods are considerably drier or wetter than others. These wet and dry cycles have significant implications for the management of land and water resources systems, where several decades of sufficient water are followed by droughts clustered over the following decades" (Chiew 2006). The length of most hydroclimatic cycles approaches or exceeds the length of gauge records. This low-frequency variability is best observed with proxy hydroclimatic records. They provide water resource planners and engineers with a historical context for standard reference hydrology to evaluate baseline conditions and water allocations, and a broad perspective on the variability of water levels to assess the reliability of water supply systems under a wider range of precipitation and flow regimes than recorded by a gauge.

Tree rings are the preferred proxy for records of climate variability at annual to multi-decadal scales spanning centuries to millennia (Briffa 2000). They are the source of both hydroclimate information and a chronology with absolute annual resolution. Annual variations in tree-ring width reflect daily and seasonal growth-limiting processes. Where available soil moisture limits tree growth, standardized tree-ring widths correlate with hydrometric variables. Streamflow records correlate with moisture-sensitive tree-ring chronologies, because streamflow and tree growth have a similar muted response to episodic inputs of rainfall and snow-melt water.

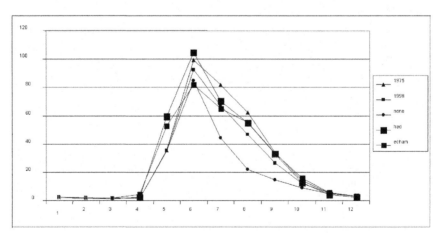

Figure 3.6 Comparison of 10-year monthly flow estimates from WATFLOOD for the Bow River at Banff, derived from both climate change and glacier change project (after Pietroniro *et al.* 2006).

Hydrological peaks are usually underestimated by tree rings, given a physiological limit to the growth response to fluctuations in soil moisture. Therefore, proxy records do not provide precise volumes of streamflow, yet they capture the timing and duration of periods of high and low flow. Tree rings are an especially good indicator of drought; dry years produce narrow rings.

Until recently, networks of moisture-sensitive tree-ring chronologies have been lacking for western Canada, and streamflow has been reconstructed using just a few chronologies (Case and Macdonald 2003). Researchers at the University of Regina Tree Ring Lab (www.parc.ca/urtreelab) have established a network of tree-ring chronologies to infer long-term moisture and streamflow variability from a pool of predictor chronologies that capture a larger range of the regional climatic variability than data from one or a few sites. Nearly all of these collections are from open-canopy forests on ridge crests, south- and west-facing slopes, and/or rapidly drained soils. At these dry sites, tree growth is limited by available soil moisture and therefore our tree-ring chronologies are proxies of summer and annual precipitation, soil moisture and runoff.

Here we present a streamflow reconstruction to illustrate interannual to multi-decadal hydroclimatic variability since 1602 and to provide a historical context for the gauge record from the twentieth century. The mean annual flow of the Oldman River at Waldron's Corner, Alberta (gauge AA023) was reconstructed by Axelson (2007) from tree-ring chronologies from five sites within 50 km of the gauge. The tree-ring model of streamflow was built by entering standardized and lagged tree-ring index data into a stepwise multiple regression. The predictand is the stream gauge record. The best model explains maximum variance in the predictand with the fewest predictors and least standard error. The validity of our tree-ring model for the Oldman River is indicated first by a reduction of error (0.45) that is comparable to the squared correlation coefficient (0.55) (Fritts *et al.* 1990), and secondly by similar values of the standard error (2.9) and root-mean square error of validation (3.07), measures of the uncertainty in predicted values over the calibration and validation periods. When the R^2 is adjusted for the number of predictors (lost degrees of freedom) the explained variance (R^2_a) is 51 percent. Most of the unexplained variance is attributable to the larger amplitude of observed versus reconstructed flows. On the other hand, the tree-ring records capture the timing of low flows and, thus, we are confident that the full reconstruction in Figure 3.7 spanning 1602–2004 gives the timing and duration of drought.

The proxy streamflow data in Figure 3.7 are plotted as departures from the median of the instrumental record. This plot reveals the impact of the droughts of the 1980s on the flow of the upper Oldman River. This sequence of low flows, however, is certainly not the worst streamflow scenario. For almost five decades from the 1830s to 1880s, just before the region was settled by EuroCanadians, there were only nine years of above-average flow. The regional water balance would have been seriously depleted by these sustained dry conditions. Similarly in most years between 1640 and 1720 the tree-rings record below-average flow. Since these droughts are relatively recent, there are historical observations of the water scarcity and its impacts, including evidence of sand dune activity (Wolfe *et*

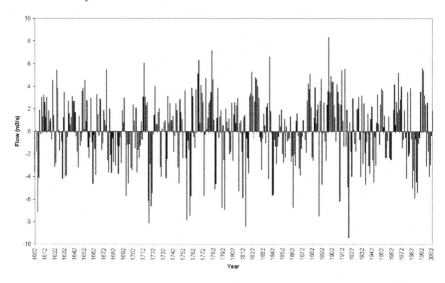

Figure 3.7 The full tree-ring reconstruction of mean annual flow of the Oldman River at Waldron's Corner for the period 1602–2004. These proxy streamflow data are plotted as departures from the median of the reconstruction.

al. 2001) from a lack of soil moisture and flows in the North Saskatchewan River at Edmonton that were so low that furs could not be moved by canoe (Sauchyn *et al.* 2002, 2003).

The proxy streamflow record reveals periodic shifts in the variance of the hydroclimatic regime. Extended wet and dry intervals (low-frequency variability) represents a different challenge for water management than predominately year-to-year (high frequency) variability. In general, natural and socioeconomic systems are able to recover from severe drought of short duration. Sustained drought has cumulative impacts on water balances and ecosystems resulting in significant, sometimes irreversible, impacts. Current water policy and management does not account for sustained dry spells lasting a decade or longer because droughts of this duration did not occur in the twentieth century.

3.3 Discussion

In Canada's western interior, the most serious risk from climate change is a shift in the distribution of water supplies and the potential for water scarcity (Schindler and Donahue 2006; Sauchyn and Kulshreshtha 2008). The region is losing the advantage of a cold winter: snow and ice, the most reliable and predictable source of runoff. The impacts of climate change on economies and communities are necessarily adverse because resource management practices and policies have assumed a stationary hydrological regime. Data presented in this chapter demonstrate that water usage, policy and management were established during a period of fairly stable and reliable water supplies, as compared to preceding and projected hydrological regimes. These data include tree-ring and historical evidence of prolonged drought, recent trends (glacier wastage, declining snowmelt runoff and summer flows), and GCM-based scenarios of precipitation and runoff.

The analysis of recent and future flows in the North and South Saskatchewan River basins showed the important contributions of glacier runoff to the headwater catchments and the diminishing influence downstream and with time. Overall, the evidence indicates large changes in glacier extent with decreasing streamflow in glacierized basins; however, no discernible trend to this point has been found in non-glacierized catchments. Given the uncertainty associated with GCM scenarios, hydrological models and current observation networks, it is difficult to quantify the exact magnitude of change. However, it appears that we are experiencing significant reductions in glacier extent and this is manifest in decreasing streamflow, both annually and in the late summer periods. The changes will likely affect water resources in low-snowfall years, particularly during the transition to base flow (TBF) period of dry late-summer conditions. However, projected increases in precipitation may very well offset these reductions in mean annual flow, resulting in an increasing spring snowmelt peak, but less water availability in the TBF period due to the lack of natural storage. These impacts will be particularly acute in mountain headwater basins.

Flow contributions from glacier sources should increase in the short to medium term, and decrease in the long term (IPCC 2001). In the eastern slopes of the Rocky Mountains, there already is evidence during critical periods of a reduction in yield with reduced glacier area. This is among the strongest signals of the impacts of global warming in western Canada. Underlying this trend is the natural variability in hydroclimate represented here with a proxy record of streamflow derived from moisture-sensitive tree-ring records. These data illustrate the significant multi-decadal variability in the hydrologic system and suggest that future surface water supplies very likely will be subject to a drought of longer duration than the most serious droughts experienced since EuroCanadian settlement of the region.

Notwithstanding the uncertainty in climate projection, particularly estimates of precipitation, the science presented here has significant implications for water policy and management in western Canada. Agriculture is particularly sensitive to climate variation and the irrigation sector in southern Alberta and southwestern Saskatchewan is vulnerable given its dependence on streamflow to overcome soil moisture deficits (Alberta Environment n.d., de Loë *et al.* 2001). About 70 percent of the irrigated farmland in Canada (400,000 hectares) is in southern Alberta (Statistics Canada, Ottawa, www.statcan.ca). This is four percent of the cultivated land in Alberta, yet it produces 18 percent of the province's agri-food gross domestic product. In the South Saskatchewan River Basin, about 75 percent of the allocated water is used for irrigation (Alberta Environment n.d.). This percentage rises to 86 in the Oldman River sub-basin. Between 20 and 30 percent of withdrawals are returned to the river system.

3.3.1 Implications for water management

Adapting to the impacts of climate change on water resources requires adjustments to practices, polices and infrastructure so that economic development can be sustained by accommodating shifts in mean hydroclimatic conditions and variability. Management strategies and structures have evolved to limit exposure to a historical range of hydroclimatic variability. Paradigms and practices of water management must be adjusted to manage a hydrological cycle that may be increasingly sensitive to the timing and frequency of rainfall events, with less buffering from glacier ice and late-lying snow at high elevations. Current sensitivity to drought suggests that our communities and institutions are not adequately adapted to climate variability, even in the absence of climate change that could produce shifts in the amplitude and frequency departures from an average climate. The principles of adaptive, anticipatory and integrated water resource management, which include monitoring and scientific discovery, would seem to provide the framework for adapting to the greater range of hydroclimatic variability anticipated for the twenty-first century: "Adaptive management explicitly accepts indeterminacy, ignorance, uncertainly and risk; the inevitability of surprise and turbulence; and the need for flexibility." (Mitchell and Shrubsol 1994: 55)

Establishing trends and variability in past and future hydroclimate is the only systematic way to understand and validate possible future scenarios. Knowledge of the current state of the climate system and systematic tracking of the gradual changes occurring in these large systems requires major investments in data collection and science. There are important economic justifications for understanding and monitoring progressive changes in support of adaptation. Operational decisions about reservoir storage, irrigation, flood and drought mitigation, and hydropower production are based on water supply forecasts from statistical and simulation models that are derived and calibrated using instrumental data from monitoring networks. This standard forecasting methodology has limited application, however, to longer-term water planning and policy making, because most instrumental records generally are too short to capture the decadal and lower-frequency variation in regional climate and hydrology. Some drivers of climate variation have a periodicity that approaches or exceeds the period of instrumental records, during which a stationary climate has or can be assumed. Developing adaptive strategies in anticipation of impacts of climate change requires that current science-based water management and planning be augmented with the types of data and information described in this paper, that is, scenarios of future hydroclimatic variability and proxy (pre-instrumental) sources of hydroclimate data. This provides a much broader perspective on the variability of water levels to assess the reliability of water supply systems under a wider range of flows than recorded by a gauge. It requires, however, that water resource managers and agencies accept and accommodate a lesser degree of determinacy, certainty and stationarity.

The adjustments to water management practices necessary to sustain water use, allocation and apportionment under a changed hydrologic regime represents a knowledge gap that may be constraining the planning of adaptation to climate change in the water resource sector. Institutional adaptive capacity will be enhanced by addressing constraints and opportunities (entry points) for the operational use of scenarios of long-term hydrological variability and by lowering resistance stemming from perceptions of uncertainty and the training required for the application of this new scientific information. Incorporating hydrologic scenarios and paleo-hydrologic data in the forecasting and managing of water supplies requires 1) moving knowledge from one organizational context to another: from research labs to facilitative research centers to water management agencies, 2) training a subset of water managers (innovators) who then influence decision-making in their organizations, 3) identifying benefits of changes in water management strategy, 4) facilitating change in operational or policy environments by collaborating with practitioners who are willing to move away from the status quo, 5) mainstreaming considerations of hydroclimate change and variability into existing management plans and policy processes, and 6) engaging the end users in the translation, delivery and application of the science.

Acknowledgements

Research described here was funded by the Natural Sciences and Engineering Research Council of Canada, Manitoba Hydro, Alberta Environment, Environment Canada and the Geological Survey of Canada. For assistance and guidance, we thank Jodi Axelson, Antoine Beriault, Jan Mydynski, Nick Kouwen, and Don Burn.

References

Alberta Environment. (2003) *Water for life: Alberta's strategy for sustainability.* Alberta Environment Pub No. I/955. Edmonton: Government of Alberta.

Alberta Environment. (nd) *Background information for public consultation on the South Saskatchewan River Basin draft water management plan.* Edmonton: Government of Alberta.

Arnold, P. E. (2005) Managing scarcity: water policy administration in the American West In *The institutional arrangements for water management in the 19th and 20th centuries* (ed.) J. C. N. Raadschelders, Cahier d'Histoire de l'Administration No. 8, Volume 24. International Institute of Administrative Sciences Monographs. Amsterdam: IOS Press, pp. 159–178.

Axelson, J. (2007) *Historical streamflow variability in the south Saskatchewan River Basin inferred from a network of tree-ring chronologies.* M.Sc. thesis, University of Regina.

Briffa, K. R. (2000) Annual climate variability in the Holocene: interpreting the message of ancient trees. *Quaternary Science Reviews,* 19: 87–106.

Case, R. A. and MacDonald, G. M. (2003) Tree ring reconstructions of streamflow for three Canadian rivers. *Journal of the American Water Resources Association,* June 2003: 703–16.

Chiew, F. H. S. (2006) Modelling hydroclimatic variability for water resources management. *Geophysical Research Abstracts,* 8: 1607–7962/gra/EGU06-A-01791.

Demuth, M. N. (1996) Effects of short-term and historical glacier variations on cold stream hydro-ecology: a synthesis and case study. *Ecological Monitoring and Assessment Network 2nd National Science Meeting.* January 1996, Halifax, Canada. National Hydrology Research Institute Contribution Series CS-96003.

Demuth, M. N. and Pietroniro, A. (2003) The impact of climate change on the glaciers of the Canadian Rocky Mountain eastern slopes and implications for water resource adaptation in the Canadian prairies. CCAF – Prairie Adaptation Research Collaborative, *Final Report Project P55*, plus Technical Appendices.

Environment Canada. (2003) HyDat for Windows, Canadian Hydrological Data, Environment Canada HyDat CD.

Fritts, H. C., Guiot, J. and Gordon, G. A. (1990) Tree-ring standardization and growth-trend estimation. In Cook, E. R. and Kairiukstis, L. A. (eds.) *Methods of dendrochronology: applications in the environmental sciences*, Dordrecht: Klumer Academic Publishers, pp. 178–185.

IPCC (Intergovernmental Panel on Climate Change). (2001) Climate change 2001: Impacts, adaptation, and vulnerability technical summary. *A Report of Working Group II of the Intergovernmental Panel on Climate Change 2001*, WMO and UNEP.

Kharin, V. V. and Zwiers, F. W. (2000) Changes in the extremes in an ensemble of transient climate simulations with a coupled atmosphere-ocean GCM. *Journal of Climate,* 13: 3760–3788.

Kouwen, N *et al.* (1993) Grouped response units for distributed hydrologic modelling. *Journal of Water Resources Planning and Management*, ASCE, 119 (3): 289–305.

Lapp, S., Byrne, J., Townshend, I. and Kienzle, S. (2005) Climate warming impacts on snowpack accumulation in an alpine watershed. *International Journal of Climatology,* 25(4): 521–536.

de Loë, R., Kreutzwiser, R. and Moraru, L. (2001) Adaptation options for the near term: climate change and the Canadian water sector. *Global Environmental Change,* 11: 231–245.

Mitchell, B. and Shrubsol, D. (1994) *Canadian water management: visions for sustainability.* Cambridge: Canadian Water Resources Association.

Pearce, F. (2006) *When rivers run dry: journeys into the heart of the world's water crisis.* Key Porter Books.

Pietroniro, A. *et al.* (2006) *Streamflow shifts resulting from past and future glacier fluctuations in the eastern flowing basins of the Rocky Mountains.* NWRI Internal Publication, Contribution Number, 06–026.

Quinn, F. *et al.* (2004) Water allocation, diversion and export. Chapter 1 in *Threats to water availability in Canada*. Burlington, Ontario: National Water Research Institute. NWRI Scientific Assessment Report Series No. 3 and ACSD Science Assessment Series No. 1.

Sauchyn, D. and Kulshreshtha, S. (2008) The prairies. Chapter 7 in D.S. Lemmen, F. J. Warren, J. Lacroix and E. Bush (eds.) *From impacts to adaptation: Canada in a changing climate 2007*. Ottawa: Government of Canada.

Sauchyn, D. J, Barrow, E., Hopkinson, R. F. and Leavitt, P. (2002) Aridity on the Canadian plains. *Géographie physique et Quaternaire*, vol. 56(2–3): 247–259.

Sauchyn, D. J., Stroich, J. and Beriault, A. (2003) A paleoclimatic context for the drought of 1999–2001 in the northern Great Plains. *The Geographical Journal,* 169(2): 158–167.

Schindler, D. W. and Donahue, W. F. (2006) An impending water crisis in Canada's western prairie provinces. *Proceedings of the National Academy of Sciences*, Available online at http://www.pnas.org_cgi_doi_10.1073_pnas.0601568103.

Sprague, J. B. (2006) Great wet north? Canada's myth of water abundance. In K. Bakker (ed.), *Eau Canada: The future of Canada's water*. Vancouver: UBC Press. Ch. 2.

Statistics Canada, Ottawa. Available online at http://www.statcan.ca, accesseed September 11, 2008.

Töyrä, J., Pietroniro, A. and Bonsal, B. (2005) Evaluation of GCM-simulated climate over the Canadian prairie provinces. *Canadian Water Resources Journal,* 30(3): 245–262.

Wheaton E., Kulshreshtha, S. and Wittrock, V. (2005) *Canadian droughts of 2001 and 2002: climatology, impacts and adaptation.* Volumes I and II. Saskatchewan Research Council Publication No. 11602–1E03.

Whitfield, P. H. *et al.* (2004) Climate variability and change – rivers and streams. Chapter 11 in *Threats to water availability in Canada.* Burlington, Ontario: National Water Research Institute. NWRI Scientific Assessment Report Series No. 3 and ACSD Science Assessment Series No. 1.

Wolfe, S. A. *et al.* (2001) Late 18th century drought-induced sand dune activity, Great Sand Hills, Saskatchewan. *Canadian Journal of Earth Science,* 38: 105–117. Young, G. J. (1991) Hydrological interactions in the Mistaya Basin, Alberta, Canada. In H. Bergmann, H. Lang, W. Frey, D. Issler and B. Salm (eds.) *Snow, hydrology and forests in high alpine areas: proceedings of a symposium held during the XX Assembly of the International Union of Geodesy and Geophysics at Vienna, August 1991,* IAHS-AISH Publication No. 205, 237–244.

4 Hydrological models to support water policy

The case of Lake Kinneret watershed, Israel

Alon Rimmer

Analysis of climate change scenarios in the Middle East region reveal changes of rainfall distribution and increase of evaporation throughout the seasons. These changes are expected to affect both water availability in the upper catchments of the Jordan River, and the salinity of Lake Kinneret, the source of 30 percent of Israel's water supply. By application of the system modeling approach to both problems, we learned the nature of each system and used it to predict future scenarios of water availability and salinity under various climate change scenarios. The issues of water availability and salinity in the Lake Kinneret watershed are presented in this chapter. We describe here the problem, the various models that were proposed to address the problem, the basic structure of the proposed model, the results of the prediction analysis, and the conclusions regarding future operation policy and feasibility of interventions.

4.1 Introduction

4.1.1 Lake Kinneret watershed in the Israeli water supply system

The main sources of the Israeli National Water Supply System (NWSS) are Lake Kinneret (also known as the Sea of Galilee), which supplies 30 percent of the water in Israel and the Palestinian Authority; the Mountain Aquifer; and the Coastal Aquifer. These sources are known jointly as the "Three Basin System." About 60 percent of Lake Kinneret recharge comes from the Hermon Aquifer.

Analysis of climate change scenarios in the Middle East region reveal changes of rainfall distribution and an increase in evaporation throughout the seasons (Kunstmann *et al.* 2007). Such changes are expected to cause new distribution of runoff during the rainy season and to lower aquifer replenishment and spring discharge.

While changes in rainfall distributions are expected to change the availability of water in Lake Kinneret, the natural replenishment of karst aquifers, such as the Hermon Aquifer, are highly non-linear processes and difficult to predict. Variability in water replenishment creates a challenge in supplying adequate amounts of water, especially during several sequential dry seasons. Attempts to assess the replenishment process under ongoing climate changes are difficult, since using statistical analysis based on historical data is of little relevance. New means and tools, which were developed and applied for this purpose, will be presented in the section of this chapter titled "Karst hydrological system of the Hermon Mountain."

Together with projected increases in future water demands, increased stress on the Israeli National Water Supply System is expected, due to further deterioration of water quality in both surface and groundwater sources. A major concern is the enhanced salinization process. The documentation of salinity variations of Lake Kinneret in the past (Rimmer and Gal 2003) enabled the development and application of a new analytical model that assesses the salinity of the lake under various future climate change scenarios. This issue will be elaborated upon in the section titled "Salinity of Lake Kinneret."

These water availability and quality changes are likely to drive desalination into becoming an important element in the water supply system. Desalination has already been initiated, and the first plant has been supplying 100 Mm^3 y^{-1} since 2006. While this source of supply is practically infinite, it requires more space on valuable beachfront property, and is more costly than can be afforded by the agricultural industry. Natural water will therefore remain a critical and important source. Efforts must be made to predict the future availability and quality of water, while protecting and using it effectively.

The objectives of this chapter are to:

- use hydrological models to predict spatial and temporal patterns of water replenishment, water availability, and water quality (salinity) in the Lake Kinneret watershed; and
- explain how these models may contribute to improving the water management of hydrological systems that are affected by climate change.

4.1.2 The Lake Kinneret watershed

The Lake Kinneret watershed, located in the northern part of the Jordan Rift Valley (Northern Israel, Figure 4.1a), is the most important surface water resource in Israel. The area of the watershed can be generally divided into three regions (Figure 4.1b): the major water source of Lake Kinneret is the upper catchments of the Jordan River (UCJR) with an area of ~1700 km^2 (of that area, ~920 km^2 is in Israel, and the rest is in Syria and Lebanon). The other two regions that discharge into Lake Kinneret originate from the direct watershed, located in the immediate vicinity of the lake. The direct watershed area is ~1100 km^2, of which 750 km^2 is in the southern part of the Golan Heights, east of Lake Kinneret, and the other 350 km^2 is part of the Eastern Galilee Mountains, west of Lake Kinneret. Water from the lake is heavily deployed through the National Water Carrier (NWC) – the national water supply system that takes water from Lake Kinneret (near Tabgha, Figure 4.1d) and distributes it to other parts of the country. The average area of the lake surface is 166 km^2, the average volume is 4,100 Mm^3, and the average renewal period is ~8.3 years.

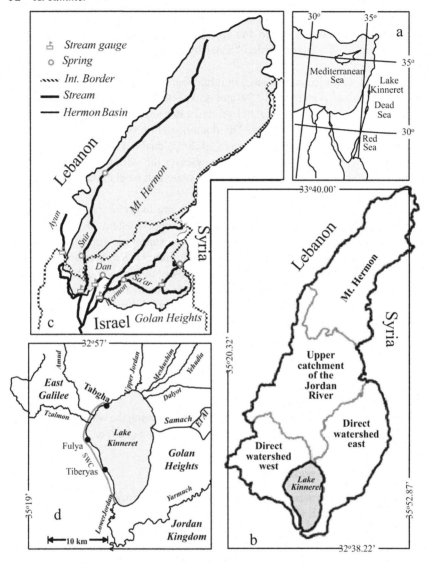

Figure 4.1 a. Orientation map of the east Mediterranean. b. The direct watershed of Lake Kinneret (dark) and the upper catchments of the Jordan River. c. Mt. Hermon area and the Dan, Hermon, and Senir watersheds. d. Lake Kinneret area with the location of Tabgha, Fuliya, and Tiberias springs, and the saline water carrier canal.

In this chapter, we focus on two models that were developed for the analysis of hydrological problems in the Hermon Aquifer and Lake Kinneret. These models are first, a hydrological model of the rainfall-streamflow relations of the Jordan River sources, and how it may be used to predict long-term rainfall-runoff relations in the Jordan River under climate change scenarios; and second, long-term predictions of Lake Kinneret salinity changes in response to operational and natural changes, including climate change scenarios. The connection between the two systems will be revealed in the following sections.

4.2 Karst hydrological system of the Hermon Mountain

4.2.1 Description of the problem

An average of 480×10^6 m^3 of water is contributed annually (1969–2006) to the Israeli water system through the karstic springs and surface flow of the Mt Hermon region, an elongated, 55 kilometer long and 25 kilometer wide anticline of mostly karstic limestone. Only seven percent of the range lies in Israel, while the rest is divided equally between Syria and Lebanon. The Hermon high regions (greater than 1000 m above sea level) receive the most precipitation in Israel (more than 1300 mm year^{-1}), restricted to the wet season from October to April. Rainfall and snowmelt of Mt Hermon recharge the main tributaries of the upper catchments of the Jordan River (Figure 4.1c): Dan (255×10^6 m^3 annually); Snir, also known as Hatzbani (118×10^6 m^3); and Hermon, also known as Banyas (107×10^6 m^3) (*see* Figure 4.2).

At present, the natural water sources in Northern Israel are deployed almost to the maximum. The three main tributaries are used not only as sources of water for Lake Kinneret, but also for local irrigation and domestic use, as well as being a

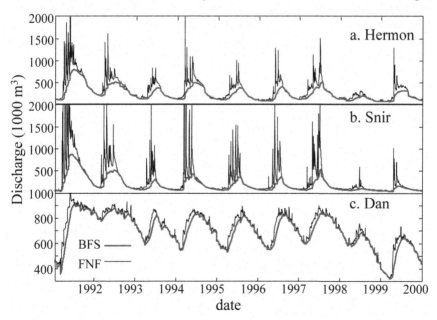

Figure 4.2 Full natural flow (FNF) of the Dan, Hermon, and Snir streams, and the application of the baseflow separation technique (BFS).

tourist attraction. Rainfall-streamflow relations are therefore of vast importance for decision making on an annual time scale (development of future new water sources such as desalinization, water treatment plants, import of water), on a monthly scale (predictions of water availability in the Jordan River and Lake Kinneret), as well as on a daily scale (predictions of peak flows during winter and low flows during summer).

The upper catchments of the Jordan River (UCJR) are an extremely important source for the Israeli water system, so a rainfall-runoff model was needed in order to characterize water availability of this natural water system in various time scales. Rainfall-runoff models applied to the UCJR in the past (Simon *et al.* 1978; Berger 2001; Rimmer and Salingar 2005; Kunstmann *et al.* 2006) were partly based on physical considerations. Although all models showed good agreement ($r^2 \geq 0.8$) between predicted and measured flow in the Jordan River, they were incapable of predicting the streamflow in the three sources of the Jordan River simultaneously, due to the karstic nature of the system. A targeted effort to characterize the monthly discharge of Mt Hermon springs was conducted by Simpson and Carmi (1983), Gilad and Bonne (1990), Kessler (1999), and Gur *et al.* (2003). Nevertheless, we found that their reported hydrological parameters were insufficient to be used in a daily rainfall-streamflow model for the entire Hermon catchment. Other studies also did not grasp the physical nature of the entire karstic system.

These past efforts highlighted the need to better represent the physical nature of the Mt Hermon hydrological system. Special attention was required to determine: 1) uncorrelated base and surface flow (Figure 4.2); 2) various types of flow regime of the Mt Hermon springs; 3) the large-scale preferential flow to groundwater; and 4) simultaneous calculations of the three main tributaries that originate from the karst region of Mt Hermon, which form nearly the entire flow of the Jordan River. The model that we developed and used is elaborated below.

4.2.2 Hydrological model for karst environment

The main equations for the model are part of a conceptual HYdrological Model for Karst Environment (HYMKE, Rimmer and Salingar 2006), consisting of three surface flow catchments, and four regional phreatic aquifers. HYMKE is made of four modules (Figure 4.3): the surface layer (0), the vadose zone (1), groundwater (2), and surface flow (3). In the conceptual model, the earth surface of the entire geographical basin is recharged by precipitation and dried by evaporation, surface runoff, and percolation to deeper layers. The karst nature of the landscape was introduced similarly to Jeannin and Grasso (1997), with a surface layer ("epikarst") composed of both low- and high-permeability sections that feed the karst network. The surface layer is drained continuously as a function of moisture content. Saturation excess is generated when the surface layer is saturated. Part of the excess saturation is then transformed into surface flow (module 3), while the other part forms a downward preferential flow component. Therefore, the percolation into the vadose zone (module 1) includes both a "slow flow" component through the matrix, and "quick flow" through the high permeability section, which is effective mainly

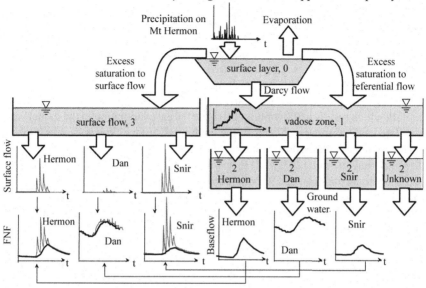

Figure 4.3 Schematic description of the Mt Hermon conceptual hydrological model: Module 0 is the surface layer, Module 1 is the vadoze zone, Module 2 consists of four groundwater reservoirs, and Module 3 simulates the surface flow. The calculated baseflow and the surface flow components of each tributary result in their full natural flow.

during the peak of the wet season. The output from the vadose zone (module 1) feeds the groundwater reservoir (module 2). However, the differences between the groundwater discharge patterns require the separation of module 2 into four groundwater reservoirs. In the case of Mt Hermon, three reservoirs feed the Dan, Snir, and Hermon baseflow component, and one reservoir contributes the residual flow of groundwater to springs in the east part of Mt Hermon in the area of Syria. The accumulating output from the surface runoff (module 3) and the baseflow (module 2) for each tributary result in the full natural flow. The sum of all three tributaries creates the flow in the main stream, the Jordan River.

4.2.3 Results and discussion

The full model (modules 0, 1, 2 and 3) was tested by reconstruction of both the surface and baseflow during a continuous period from 1 January 1986 to 30 September 2000. It was then verified by applying the calibrated parameters to the periods 1 January 1970 to 31 December 1985, and 1 October 2000 to 30 September 2006.

Beyond the successful calibration (Rimmer and Salingar 2006), several important practical results were identified during this study:

4.2.3.1 Model simultaneously the mass balances of the three main UCJR sources

The comprehensive model approach allowed us to calculate systematic mass balance. It was based on setting the entire catchment area as $A = 783$ km^2. Annual average precipitation on the entire Hermon region was calculated as ~958 mm. The entire annual precipitation is equivalent to 783 km^2, multiplied by 0.958 m of rainfall, which results in 750 million m^3 (Mm^3). Real evaporation in the model was calculated as 226 mm (~177 Mm^3); the calibrated surface flow was only 90 mm (70 Mm^3); the calculated downward flux includes 275 mm (215 Mm^3) from Darcian slow flow and 367 mm (287 Mm^3) from preferential flow, which sums to 502 Mm^3 according to the model, and 393 Mm^3 according to the measured streamflow in the Israeli area. The ~109 Mm^3 difference is probably attributable to the east part of Mt Hermon, such as the Beit Jinn and Sabarani springs in Syria, as was suggested by previous studies (Gur *et al*. 2003, and others).

4.2.3.2 Nature of flow of the Dan Spring

Usually when the recession of a spring flow is calculated using a simple linear reservoir model, the discharge Q during the dry season follows an exponential decay of the type:

$$Q = Q_0 \exp (-t/K) \tag{1}$$

where K stands for the recession constant. Previous publications (see Rimmer and Salingar 2006 for more details) concluded that the K parameter of the Dan Spring was two times larger than the recession constant that we found in this model (~600 compared to ~300 days respectively). It means that while according to previous analysis the Dan Spring may dry up only after five sequential "dry" years, according to HYMKE it would take less than three sequential "dry" years. Past overestimation of the K mislead water policy makers to believe that the discharge of the Dan Spring is far more stable than it really is. Although this finding is not completely new, the development of the HYMKE model verified it, with its physical rationale.

4.2.3.3 Predictions of climate change scenarios

HYMKE may be developed further to predict long-term stream flow, given the predicted changes in characteristics of future rainfall and evaporation. An example of "predicted" stream flow under reduction of 20 percent in daily rainfall, and increase of evaporation by 20 percent (Figure 4.4), shows that in the Dan Spring we expect a constant daily reduction of ~300,000 m^3, which is equivalent to 110 million m^3 annually – nearly 43 percent of the annual spring discharge. Figure 4.5 illustrates the average monthly flow in the Jordan River, separated into base and surface flows, under 100 percent, 90 percent, 80 percent, 70 percent, and 60 percent of the current annual rainfall amounts on Mt Hermon. An obvious

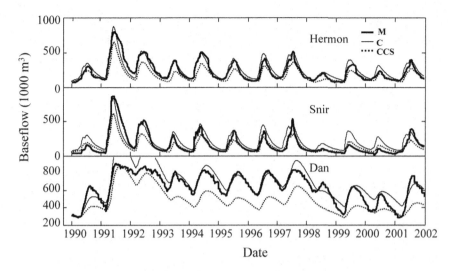

Figure 4.4 The baseflow of the Mt Hermon tributaries from separation analysis (M) for the years 1990 to 2002, compared with the baseflow calculated by HYMKE for the current situation (C), and under climate change scenario (CCS), in which rainfall was reduced by 20 percent and evaporation increased by 20 percent.

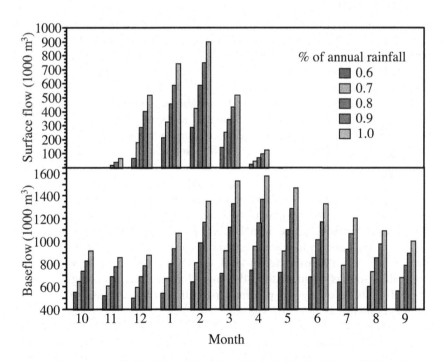

Figure 4.5 Average daily baseflow and surface flow in the Jordan River, calculated by HYMKE for five scenarios, in which rainfall was 100 percent, 90 percent, 80 percent, 70 percent, and 60 percent of the current situation.

outcome of this prediction is the clear reduction of the surface flow component to much lower percentages than the reduction of the rainfall. This component is responsible for the fast recharge of Lake Kinneret during the winter months and, therefore, we expect much lower annual recharge than the relative reduction in rainfall. Another result, which was verified by the model, is a delay in the occurrence of high recharge events for base and surface flows.

The model can be further developed and adapted to include more predictions, under various climate change scenarios from climatic models.

Recently, the Israeli Hydrological Service (IHS), decided to use HYMKE as a decision-making tool, which will be operated parallel to other, statistically-based models. HYMKE is now under continuous process of improvements.

4.3 Salinity of Lake Kinneret

4.3.1 Description of the problem

An obvious outcome of the expected reduction of water inflows to Lake Kinneret is the increased salinity of the lake. In this section we present a model that efficiently predicts this effect, together with the influences of other components of the hydrological system (water outflows, evaporation, solute inflows, lake level).

The salinity of Lake Kinneret (190–280 mgCl L^{-1}) is significantly higher than the salinity of the Jordan River, and other surface streams that flow into the lake (~30 mgCl L^{-1}). The lake water is pumped by the national water carrier to the coastal area of Israel, where it is used for drinking, irrigation and reuse in the populated areas above the coastal aquifer. Its extensive usage for agricultural irrigation, both as original Lake Kinneret water and as reused water, poses a threat to the future sustainability of the groundwater and agricultural soils in the coastal areas. The salinity of the reused water from the Lake Kinneret source may increase to ~400 mgCl L^{-1} – a rather problematic concentration for most irrigated crops. Limiting the Lake Kinneret water salinity is therefore of high national interest.

The salinity of the lake is derived from the mixture of fresh stream water from the Jordan River and other tributaries, and saline groundwater that emerges through springs, mostly along the northwest coast of the lake (Tabgha, Fuliya and Tiberias springs, Figure 4.1d). Some of these springs emerge inside the lake (off-shore springs) and some come from the shore around the lake (on-shore springs). Most of the on-shore springs are diverted to the canal of the saline water carrier (SWC, Figure 4.1d). Constructed in 1964, the SWC diverts the northwestern on-shore saline springs down south to the lower Jordan River, reducing the lake's potential solute inflow by ~30 percent. Originally, the solute mass inflow to the lake was evaluated as ~160×10⁶ kg×year⁻¹ by several researchers (Benoualid and Ben-Zvi 1981; Simon and Mero 1992; and Rimmer 1996). However, after the operation of the national water carrier and the diversion of ~55×10⁶ kg×year⁻¹, the average annual solute inflow reduced to ~105×10⁶ kg×year⁻¹. Currently, the main contribution to the solute mass in the lake comes from the off-shore, unmonitored springs (Kolodny *et al.* 1999; Dror *et al.* 1999), which contribute only 10 percent of the water inflows but nearly 90 percent of solute inflow to the lake (Rimmer and Gal 2003).

4.3.2 The Lake Kinneret salinity model

This section describes a systematic method with regard to the Lake Kinneret water and solute balances. The system contributes quantitative estimation of the salinity and helps in making decisions regarding the management of water in Lake Kinneret and in the surrounding aquifers.

Four long-term changes may cause simultaneously significant increase or decrease of salinity in Lake Kinneret. They are solute inflows to the lake; the quantity of freshwater inflows from the Jordan River and other streams from the Lake Kinneret direct watershed; the quantity of water pumped and released from the lake; and evaporation.

In the past, several models were used to support decisions regarding the operation of the lake as a water resource. Mero developed in the late 1970s a model for the effect of operational aspects, such as pumping and diversion of the saline spring, on the salinity of the lake (Mero and Simon 1992). Benoualid and Ben-Zvi (1981) developed a model that connected the solute inflow to the semi-annual water discharge and rainfall. Assouline *et al.* (1994) suggested a monthly-based model for the same purpose, and Berger (2000) further developed Assouline's model into a general operational model for the Lake Kinneret system. All of the proposed models were based on statistical analysis of monthly inflows and outflows to and from the lake, and monthly solute discharge from the saline spring's system, and therefore were rather complicated to operate.

The system approach model, proposed by Rimmer (2003) and Rimmer *et al.* (2006) is a lake-wide model for the salinization mechanism, based on the main components of the water and solute balance. However, unlike previous statistical models, it proposes that, with the appropriate assumptions, the Lake Kinneret salinization mechanism can be described by a simple physically based model (complete mixing Figure 4.6) and therefore can be solved analytically. The solution allows us to easily examine the influence of each component of the solute balance on the expected salinity changes.

The objective of this model was to predict long-term changes of chloride concentration in Lake Kinneret. To that end, the theoretical complete mixing mechanism was tested against special cases of long-term salinity changes in Lake Kinneret in the past (Rimmer 2003), and then was used to predict the long-term influence of future climate change scenarios or operation policies on lake salinity. The model includes both a deterministic component, which results in the "exact prediction" under a certain input, and a stochastic component, which shows the possible range of the prediction.

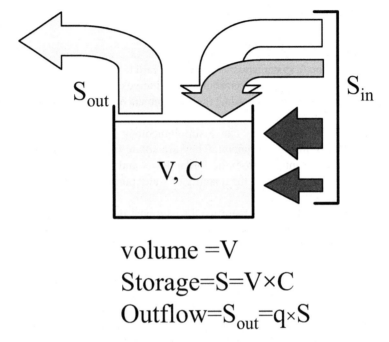

volume =V

Storage=S=V×C

Outflow=S$_{out}$=q×S

Figure 4.6 The complete mixing concept: C the salinity of the lake (ppm Cl⁻), V volume
(Mm³), S the solute mass in the lake (kg), S$_{in}$ and S$_{out}$ the inflow (tributaries,
springs) and outflow (pumping and water release) of solute, respectively
(kg × year⁻¹).

4.3.3 Description of the model

The theoretical development of the complete mixing model consists of a simple
differential equation for the mass of an inert solute in the lake, as was described
in detail by Rimmer (2003):

$$\frac{dS(t)}{dt} + q(t)S(t) = S_{in}(t) \quad \text{S.T.: } S\big|_{t=0} = S_0$$

$$q(t) = \frac{Q_{out}(t)}{V(t)} \quad ; \quad S_{in}(t) = Q_{in}(t)\overline{C}_{in}(t)$$

(2)

In this equation $S = C_{lake} V$ the solute mass in the lake (kg) is represented by
multiplying the average solute concentration in the lake C_{lake} (ppm) by the lake
volume V (Mm³); "t" represents a time unit (year), Q_{in} is the inflow discharge
(Mm³×year⁻¹) (including direct rainfall), Q_{out} is the outflows from the lake
(Mm³×year⁻¹), and S_0 is the initial mass of solute in the lake (kg) at t=0; q(t)
represents the leaching ratio, the ratio of outflows to lake volume, which is the
reciprocal of momentary water residence time (Wetzel 1983), and $S_{in}(t)$ stands for
variations of annual solutes inflow in time. The averaged solute concentration of

the incoming solute flux $\overline{C}_{in}$ (ppm) is an integrated value of all solute contributors from the lake exterior, which consists of the lake floor (streams, on and offshore springs) and the water surface (direct rainfall and fallout).

Equation (2) can be solved analytically. The solution shows that the changes of solute mass in the lake are the result of integration in time and space of the water, and solute inflows, outflows, lake volume, and evaporation. Moreover, the solution of Equation (2) assumed that all variables were deterministic values for a given period. However, in the real world, water and solute inflows, as well as evaporation and lake level, may change randomly from one year to another. These fluctuations are subject to natural conditions, such as various seasonal rainfall amounts, lake volume oscillations, and various annual outflows. Other deviations from deterministic values are subject to measurement errors. It was therefore proposed that the variables in Equation (2) are better represented by a statistical distribution rather than by a single average value. To that end, an uncertainty component was added to each variable of the model, in order to estimate not only the expected long-term changes in lake salinity, but also the possible ranges of this predicted change.

4.3.4 Results and discussion

In order to produce and verify this prediction tool, the history of Lake Kinneret salinity was reviewed and the model was verified by comparison of "reconstructed" salinity results with the measured historical data (Rimmer 2003). Here, we exemplify the complete mixing model performance over the past years by comparing the calculated results of the model with the changes of solute mass from 1964 to 2005 (Figure 4.7). During this period, the solute mass of the lake decreased from an average of $1,330 \times 10^6$ kg in 1964 to 875×10^6 kg by the end of the 1980s (the salinity dropped from ~350 to ~210 ppm Cl), and then increased to ~950×10^6 kg. With the complete mixing model, we identified two dominant, long-term procedures that caused the changes of the solute mass simultaneously. The most important cause was the operation of the saline water carrier during January 1965 which caused a step reduction in solute inflows from ~160×10^6 to ~105×10^6 kg year^{-1}. However, it is the second procedure – the influence of the ongoing reduction in available water – which is more important for future predictions. Analysis of long-term annual inflows shows that available water in Lake Kinneret, which was ~550 Mm^3 during the 1960s, is currently reduced to ~450 Mm^3 (Figure 4.7). This reduction resulted in a change of the leaching ratio q (Equation 2) from ~0.15 to ~0.12 (Figure 4.7) and a significant increase in salinity during the last 20 years.

Figure 4.8 illustrates a scenario that maintains the same trend of water inflow reduction as that which occurred over the last 40 years, but maintains the same amount of solute inflows and evaporation. The results demonstrate that under these conditions the salinity of Lake Kinneret will increase significantly during the next few decades. The addition of the stochastic component was calculated, and the possible deviations from the average solution are also illustrated.

In Figure 4.9, we tested seven scenarios of various quantities of available water, together with changes in solute inflows. The results are predictions of the expected

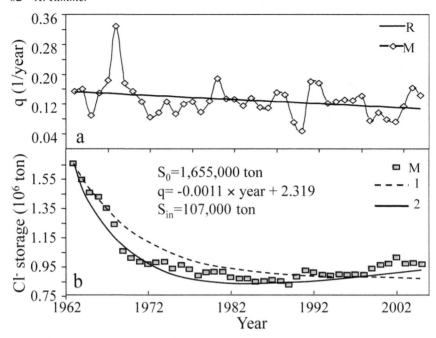

Figure 4.7 a. Gradual linear decrease in past water inflows to Lake Kinneret expressed
by linear decrease of q (R-linear regression, M-measured). b. The actual
salinity of the lake on 1 October for each year, compared to the model results
of two cases using the CM model: 1. Step reduction of solute inflow in 1964,
with constant water inflow/outflow, and 2. Step reduction of solute inflow in
1964, together with linear reduction of inflow/outflow.

Lake Kinneret salinity for the next 40 years. While the solute inflow will reduce,
the lake salinity may increase significantly as a result of much lower freshwater
inflows.

The proposed system brings into consideration the effects of human intervention.
Several practices for artificial reduction of Lake Kinneret salinity are under
consideration. Each practice has its own cost, as well as its predicted effect on the
lake salinity. The advantage of the proposed system analysis is that it can bring into
account simultaneously several variables that effect lake salinity. For example, we
may employ an expensive practice that theoretically will reduce the solute inflows
to the lake by five percent. However, if at the same time fresh water inflows from
the upper catchments of the Jordan River will be reduced by 20 percent, the effect of
this practice will vanish quickly and we may not even be able to notice it. The result
of this understanding leads to three current policy implications. The first of these
is that activity to reduce Lake Kinneret salinity alone is insufficient. It must have
another beneficial purpose, like additional freshwater pumps from the contributing
aquifers. The second is that three wells were dug to the upstream aquifers, and the
monitoring system of Lake Kinneret salinity was farther developed to include them.

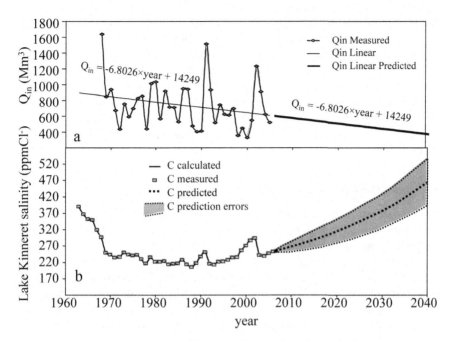

Figure 4.8 a. Prediction of inflows reduction, assuming the same trend as during the last 40 years. b. Predictions of future lake salinity, including the stochastic component, if the same reduction of inflows continues, while all the other conditions remain constant.

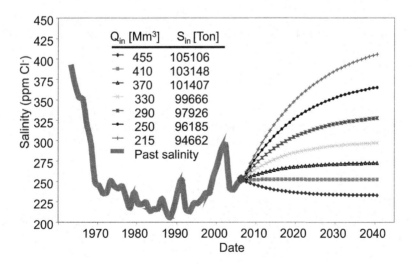

Figure 4.9 Seven scenarios of lake salinity changes as a result of various amounts of available water, together with changes in solute inflows.

The third is that the reduction of inflows to Lake Kinneret is considered today as a water quality problem, rather than "just" a quantity problem.

The above complete mixing approach was developed into a user-friendly decision support system (DSS) for the Israeli Hydrological Service. It includes long-term predictions of Lake Kinneret salinity for a variety of problems, such as reduced inflows and/or outflows, changes in evaporation, changes of solute inflows, changes of lake volume, and more. All deterministic calculations were escorted with the stochastic approach results; bringing a degree of certainty into the predictions.

4.4 Conclusion and policy implications

The models that were introduced in this chapter are part of a growing effort to develop analytical tools in order to construct a comprehensive Decision Support System to manage the water sources in the upper catchments of the Jordan River and Lake Kinneret. The two models were constructed separately as a result of the specific needs of the water management authorities. Each model was based on a different time scale, was constructed according to certain assumptions, and verified according to its own datasets. Moreover, these two are only part of a group of models that operated separately to improve water management in the region. However, both models are used to predict the hydrological situation in the Lake Kinneret watershed and, as such, they should be further developed to integrate both the rainfall-streamflow of the Jordan River sources, and the salinization mechanism of Lake Kinneret.

Figures 4.4, 4.5 and 4.9 provide a simple example of how each model may be integrated with others, as well as ways in which one model can solve problems by using the output of another model. Given a certain long-term climate scenario, the first model (HYMKE) should be used to predict the future daily flows into the Jordan River (see example in Figure 4.4). The monthly and annual predicted flows can then be summarized, and together with the predicted changes of annual evaporation, may serve as an input to the second model (complete mixing in Lake Kinneret), which predicts future changes of Lake Kinneret salinity (as shown in Figure 4.9).

The process of integrating several models in the Lake Kinneret catchments is currently in its embryonic stage, but it will certainly gain momentum in the near future, due to the severe water availability and salinity problems expected in the future.

Acknowledgment

This research was partly supported by GLOWA – Jordan River Project, funded by the German Ministry of Science and Education (BMBF), in collaboration with the Israeli Ministry of Science and Technology (MOST).

References

Assouline, S., Shaw M., and Rom M. (1994) *Modeling the solute and water components in Lake Kinneret system.* Watershed Unit, Mekorot, Sapir Site, Israel. (in Hebrew).

Benoualid S. and Ben-Zvi, A. (1981) *A model to predict the Lake Kinneret salinization and the solutes reservoir.* Jeruasalem: Israel Hydrological Service report (1981/5) (in Hebrew).

Berger, D. (2000) *Operational model for the Lake Kinneret system.* Watershed Unit, Mekorot, Sapir Site, Israel (in Hebrew).

Berger, D. (2001) *Estimating the natural flow in the upper catchment of the Jordan River.* Watershed Unit, Mekorot, Sapir Site, Israel (in Hebrew).

Dror, G., Ronen, D., Stiller, M. and Nishri, A. (1999) Cl/Br ratios of Lake Kinneret, pore water and associated springs. *Journal of Hydrology,* 225: 130–139.

Gilad, D. and Bonne, J. (1990) Snowmelt of Mt Hermon and its contribution to the sources of the Jordan River. *Journal of Hydrology,* 114: 1–15.

Gur, D., Bar-Matthews, M. and Sass, E. (2003) Hydrochemistry of the main Jordan River sources: Dan, Banias, and Kezinim springs, north Hula Valley, Israel. *Israel Journal of Earth Sciences,* 52: 155–178.

Jeannin, P-Y. and Grasso, D. A. (1997) Permeability and hydrodynamic behavior of karstic environment. In G. Gunay and A. I. Johnson (eds) *Karst waters environmental impact.* Rotterdam: A.A. Balkema, pp. 335–342.

Kessler, A. (1999) *Hydrologic model of Dan Spring monthly flow using a conic linear reservoir.* Submitted to the Israeli Water Commission (in Hebrew).

Kolodny, Y. *et al.* (1999) Chemical tracing of salinity sources in Lake Kinneret (the Sea of Galilee, Israel). *Limnology and Oceanography,* 44: 1035–1044.

Kunstmann, H., Suppan, P., Heckl, A. and Rimmer, A. (2007) *Quantification and Reduction of Predictive Uncertainty for Sustainable Water Resources Management* (Proceedings of Symposium HS2004 at IUGG2007, Perugia, July 2007). IAHS Publ. 313.

Mero, F. (1969) An approach to daily hydro-meteorological water balance computations for surface and groundwater basins, *Proc. ITC-UNESCO Seminar for Integrated River Basin Development,* Delft: ITC-UNESCO.

Mero, F. and Simon, E. (1992) The simulation of chloride inflows into Lake Kinneret. *Journal of Hydrology,* 138: 345–360.

Rimmer, A. (1996) The salinity of Lake Kinneret: estimation of the un-measured saline springs inflow characteristics. Watershed Unit, Mekorot, Sapir Site, Israel (in Hebrew).

Rimmer, A. (2003) The mechanism of Lake Kinneret salinization as a linear reservoir. *Journal of Hydrology,* 28: 177–190.

Rimmer, A. and Gal, G. (2003) The saline springs in the solute and water balance of Lake Kinneret, Israel. *Journal of Hydrology,* 284: 228–243.

Rimmer A. and Salingar, Y. (2005) *Developing a dynamic river basin model for contaminants transport in the UCJR using GIS. Final researches report.* Submitted to BMBF-MOS Cooperation in environmental research-GLOWA. IOLR report T22/2005.

Rimmer A. and Salingar, Y. (2006) Modelling precipitation-streamflow processes in Karst basin: the case of the Jordan River sources, Israel. *Journal of Hydrology,* 331: 524–542.

Rimmer, A., Boger, M., Aota, Y. and Kumagai, M. (2006) A lake as a natural integrator of linear processes: application to Lake Kinneret (Israel) and Lake Biwa (Japan). *Journal of Hydrology,* 319: 163–175.

Simon, E. and Mero, F. (1992) The salinization mechanism of Lake Kinneret. *Journal of Hydrology,* 138: 327–343.

Simon, E., Ben Zvi, A., Atzmon, B. and Veber Y. (1978) *Synthetic timeseries of flows in the upper catchment of the Jordan River.* Tahal publication # 01/78/09.

Simpson, B., and Carmi, I. (1983) The hydrology of the Jordan tributaries (Israel). Hydrographic and isotopic investigation. *Journal of Hydrology,* 62: 225–242.

Wetzel, R. G. (1983) *Limnology.* Fort-Worth: Saunders College Publishing.

5   Combined impacts of development and climate change on the Rhône River (Switzerland and France)

Jean-Paul Bravard

Most of the total discharge of the Rhône River at the mouth ($1700 \, m^3.s^{-1}$) originates in the Alps. Climatic models anticipate a decrease of total discharge, a marked decrease of summer discharge, an increase in winter discharge, and a decrease in ice and snow cover, inducing a change in the river flow regime. However, the high level of economic development in the entire watershed has triggered complex impacts on river and lake hydrosystems. These already registered changes foreshadow predicted changes and provide insights into the future of aquatic ecosystems that will suffer the impacts of warmer temperatures. An attempt was made to summarize the possible impacts on the future uses of water. Hydro and thermal power will be affected by changes in hydrological regime and reduction in the cooling capacity of the Rhône River. Also, tourism will experience a reduction of snow cover in winter; agriculture, a reduction of water availability in summer; human health will face threats of new kinds of parasites; and last, the level of flood risks may increase in valley bottoms following deposition of sediments and increased water levels.

5.1 Introduction

During the last 10 years, many detailed studies and general reports (IPCC 2002; Deneux 2002; Redaud *et al*. 2002; Pont 2003; Husting 2005; OcCC 2003) have been devoted to the impacts of predicted climate change in Europe, and notably in the Alps, and on the Rhône River in particular. These reports deal mostly with probable changes in the hydrological regime of the Upper Rhône River in Switzerland, and with the hydrological and ecological changes of the Rhône River downstream of Geneva. This chapter will present a summary of the main results, which combine past, present, and future changes of natural components of hydrosystems, as well as the complex interactions of natural- and human-induced changes. The approach will take the complete hydrosystem into account, from upland ecosystems down to the delta of the Rhône, with some insight into the tributaries. We follow the proposal made by Leblois and Grésillon (2005) to draw a distinction between "effects" and "impacts." "Effects" are changes, or direct consequences of climate change on hydrosystems, while "impacts" are consequences of the latter on human uses of water or instream uses of water (ecological requirements).

While much research has been done on river discharge, few studies have dealt with water as a resource, subject to locally intensive uses and sensitivity to climate change.

5.2 Studied area and methods

5.2.1 The Rhône River basin

The Rhône river watershed covers a surface area of 98 000 km², including 10 000 km² in Switzerland (Figure 5.1). The Swiss Rhône in the county of Valais

1. Lake Geneva
2. Annecy Lake
3. Bourget Lake
4. Portes Pass
5. Porte de Sax
6. Bugey
7. Saint-Alban
8. Tricastin
9. Mauvoisin
10. Rousset
11. Morzine
12. Serre-Ponçon dam
13. Etang de Berre
14. Camargue
15. Grand Rhône
16. Petit Rhône
17. Saint Gervais
18. La Clapière

Figure 5.1 Location of place names in the watershed of the Rhône River.

is affected by mountain climate. Its natural regime is characterised by low winter discharge due to snow retention, and high spring and summer discharges due to melting of the snow and ice. Like other subalpine lakes, Lake Geneva smoothes flood peaks downstream, similarly to Lake Annecy for the Fier River, and Lake Bourget for the Rhône. The tributaries of the Rhône, between Geneva and Lyon (notably the Arve, Fier, Guiers and Ain rivers), drain lower ranges but preserve the snow-melt regime, while the glacial influence is strongly attenuated. The Saône River, which joins the Rhône in Lyon, has a typically oceanic regime with high discharge during the cold season and low discharge during the warm season, due to evapotranspiration. As a consequence, downstream of Lyon, the mountain regime, "compensated" by tributaries of different origins (oceanic, Mediterranean), is more regular (Pardé 1925). Flowing from the Alps, the left bank tributaries regenerate the snow-melt influence, while right bank tributaries and the Durance deliver high discharges during the fall and the spring, under Mediterranean climate influence. At Beaucaire, the regime is characterized by low flow from September to November, along with risks of marked low flow.

5.2.2 Observed climate and hydrological change since the nineteenth century

Climate is widely considered to have changed since the late nineteenth century, particularly during the last decades. Climate change may have affected both temperatures and precipitation. Change in temperature is not documented before the mid-twentieth century in the hydrosystem of the Rhône. Temperature of large subalpine lakes, such as Lake Geneva, has been proved to have increased by 1°C since the 1960s.

Concerning river discharge, statistical tests applied to eight gauging stations of the Rhône River downstream of Geneva demonstrated that hydrology is stationary. However, two types of ruptures are apparent: one locally in 1891, due to artificial developments at the outlet of Lake Geneva; and a second one at the end of the 1970s, with the occurrence of wet decades throughout the basin, following a period (1940–1975) of quiet hydrology. A new cycle, rich in strong floods, has occurred in recent years, similar to the late nineteenth century period, but no effects of global change have been detected yet (Sauquet and Haond 2003). Moreover, changes in hydrosystems incorporate human-induced changes, particularly in highly developed watersheds. Indeed, the control of upland hydrology has been a long-lasting process in the Alps, changing the hydrology of rivers. Also, thermal plants have been located along the Rhône River to benefit from cooling by its waters, thereby inducing an increase of water temperatures with marked consequences on aquatic ecosystems.

5.2.3 Modeling the changes

The assessment of climatic change has been traditionally based on General Circulation Models (GCM) which typically have a resolution of 2.5° latitude and 3.75° longitude. In the watershed of the Rhône, the scenarios concerning precipitation and temperatures of the General Circulation Model (IPCC 1992 and 2002) has been used. It projects that expected climate warming will result in higher precipitation in winter, higher rates of evaporation and decreased precipitation in summer and during the fall. Two scenarios have been tested:

- B2: average temperature would increase by 2–2.5°C in one century
- A2: average temperature would increase by 3–3.5°C

To complement the predictions from preceding programs, the ECLAT-2 project (1998–2001), funded by the Climate and Environmental Program of the DG12 of the European Commission (EC) was launched. Computations were made in the Swiss Alps, using a high-resolution model (20 km × 20 km). Downscaling techniques were applied to the Rhône basin (Noilhan *et al.* 2000), using selected GCM ouputs in the basin for doubled CO_2 concentration conditions. These studies explored the sensitivity of the production functions of the hydrological model to anomalies in precipitation and temperatures for selected sub-basins during the period 1981–1985. The ECLAT-2 program provided the first evaluation of predictable climate change effects in the basin in different components of the water budget, such as runoff, and snow and soil moisture availability for the interface between soil and atmosphere. It was based on the GEWEX-Rhône program, which used the macroscale Coupled ISBA MODCOU (CIM) model for the 1981–98 time series. This model was calibrated with present-day conditions using atmospheric forcing, land surface types, soil freezing, surface runoff, evapotranspiration, river flow series and snow depth in the Alps. The model was run over 15 years for spatial resolutions ranging from 1 to 8 kilometers. Indeed, it was recognized that the model could be used for testing the GCM anomalies (Habets *et al.* 1999; Etchevers *et al.* 2001). Research was continued through the programme GICC-Rhône (1999–2004), with the hypothesis of a doubling of CO_2 concentrations in 2050 (Leblois and Grésillon 2005).

5.3 Predicted changes of the natural components of the hydrological cycle

5.3.1 Climatic change

5.3.1.1 Present and predicted changes in air temperature

During the twentieth century, the average temperature of the globe increased by 0.6 +/–2°C (IPCC 2002). The Alps experienced a warming of temperatures of between 1° and 2°C. However, more than 1°C out of the strong recent increase, which occurred since 1990 (along with a decrease in precipitation), could be related to positive values of the NAO (North Atlantic Oscillation, a measure of the intensity of westerly flow and associated storm tracks) according to Beniston and Jungo (2002). These authors propose that warming would have been weaker without the

NAO effect and suggest that the performance of models should be improved in simulating NAO decadal-scale variability.

During the twenty-first century, global temperature could increase by 1.4 to 5.8°C (IPCC 2002 and 2007). The GICC-Rhône study predicts an average yearly increase of 2.5°C and an increase in July of 4°C, for the doubling of CO_2 concentration.

5.3.1.2 Changes in precipitation

According to GIEC models applied to France, with the B2 scenario precipitation would increase in the winter, while it would be reduced by 5 to 25 percent in the summer. According to the A2 scenario, summer droughts would be more severe, with a decrease of 20 to 35 percent in summer rainfall. In the Swiss Alps, Beniston (2003) has shown that "milder winters are associated with higher precipitation levels than cold winters, but with more solid precipitations at elevations exceeding 1700–2000 m above sea-level, and more liquid precipitations below." With expected climate warming, the average predicted precipitation would not change, but summer precipitation should decrease, while winter precipitation would increase (Figure 5.2a). Modeling of winter storms suggests a stronger frequency of southern flows from the Mediterranean and heavy storms (Beniston 2004). Also, periods of drought could be more frequent, as could periods of heavy rainfall. Higher snowfalls at high altitudes would not compensate for increased ice melting. In France, the ECLAT-2 program predicted a minimum of precipitations in summer months (from –45 percent to +8 percent), and increased precipitations in winter of up to 5 to 30 percent.

The changes associated with an increase in global temperature are rendered more

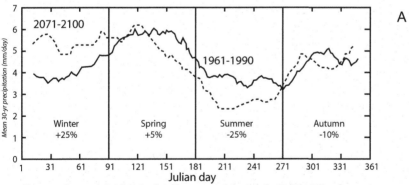

Changes in precipitation in the Alps, averaged over the 1961-1990 reference period (solid line) and the 2071-2100 future simulated period (dotted line). Figures refer to the shifts in precipitation amounts by season, in %.

Figure 5.2a Observed and predicted precipitation changes in the Swiss Alps (after Beniston 2005, modified).

complex by interactions with the NAO shifts. Indeed, the amounts of precipitation are influenced by the NAO. Beniston *et al.* (1997) correlated thick snow cover and long duration in the Swiss Alps with a high NAO index because during these episodes winter temperatures shift toward higher values. The frequency of temperatures exceeding the freezing point should double above 1000 metres, thus enhancing the potential for early snowmelt.

5.3.1.3 Changes in the depth and duration of snow cover

The depth of snow cover is influenced by temperature. At Portes Pass (Northern French Alps, alt. 1320 m), snow depth in February has decreased during the last 40 years. The strong reduction in the last 10 years is "probably related to climate warming" (Etchevers and Martin 2002). A reduction of snow cover by three to four weeks was observed in the Swiss Alps during the late 1980s and the early 1990s. An average increase in temperature of 4°C, forecast by several regional models for this area of Europe, would reduce the volume of snow by approximately 50 percent. For every degree Celsius increase in temperature, the snow line will rise by about 150 metres, so regions in which snowfall is the current norm will increasingly experience precipitation in the form of rain (Beniston 1997). According to the scenario of Météo-France (Martin and Durand 1998), assuming an increase in temperature of 1.8°C at an elevation of 1500 metres, the average length of snow cover, presently between 160 and 180 days in the Northern French Alps, could decrease to 125 to 135 days. In the Southern Alps, it could decrease from the present 100 to 130 days to 55 to 80 days a year. This means one month less of snow cover than occurs today (SAFRAN-CROCUS snow model, in French ARPEGE GCM – Equipe Climate Modelling and Global Change). According to the GICC-Rhône study, the depth of snow may be reduced by 50 percent at low altitudes, but is less affected at higher altitudes (1800–2000 m). In the different scenarios, the areas covered by snow would decrease by 25 to 40 percent (Etchevers and Martin 2002; Lebois and Grésillon 2005).

As a result of climate change, glaciers have already retreated because they stand close to the freezing point. Haeberli (1994) considers that past and present fluctuations of glaciers and permafrost are proofs of past and present climate changes through the changes in energy balance. Due to the greenhouse effect, the velocity of observed changes exceeds the changes monitored during the Holocene. Haeberli (1995) and Haeberli and Beniston (1998) have shown that the glaciers of the European Alps have lost about 30 to 50 percent of their surface and about half of their volume. According to these authors, about 30 to 50 percent of existing mountain glacier mass could disappear by 2100 if global warming scenarios in the range of 2–4°C indeed occur. With an upward shift of 200–300 meters in the altitude of the line of equilibrium, the reduction in ice thickness could reach 1–2 meters per year (Maisch 2000). The sensitivity of the line of equilibrium to temperature is between 60 and 120 m/°C, according to different authors (Green *et al.* 1999; Maisch 2000; Vincent 2002). According to Vincent (2002), glaciers of the French Alps retreated during two periods:

- from 1942 to 1953, due to low winter snow falls and to a high rate of retreat in summer
- from 1982 to 1999, due to a high level of summer melting (from 1.9 metres to 2.8 metres at 2800 metres elevation). This is due to a strong increase of the energy balance.

The difference in mass balance between 1800–50 and 197–80 stands between 0.50 and 1.00 metres in water equivalent for the glaciers of the French Alps (Vincent 2002). Six *et al.* (2002) proposed that the mass balance of Alpine glaciers could be negatively correlated to the oscillations of the NAO index for periods of warm temperature and low precipitation.

5.3.2 Present and predicted changes of discharge

5.3.2.1 Vegetation, soils and water balance in mountain ecosystems

Changes in direct water consumption by existing vegetation will occur. They will be due to changes in forest cover and to changes in the amount of evapotranspiration. If an increase in water consumption can be predicted, then a decrease of river flow is logical. At the basin scale, the GICC study predicts that the pattern and the spatial extension of natural vegetation would not change significantly, so hydrology would not be affected by this parameter. However, in the long term, vegetation would colonize the upper slopes of the Alps. In the Southern regions, the decrease of water content in soils and vegetation would increase the stress on vegetation, induce a higher sensitivity to fires during the driest periods of the year, and increase exposure to soil erosion (IPCC 2002). For instance, the 2003 summer drought provoked several fires in the Vercors, a wet massif of the Northern Prealps, which had not experienced any fire in the previous 30 years at least.

5.3.2.2 River discharges

The statistical study of river discharges in France did not detect any significant change in the number and the intensity of floods since the mid-twentieth century Also, it is impossible to confirm any change in low discharges, mostly because of heavy human impacts on rivers (Lubès-Niel and Giraud 2003). However, in the mid-twenty-first century, the situation could be different, especially concerning the regimes of mountain rivers. Indeed, the specific annual discharge of mountain rivers is higher than the specific discharge of extended watersheds including lowland areas. This results from higher precipitation, low evaporation rates, and by conditions favoring runoff. Being strongly influenced by water accumulation in the form of snow and ice, the hydrological regime results in a pronounced annual cycle of discharge (Horton *et al.* 2005). The recent increase in temperatures may have had some consequences on river regimes.

In Switzerland, shifts in snow-pack duration and amount should be crucial factors in water availability for runoff, according to Beniston (2003). The increase in winter temperatures will have clear consequences on the beginning of snowmelt and on the reduction of flow during the spring at low altitudes and on summer flow at the highest altitudes. The reduction of snow cover below 1000 m will reduce runoff. These shifts will affect river regimes with higher winter discharges (Figure 5.2b). However, increased evaporation in winter may partly reduce runoff and river discharge. Climate warming will increase the average discharge of rivers flowing from glaciers at first during the period of retreat, but then will decrease summer discharge, as rivers will progressively lose their glacial-type hydrological regime. A detailed study has been performed on the potential impacts of climate change on the runoff regimes of 11 small catchments having glacier surfaces between 0 and 50 percent, at altitudes ranging between 1340 and 2940 metres, under different hydrological regimes (Horton *et al.* 2005; Schaeffli, 2005). Predictions were developed for a scenario of +1°C (expected for 2020–49) and two scenarios considering two increased greenhouse gas emissions (period 2070–99: + 2.4 to +2.8 °C and +3.0 to +3.6°C, with rates higher in summer than for the average). The following effects are expected for the +1°C scenario:

• a decrease of annual precipitation;
• an increase of winter precipitation, with the risk of higher flood peaks;
• a decrease of summer precipitation;
• a strong decrease of ice-covered areas, due to the strong increase of summer temperatures. The regimes will be mainly driven by snow-melt during the late twentieth century (Braun *et al.*, 2000; de Jong *et al.*, 2005; Schaefli, 2005; Zierl and Bugmann, 2005).

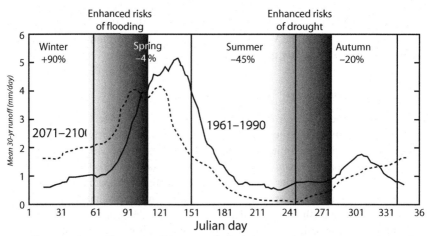

Changes in surface runoff in a typical alpine catchment area, such as the Rhône and the Rhine, averaged over the 1961–1990 reference period (solid line and the 2071–2100 future simulated period (dotted line). Figures refer to the shifts in runoff by season, in %.

Figure 5.2b Observed and predicted surface runoff changes in the Swiss Alps (after Beniston 2005, modified).

- a decrease in the amplitude of discharge;
- a significant decrease of annual discharge (5–15 percent for the +1°C scenario) due to the reduction of precipitation, the increase of evapotranspiration, the long-term decrease of glacier surface and discharge.

Horton *et al.* (2005) predicted "a significant decrease of the total annual discharge and a shift in the monthly maximum discharge to earlier periods of the year, due to the temperature increase and the resulting impacts on the snow-melt processes," while at lower altitudes "the influence of precipitations is more pronounced and the variability of the predicted climate change impact is mainly due to the large range of predicted regional precipitation change" (Figure 5.3).

In France, a statistical analysis of discharges at 140 gauging stations from 1975 to 1990 shows a reduction of snow-melt regimes to the benefit of "transitional" regimes and to a marked irregularity in the seasonality of regimes. With the warming of climate, minimal and maximal discharges will be observed more frequently than in present times during other periods of the year than it is presently expected (Krasovskaia *et al.* 2002). In others words, prediction will be more difficult and the authors recommend the adoption of a probabilistic approach. However, some specialists consider that discharge regimes have not changed enough to justify any forecast change in the policy of dam management (Lubiès-Niel and Giraud 2003; Duband 2007). The coupled ISBA MODCOU model was used in three sub-watersheds and on the entire Rhône basin for a selected warm year, then tested for the prediction of change (Noilhan *et al.* 2000; Etchevers *et al.* 2001; Etchevers and Martin 2002; Leblois 2002; Leblois and Grésillon 2005):

- In the Doubs basin, the snow-rain regime should shift to rain regime with an increase of discharge in December and January, and a decrease in spring, without a significant change of the total yearly discharge.
- In the Saône basin (Mâcon), the rain regime should remain the same, but discharges should decrease in summer.
- In the Isère basin (Northern Alps), the maximum should shift from April to March, the winter maximum increase, and the summer minimum decrease by 50 percent.
- In the Southern Alps, the simulated change forecasts an annual reduction of river discharge and of soil moisture, decreasing by as much as 30 percent below the present values. The reduction of snowfall and earlier snow melting (due to increased air temperature) should induce a decrease of the average snow depth by 50 percent and of the snow duration by more than one month. Snow pack at high altitude should be less affected because the average air temperature would remain below 0°C.

The GICC-Rhône program extended these conclusions drawn from sub-waterheds to the larger area of the French part of the Rhône basin (Leblois and Grésillon 2005):

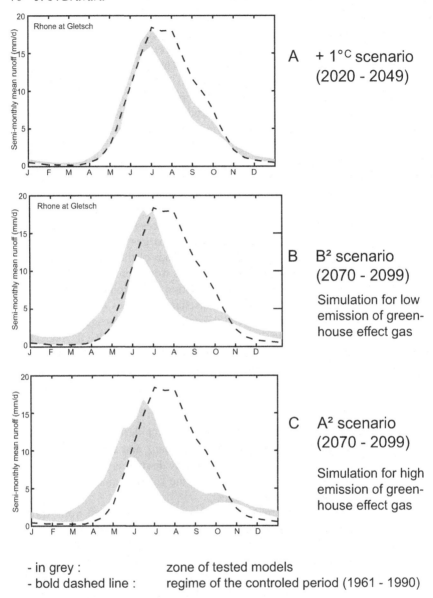

A   + 1°C scenario
     (2020 - 2049)

B   B² scenario
     (2070 - 2099)

     Simulation for low
     emission of green-
     house effect gas

C   A² scenario
     (2070 - 2099)

     Simulation for high
     emission of green-
     house effect gas

- in grey :   zone of tested models
- bold dashed line :   regime of the controled period (1961 - 1990)

Figure 5.3 Predicted changes of the hydrological regime of the upper Rhône at Gletsch,
           Switzerland (glacial discharge regime) (after Horton *et al.* 2005, modified).

- average yearly discharge and low flows decrease (from May to November),
  but high discharges increase. Low flows may be reduced by 40–50 percent
  near the outlet of the Rhône.
- spring flow related to snow melt decreases, since the warming of the climate

reduces snow depth and the duration of snow cover, and snow melt occurs one month earlier.

- the behavior of rivers in the winter depends on the different scenarios, but generally the increase of winter rainfall induces an increase of winter discharges.

5.3.2.3 Interactions between sediment supply and floods

Winter peak flows should interact with changes in sediment fluxes and, locally, with the hydraulic geometry of rivers, increasing waterborne risks. The increased elevation of permafrost, due to increased temperatures, will decrease the cohesiveness of soils and trigger mass movements (Haeberli *et al.* 1990). Extreme rainfall and increased average winter temperatures, and increased alternations of freezing and warming in weak rocks will increase landslides and rockfall hazards. However, recent catastrophic events occurred in the Mattertal (Valais region) in 1987, 1993, and 2000. In fact, recent concenrations of events may be explained by insufficient and short archival data, because paleo-environmental studies prove that the occurrence of events was similar in the past to what it is now (Stoffel *et al.* 2005).

These changes in slope processes will increase sediment inputs into rivers, will induce deposition and raise the level of floods, interacting with land occupation issues along valley floors. This trend could affect northern regions of the basin, as predicted by Beniston *et al.* (1995).

5.4 Observed current human impacts on the hydrological variables

5.4.1 Hydrological impacts of high-altitude reservoirs on the river regimes

The effects on river regimes of the ongoing natural warming of climate are rendered more complex by the impacts of the management of Lake Geneva and of upland reservoirs. The economic use of Lake Geneva has slowly changed since the late nineteenth century to the benefit of tourist activities predominantly, which require a constantly high water level during the warm season. The development of the tourist industry has imposed a reduction in the amplitude of vertical variations in Lake Geneva, inducing a reduction in flood control and difficulties for the optimal use of water at the outlet (Coulouvrenière dam). The Rhône, at the outlet of Lake Geneva, was initially developed to maximize the efficiency of energy production, through strong variations in the level of the lake, and then unpredictable variations downstream. However these variations have decreased with time, since the conservation volume of the lake, which peaked in the 1850s (810 hm^3), was reduced to meet the needs of tourism (i.e., stability) of the Vaud and Valais cantons (330–340 hm^3 after 1892). The artificial regime of the lake decreased the discharge of the Rhône from July to October (to preserve a capacity of storage in case of a summer drought) and increased it in the winter for the production of energy (Bravard 1986).

These changes interfered with the impacts of the development of energy production in the Alps. Indeed, the fast development of water storage in high-altitude reservoirs of upper Valais since the 1950s has impacted the filling up of Lake Geneva because more and more water was used in the inner Alps during the spring. This delays the filling up of Lake Geneva and affects the hydrology of the Rhône downstream of Geneva, high summer discharges being reduced when compared to natural discharges. At the end of the 1960s, the cumulated conservation storage was up to 1,400 hm³, i.e., three times the conservation storage of Lake Geneva (Bravard 1986). Vivian (1989) insisted on the impacts of Valais dams on the regime of the Rhône River. During the winter season, the production of high-priced energy in Valais increases river discharge (deep waters of reservoirs do not freeze and may be turbined). These impacts trigger a change in the regime of the Rhône River at Porte de Scex, which loses part of its mountain characteristics (ice-fed and snow-fed regime toward a regime artificially similar to a rain-fed regime). This change, which is still visible at Valence, allowed Vivian to state that the hydrological regime has become an oceanic type. Upstream of Lyon, low flow no longer occurs in winter. It occurs during the fall, while the winter high flow downstream of the confluences with the Ain and the Saône increases ("exaggeration of the natural regime"). Similar changes have been noticed in the Isère watershed, since modeled discharges differ significantly from gauged discharges. It is worth noticing that reservoir construction upstream of Saint-Gervais strongly decreased spring discharges to the benefit of all the winter months. Thus, the predicted increase of winter flow is already anticipated by the artificial increase linked to the production of hydro-energy.

In conclusion, the impacts of Lake Geneva and mountain reservoirs are multiplied since they store water in spring and summer and decrease the Rhône discharge during these seasons and increase the discharge during the cold season. These artificial changes have anticipated the ongoing and expected impacts of climate warming, even if a higher degree of complexity in engineered flow could be taken into account. This complexity would deserve more interest and international collaborative research, considering the economic consequences along the French course of the river (running of nuclear power plants).

5.4.2 Human impacts on water temperature

The temperature of Lake Geneva has increased by 1°C since the 1960s, while the temperature of Lake Annecy has increased 1°C since the late nineteenth century. The temperature of the Rhône river increased by 1.3°C to 3°C in the different stations between 1977–87 and 1988–99. It increased notably during the spring and the summer. The former temperature at Orange is the present temperature at Lyon (Poirel 2004). This warming is due to both natural and human-induced causes.

The Compagnie Nationale du Rhône (CNR) estimated the yearly average warming impact of the chain of hydroelectric schemes at 0.14°C, due to the slower velocity of flow in the 16 reservoirs (Cottereau 1989). A far more important part of the warming must be related to the impacts of nuclear power plants. Indeed, the influence of these plants on the thermal regime has been demonstrated by Electricité de France (Desaint 2004). The theoretical impact is less than 3°C, just below the nuclear power plants 90 percent of the time, while the average warming is 1.72°C (Bugey plant), 1.03 (Saint-Alban plant), and 1.34°C (Tricastin plant). Temperatures have a strong seasonal behavior, depending on the meteorology, on the discharge of the Rhône, on the input of cool water from the tributaries (Isère River), and on the energy production of the plants. The artificial warming decreases downstream of the plants, but the warming due to the Bugey plant is still noticeable on the lower Rhône. The residual artificial warming is between 1°C and 1.5°C on the downstream course.

5.5. Complex changes of water ecosystems

5.5.1 Changes in river ecosystems: upland rivers and foreland rivers

Considering a possible reduction of discharges of 30 to 40 percent and an increase in temperature during the dry months throughout the basin, biologists (Pont *et al.* 2003) working in the GICC program propose the following preliminary results:

- a potential reduction of cryophilous and rheophilous fish species, such as the trout, the bullhead, the loach, the Planer lamprey, and the introduced sun perch. The main threshold should be a 2°C increase in temperature. This would enhance the noted reduction of these species already found in Europe, which has been caused by the physical impacts of river training (i.e., embankments, dams). Considering the impact of decreased discharges on river hydraulics and river habitat for fish, models predict the negative impact of lower summer discharges on reophilic species, such as grayling, dace, and barbel. Their abundance could decrease by 20 percent due to this factor;
- some Cyprinids will be positively affected, such as the chub, the bleak, and the perch. The most rheophilous Cyprinids will colonize the upstream river reaches;
- some families of macroinvertebrates are negatively influenced by increased temperature (e.g., Perlidae, Odontoceridae). In fact, several physical and chemical factors interact in a complex manner with temperature increase.

These expected tendencies would reinforce the negative impacts of river training, which have been monitored since the nineteenth century along rivers of Europe.

Also of major concern are the effects of the recent warming of the rivers. Two types of studies have documented these changes:

- the average yearly temperature of the Saône River increased by 1.5°C between 1987 and 2003. The 2003 summer heat wave could exemplify future years, since temperatures reached the highest recorded since 1500. Mouthon and

Daufresne (2006) studied the response of mollusc communities between 1996 and 2004. The resilience of these communities to high temperatures is low, particularly for *Pisidium*. More than half the mollusc species currently inhabiting the potamic area of the Saône and Doubs rivers could be directly threatened with extinction;

- the effects of a 1°C increase on macro-invertebrates of the Rhône since 1985 has been studied. While improvement in water quality did not introduce significant changes in community structure, temperature was proven to be affected by local development schemes, such as hydropower schemes and nuclear power plants. The period was characterized by the progressive development of invasive species and progressive changes in native community structure, due to gradual environmental changes (Daufresne *et al*. 2004). Moreover, large recent floods (pulse disturbance) and the 2003 heat wave triggered rapid shifts. They were beneficial to eury-tolerant and invasive taxa in the downstream and middle river reaches. No sign of recovery was observed after disturbances, and the sensitivity of community structures seemed to increase with time, due to catastrophic bifurcations (Fruget 2007).

5.5.2 Changes in lake ecosystems

The effects of the increase in temperature in the large subalpine Lake Geneva have been studied for the current conditions, which provide some insights into predictable changes linked to global warming. Temperature increased by 1°C along the vertical profile during the last 30 years (Figure 5.4). The thermal stratification sets up one month earlier in the epilimnion, along with the primary production and the growth of herbivorous zooplankton. Complementing the human-controlled decrease in the concentration of phosphorus, the spring mixing of water, the availability of nutrients, and the structure of phytoplankton and grazers were influenced by the winter warming of the lakes, which in turn is linked to the NAO (Anneville *et al*. 2005). The different fish species were also affected by the warming of water (Gerdeaux 2005):

- the arctic chars (*Salvelinus alpinus* and *Coregonus lavaretus*) are endemic species adapted to the cold deep waters of the hypolimnion since the Late Glacial Period, similarly to Arctic areas. They have a strong importance in the fishing economy of the lake. These species spawn in winter when photoperiod and temperature both decrease. The registered warming of the lake delayed spawning in December, reducing the development of embryos so that larvae were hatching a few days earlier than before, and are benefited from warmer waters and plenty of food from plankton. Then moderate warming benefited the arctic chars, catches of which increased from 50 tons in the 1970s to 300 tons since the late 1990s. Bottom temperature increased from 4.5°C to 5.5°C during the last 30 years. When temperature reaches 7°C, ovogenesis of females will be halted and these species will not be able to adapt;
- the roach is a cyprinid, living in the warmer epiliminion, which spawns in

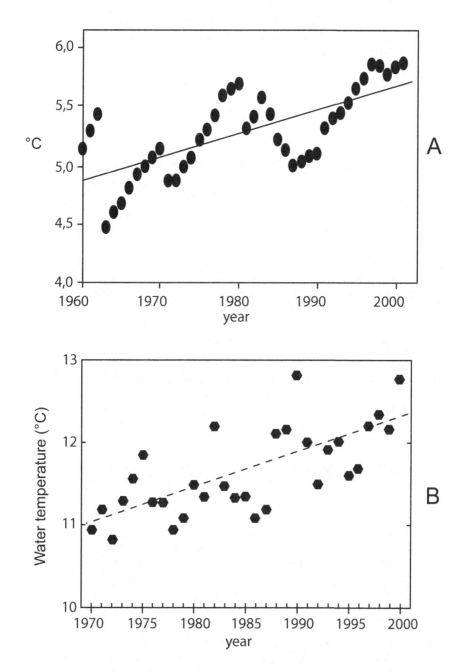

Figure 5.4 Measured changes in water temperature of Lake Geneva. Bottom from 1960 (A), 5m depth from 1970 (B) (after Gerdeaux, 2003 and 2004, modified).

May, one month earlier than before. Generally speaking, white fish have benefited from the recent warming of the lake through better survival of larvae due to increased plankton food supply;
* the perch, which lives deeper in the lake (i.e. below the epilimnion), does not benefit from the earlier warming of water. Since the reproduction of perch does not occur earlier, the alevins no longer benefit from the presence of roach larvae and experience a slower growth.

In the future, the lakes will experience a warming trend from warmer air temperatures and tributary waters. Earlier snow melting and peak flows from the Alps will increase spring warming of the lakes. Also, the reduction of glacier mass will reduce the cooling by tributaries in late spring and summer. This impact of warmer waters on the vertical profile will depend on the future influence of stratification and on tributary inputs. Danis *et al.* (2004) have studied the future conditions of water mixing behavior, using a thermal model. For example, Lake Annecy experiences one full mixing when air temperature cools surface waters to a maximum density of 4°C. As a result, the temperature of the surface of Lake Annecy will increase 2.2°C in one century. The temperature of deep layers will experience the same change due to the high transparency of water, which allows the absorption of solar radiation. The regular overturning will then be preserved. However, as in Lake Geneva, the arctic char will disappear due to the increase in temperature above 7°C.

5.6 Predictable impacts on the uses of water and on humans

5.6.1 Energy

5.6.1.1 Hydropower

The general reduction in runoff will affect the production of hydraulic energy throughout the Alps – particularly in the Southern Alps, which should experience the strongest reduction. In Switzerland, the scenarios of change predict a reduction of the mean annual hydroelectricity potential due to a significant decrease of mean annual discharges. After 2050, the reduction of summer discharge will reduce the differences in seasonal discharges, inducing an easier management of energy production. The winter discharges will increase in response to earlier snow melt and to increased precipitation. Spring discharges will increase, but the change will be more limited. Modeling of the Mauvoisin hydropower plant production allowed Schäfli (2005) to predict a 36 percent decrease between the two periods 1961–90 and 2070–99. The same behavior is predicted in the Northern French Alps. Since the future hydrological regimes will be driven more by precipitation than by snow-melt and glacier-melt processes, the inter-annual variability of mean annual discharge is expected to increase, and may also increase the year-to-year hydroelectricity potential (Horton *et al.* 2005). High-elevation reservoirs will fill up earlier in the season, due to earlier snow melting and increased winter temperatures.

Economically, this change may coincide with the highest levels of energy demand during winter peak periods. However, the recent increase in summer consumption of energy observed during the hot months of 2003, due to the use of electric coolers, has triggered peaks of prices in the European market. This unexpected peak in demand will increase the value of summer production and may change the conditions of water storage in the Western Alps to the detriment of summer storage, which is commonly used for winter production.

5.6.1.2. Thermal power cooled by rivers

The increased temperature of the Rhône will reduce the production of thermal energy. The use of water from the Rhône to cool nuclear power plants in France is based on significant differences in temperatures between the river and the cooling system. Any warming of the river decreases the potential of energy production, since the maximum temperatures of the releases are controlled by strict rules. However, these regulations may be softened to the detriment of aquatic ecosystems, as occurred in August 2003. This policy will be all the more probable in the future, as energy prices rise during the summer months.

5.6.2 Tourism

Climate change will have impacts on tourism during different seasons. Beniston (2003) recommends drawing a distinction between direct impacts (through conditions for specific activities) and indirect impacts (through changes in landscapes and through the modified pattern of economic demand). We will consider herein the direct impacts upon tourism, based on the amount of snowfall and lake levels.

5.6.2.1 The challenge of snow cover reduction

According to Abegg and Froesch (1994) and Abegg *et al.* (1997), an increase in temperature of 2–3°C by the year 2050 will adversely affect ski resorts located at lower altitudes (below 1200–1500 metres). Warmer winters will bring less snow at these altitudes, and snow will melt faster, reducing the probability of practising skiing, a sport requiring a snow cover of 30 cm during at least 100 days. Warming would reduce the reliability of Alpine resorts in Switzerland, affecting in particular the low-altitude resorts. In Isère Department, France, the Conseil Général ordered a study of the last 29 winters. The results point to the vulnerability of the resorts, whose ski runs are lower than 1500 m in elevation. These resorts may lack the necessary snow cover to remain operational.

To avoid the headlong pursuit towards the development of artificial snow by the communities in charge of developing winter sports, the Conseil Général of Isère Department proposed a new type of contract for the lowest resorts, in order to avoid the resorts financially soliciting the Conseil Général in the event that they experience a series of winters deprived of snow. Indeed, these changes in snow cover and in the duration and quality of the winter season will have economic consequences, such as have occurred in the Morzine-Avoriaz resorts complex (Frangialli and Passaquin 2003). The lack of snow is being compensated for by costly investments in snow-making equipment, better vegetation cover on the runs, development of resorts at higher altitudes, and by investments in other types of activities. If over-frequentation may be predicted in high-altitude resorts, Christmas and Easter periods will generate less revenue, and the value of estates will decrease at the lowest altitudes. Heavy past investments may not be refunded, which would affect the finances of communes or private investors. Thousands of seasonal workers will have shorter seasons and reduced incomes.

The development of artificial snow has been precisely documented in the French Alps (Dugleux 2002). In 2002, 85 percent of the 162 ski resorts of the French basin of the Rhône produced artificial snow on 15 percent of surfaces, at mostly between 1500 and 2000 metres, but increasingly at higher and higher altitudes. This is detrimental to local water resources, since making 2 m^3 of snow requires 1 m^3 of unfrozen water, while the torrents are at low flow. In 1999–2000, 10 hm^3 of water was used at 119 resorts in Savoy, i.e. the same amount a city of 170,000 inhabitants would consume. In terms of specific consumption, artificial snow requires 4000 m^3/ha, compared with 1700 m^3/ha for the irrigation of corn in the Alpine valleys. Water for artificial snow has three origins:

- more than one-third of resorts experience shortages in water supply for domestic uses because in 25 percent of resorts, snow production competes with human uses (total volume: 2 hm^3 per year);
- 50 percent of ski resorts have built artificial tanks storing 20,000 to 150,000 m^3 (total volume: 5 hm^3 per year);
- 25 percent of resorts withdraw water from rivers during the cold season;
- making artificial snow has impacts on the aquatic environment;
- tanks are harmful to wetlands, have no hydrological impacts on rivers during the cold season, but are filled during the summer season, and may be prone to destruction by floods;
- direct winter withdrawals impact rivers at low flow, from November to February (January represents 30 percent of the total consumption);
- Dugleux (2002) proposed an indicator of pressure upon low-flow discharges. For 60 percent of resorts, withdrawal represents less than 10 percent of low-flow discharge. For 11 resorts, it represents from 30 to 49 percent of this discharge, and for two of them, more than 50 percent. As it has been said, if the present impacts are not too harmful, they will develop in the future. Since artificial snow meets major economic objectives (the survival of the resort in some cases, the maximum snow depth on all the tracks during the complete season), the phenomenon must be strictly monitored and controlled.

5.6.2.2. Water supply to southern resorts

Water supply to resorts (swimming pools, lawns) and for leisure (golf courses) will be reduced if summer precipitations decrease and if evaporation increases, notably in the southern part of the watershed (Ceron and Dubois 2003). Mountain reservoirs will be solicited, as is presently the case in the Ardèche basin where a minimum discharge guarantees the practice of canoeing in the downstream gorges during July and August.

5.6.2.3. Maintaining levels of large subalpine lakes

Tourism on large lakes will be impacted by climate change in a complex way. An early reduction of discharge will probably impact the conditions of the seasonal filling up of Lake Geneva. Lakes Annecy and Bourget have small tributaries that will be affected by earlier snow melt and by decreased summer discharge, in a context of increased evaporation, as in 2003. Due to water withdrawal for domestic uses from Lake Annecy, and withdrawal of used water collected around both lakes Annecy and Bourget, the natural inputs into the lakes have been artificially reduced. Maintaining high water levels in summer for the sake of aesthetics and tourism is a challenge, which precludes any variation for the sake of the sustainable ecology of the shores of Lake Annecy. In the case of Lake Bourget, maintaining a high and constant level would require supplying water from the Rhône to the lake, as in July 2003.

5.6.3 Pressures on the consumptive uses of water

5.6.3.1. Present consumption in the Rhône watershed (France) and along the Rhône River

The total withdrawal from the whole watershed amounts to 15,800 billion m^3/year (Table 5.1), but does not exceed 4,600 hm^3 if one excludes withdrawals from the Rhône River (most of this withdrawal is just a diversion to the cooling systems; a small proportion only is lost in cooling towers, most of the cooling systems being "closed" systems). This yearly volume must be compared with the yearly discharge of the Rhône River at the outlet, i.e., 54 billion m^3 and 15.5 hm^3 stored in the decaying Alpine glaciers.

Excluding energy uses:

- the withdrawal from the Rhône River alone stands below 850 hm^3/year (Table 5.2), i.e., it represents less than 1.6 percent of the total discharge into the Mediterranean;
- the withdrawal at the watershed scale (4,600 hm^3/y) represents 8.5 percent of the discharge into the Mediterranean;
- part of these withdrawals devoted to domestic uses, agriculture and industrial processes are not consumed and go back to the ground waters and to the river.

Table 5.1 Withdrawals in the Rhône watershed for different water uses, France only (billion m³/year)

Domestic uses	Industry	Thermal energy	Irrigation	Total
1900	0.95	11.2	1.75	15.8

Source: Agence de l'Eau Rhône-Méditerranée et Corse

Table 5.2 Withdrawals from the Rhône River only (hm³/year)

	Domestic uses	Industry	Thermal energy	Irrigation by gravity	Irrigation sous pressure	Others
Superficial water	10.4	112.1	11,200	45.6	134.8	0
Ground water	212.6	277	0.1	4.3	13,7	15.4
Total	223	390	11200	49.9	150	15.4

Source: Agence de l'Eau Rhône-Méditerranée et Corse

5.6.3.2. Irrigation in the perspective of climate change

The GICC-Rhône study (Leblois and Grésillon 2005), using the STICS model, predicts that the doubling of CO_2 concentration will induce a shorter seasonal cycle for corn cultivation (reduction by 21 percent), and a 15 percent loss of yield. The shorter cycle would induce an increase of irrigation rates, which would be accompanied with increased plant requirements due to climate warming. However, the earlier growth would reduce the intakes in August, the most difficult period for river hydrology. The GICC study predicts that agriculture will adapt through a reduction of irrigation practices to the benefit of crops less dependant on water resources.

The pressure upon water resources (superficial water and groundwater) will change in a complex way. Industrial consumption uses are decreasing, while domestic uses are stagnant, partly due to the rise of prices. Global water consumption by agriculture will be influenced by the policy of the European Union and by the global market, in ways that are difficult to predict today. It is clear that different ecoregions have different potentialities and that a unique set of rules is not recommended to overcome periods of water shortage. Beyond the modelling of river discharges, the GICC-Rhône study recommends the investigation of the different components of water balance at the scale of the geographical units. The variations of precipitation from year to year, and the variation of water volumes, should be computed for a better management of resources in situations of potential conflicts.

It is worth considering the present responses of farmers to drought, such as those conditions that occurred in 1989, 2003 and 2004, because they may indicate future massive forms of adaptation to crisis situations.

- In the "ecoregions" prone to the drying up of rivers and deprived of subterranean resources, i.e., mainly in the crystalline regions of the basin, farmers were granted permission to built tanks intercepting the headwaters and the hypodermic flow. Hundreds of tanks have been built along the eastern rim of the Massif Central during the last 30 years (Lyon and Vivarais Mounts). They induce severe reduction of summer flow and decrease winter floods during the period of infilling. As such, they have been proven to induce such severe impacts upon river hydrology and ecology that they are no longer a priority of public authorities, even if they are economically efficient.

• A kind of adaptation is the development of wells into the alluvial aquifer bordering the river. This practice is detrimental to small rivers, which are fed by the aquifer and are prone to severe and long-lasting dry spells. Authorities are reacting by delineating the riparian aquifers and by limiting the authorization of pumping from the wells (Bonhomme and Nicolas 2005).

• Most of the recent developments concerning the aquifer occurred inside the deep and rich mollassic sandstones of the Alps and Jura forelands. Water extraction is so intense that the groundwater levels are declining due to a negative balance between refilling through precipitation, and extraction during the warm season. Public authorities have recently decided to develop a network of piezometers in threatened areas, because they are sensitive to the over-exploitation of water resources (in some rare cases, water for domestic use is no longer available due to the lowering of the groundwater level). Undoubtedly, controlling the volumes that are extracted from aquifers will be a challenge.

As is shown by the above developments, human interference with the effects of climate change is increasing with regard to agricultural uses. The more rivers are affected by water withdrawal from aquifers, the more difficult it becomes to make a distinction between anthropogenic impacts and changes induced by climate change, even along large rivers like the Rhône.

While admitting that French agriculture will need more security, Redaud *et al.* (2002) recommended the reinforcement of regulations aimed at controlling irrigation in order to better respect the low-flow objectives of the EU Water Framework Directive and of the Watershed directory scheme (SDAGE) in heavily impacted basins.

5.6.3.3. Massive withdrawals from large rivers

Water intakes from large rivers in Southern France is of historical significance. In the mid-fifties, the Durance and the Rhône rivers were affected by large withdrawals for different purposes. The average yearly discharge of the Durance River was 210 m³/s at the confluence of the Rhône River. On the upstream course of the river, the Serre-Ponçon dam (1955–59), along with a complex hydraulic system on the Verdon (a tributary), allowed the diversion of 0.7 km³ for energy production and 0.2 km³ for agriculture into a lateral canal, designed to carry up to 300 m³/s. Also, part of the discharge was diverted to the cities of the Mediterranean coast in order to secure water supply during a period of growth in tourism. The lower reach of the canal pours into the Etang de Berre, to the detriment of the Rhône discharge. Downstream of Serre-Ponçon, the minimum discharge of the river is no more than 2 m³/s during most of the year (when the canal discharge is not exceeded), while the absolute minimum was 25 m³/s before 1960. Warner (2000, 2001) described the artificial river corridor as a case of artificial desertification, and suggests that with further effective reductions in precipitations and increase in temperature, sustaining these enterprises will be very difficult.

The Languedoc canal (1957–1960) was dug to divert up to 75 m³/s from the Petit Rhône, the eastern branch of the Rhône in the Camargue delta, for the sake of irrigating agriculture. However, withdrawals have never exceeded 15–20 m³/s. In 1995, the company controlling the canal and a society delivering drinkable water to the city of Barcelona proposed to divert 10–15 m³/s from the Rhône to Barcelona, using the same intake. The purpose was to secure water delivery to Barcelona and to provide better quality water. The development of tourism, and the increase of summer discharge of coastal rivers in Languedoc were other objectives. This project failed for complex political reasons, but it reveals the renewal of pressure upon the Rhône River.

5.6.4. Risks

5.6.4.1. Floods

The major apparent risk is linked to increased flood hazards. If winter floods occurring on rivers in Switzerland have negative influences on discharges in downstream countries, then these countries may ask for improved retention in the Swiss lakes and reservoirs. Such requests may have some political consequences (Schädler 2003). In the last 15 years, severe floods have occurred in the Upper Rhône, downstream of Geneva (1990 saw a 1-in-100 year flood), and in the lower Rhône (for instance in 1993, 1994, 2003). As stated above (Sauquet and Haond 2003), these events may be just a cycle of high discharges, as many have occurred in the past. Also, they may be the first signal of changed climate towards higher peak floods. However, they revealed the strong vulnerability of the Rhône valley to flooding. In 1995, the French government launched a large study called "Global Rhône study," combining hydraulics, sediment transport and land occupation, as these different topics have been recognized as complementing each other. The 2003 flood, the 1-in-100 year flood for the downstream gauging stations, motivated the French government to launch the so-called "Rhône Masterplan" (2005), which includes a series of measures to mitigate the human consequences of flooding, as well as recognizing the reduction of hydrological hazards as being impracticable. The expected risk explicitly refers to the largest past floods (1856), to extreme scenarios combining several meteorological origins (the so-called "general flood" in the sense of Pardé 1925), and to the negative impacts of the occupation of the floodplain. It is thus worth noting that the possible effects of climate change on the intensity of large floods are not taken into account, despite the increase in extreme winter events. Also, to face the expected changes, the French Ministry of Environment and Sustainable Development recommended extending the number of "Plans de Prévention des Risques" and to improve forecasting procedures (Redaud *et al.* 2002).

5.6.4.2. *The Camargue delta and the mouth of the Rhône River*

With rising sea levels, the coast dunes protecting the Camargue delta will be threatened and brackish water may extend upstream, changing the ecological conditions of the lower river. According to Provansal and Sabatier (2000), the main cause of present coastal retreat is not the rise in sea level but the decrease of sediment supply from the Rhône River, which has complex causes (sediment retention in reservoirs, impacts of embankments of the Rhône, reforestation of the watershed). The velocity of the coastal retreat should increase, particularly if sea storms and surges get more intense.

The intrusion of brackish water will affect the Grand Rhône itself. In the 1990s, an outcrop of bedrock was suppressed for the sake of navigation downstream of Arles, making the intrusion of marine water at low flow easier. The expected reduction of low flow and the expected rising sea level may induce longer periods of brackish conditions, between flood pulses, upstream of the present limit, to the detriment of human uses (domestic uses and irrigation of paddy fields inside the delta).

5.7 Conclusion: toward new policies

Changes have begun for some of the components of the hydrosystem of the Rhône River, due to the direct impacts of recent climate warming, although it is too early to disentangle the NAO effects and the effects of global warming. Documented changes due to climate warming interfere with strong human-induced changes in a highly developed watershed. If predicted changes of hydrostems linked to modeled climate change are confirmed, they may have significant hydrological, ecological, and economic impacts in the next decades, as seen above.

An important challenge will be the adaptation of societies to the direct and indirect effects of global change. In this perspective, the adaptation of present policies or the willingness to adapt future policies is an interesting topic. One of the main conclusions that may be drawn from this review is that the only significant changes in policy involve the decrease of snow cover during about the last 30 years, which is related to the warming of temperatures at low altitudes. The reluctance to subsidise snow making in these ski resorts anticipates expected changes that could worsen in the next decades.

There is much concern about river discharge and the seasonality of discharge among the producers of hydraulic and thermal energy (as long as the river is used for cooling nuclear power plants). The debate is quite open in Switzerland, but the situation is different in France because the EEC freed the energy market in 2002. Electricité de France (EDF), which was the only French producer, is no longer a state company and must compete on the European market. It is therefore understandable that information on this subject has too much value to be divulged. Hydraulic electricity from the Alpine reservoirs will be valued as sustainable energy, but the policy of the company is to reinforce its capacities in new nuclear plants. EDF is concerned about the warming of the Rhône River, which impacts the capacity for production during the warm season. The company is asking for a softening of official regulations concerning the temperature of releases during severe conditions (high temperatures combined with low flow). Also, the National Rhône C° is observing changes in discharges with much interest, since it manages all of the hydroelectric plants of the Rhône, except one.

In the future, one of the issues will be the conflict between ecology and the production of energy. The official environmental policy is to restore the river, which has been transformed into a staircase of dams. Part of this policy, which has been evident since 1995, consists of increasing the discharge of the reaches through an industrial canal in order to restore a "fast-flowing river." These measures have a cost, in terms of energy, even if small plants will turbine the discharge released on the site of the retention dam, and they will compete with the crucial need for energy in the next decades. There is no doubt that the deep willingness of local people to get back to their river will be challenged in the future.

French farmers are adapting their agricultural practices quite quickly, as demonstrated by their reactions to the 2003 drought. Some of them dig wells, and the government will have to control these practices very soon. Most of them have changed their crops back to dry cereals, such as wheat, and hay. This kind of adaptation is more acceptable because the price of wheat has rocketed. In other words, water consumption by agriculture at the watershed scale could stabilize or even decrease. However, massive withdrawals from the Rhône River will occur in order to relieve the high pressure that the tributaries will experience due to the expected decrease of summer discharges. To some extent, these withdrawals may impact the production of energy along the downstream river and, in the long term, may affect the western Mediterranean Sea as an ecosystem.

Will water authorities promote the construction of a new generation of reservoirs to store water for controlling floods and for human consumption? It is not the present policy, just as the possible increase of floods is not yet officially accepted by public policymakers. But this policy may be enacted out of necessity.

References

Abegg, B. and Froesch, U. (1994) Climate change and winter tourism: impact on transport companies in the Swiss canton of Graubünden, 328–340. In Beniston M. (ed.) *Mountain Environments in Changing Climates.* London and New York: Routledge.

Abegg, B., Koenig, U., Burki, R. and Elsasser, H. (1997) Climate impact assessment in tourism. *Die Erde,* 128: 105–116.

Anneville, O., Gammeter, S. and Straile, D. (2005) Phosphorus decrease and climate variability: mediators of synchrony in phytoplankton changes among European peri-alpine lakes. *Freshwater Biology,* 50: 1731–46.

Beniston, M. (1997) Variations of snow depth and duration in the Swiss Alps over the last 50 years: links to changes in large-scale forcings. *Climatic Change,* 36: 281–300.

Beniston, M. *et al.* (1995) Simulation of climate trends over the Alpine region: development of a physically-based modelling system for application to regional studies of current and future climate. Final Scientific Report No. 4031–33250 to the Swiss National Science Foundation, Bern, Switzerland 200.

Beniston, M. (2003) Climatic change in mountain regions: a review of possible impacts. *Climatic Change,* 59: 5–31.

Beniston, M. (2004) Extreme climatic events: examples from the alpine region. *Journal de Physique IV,* 121: 139–149.

Beniston, M. and Jungo P. (2002) Shifts in the distribution of pressure, temperature and moisture and changes in the typical weather patterns in the Alpine region in response to the behavior of the North Atlantic Oscillation, *Theoretical and Applied Climatology,* 71: 29–42.

Bonhomme, B. and Nicolas J. (2005) Bilan de la Sécheresse 2003 et 2004 en Rhône-Alpes vis-à-vis des Eaux Souterraines. Rapport final. Bureau de la Recherche Géologique et Minière, RP-54245-FR.

Braun, L. N., Weber, M. and Schulz, M. (2000) Consequences of climate change for runoff from Alpine regions. *Annals of Glaciology,* 31: 19–25.

Bravard, J.-P. (1986) *Le Rhône du Léman à Lyon.* Lyon : Ed. La Manufacture.

Ceron, J.-P. and Dubois, G. (2003) Tourisme et changement climatique: une relation à double sens. Le cas de la France. *1ère Conf. int. sur le Changement Climatique et le Tourisme,* Djerba, Tunisia.

Cottereau, C. (1989) Les problèmes d'environnement et d'impact liés à l'aménagement du Rhône. In *La Ville et le Fleuve,* colloques du Comité des Travaux Historiques et Scientifiques, 3: 73–105.

Danis P.-A. *et al.* (2004) Vulnerability of two European lakes in response to future climatic changes. *Geophysical Research Letters,* vol. 31, L21507, doi:10.1029/2004GL020833.

Daufresne, M., Roger, M. C., Capra, H. and Lamouroux, N. (2004) Long-term changes within the invertebrate and fish communities of the Upper Rhône River: effects of climatic factors. *Global Change Biology,* 10: 124–140.

De Jong, C., Collins, D. N. and Ranzi, R. (ed.) (2005) *Climate and Hydrology of Mountain areas.* Chichester: Wiley.

Deneux, M. (2002) Rapport sur l'évaluation de l'ampleur des changements climatiques, de leurs causes et de leur impact prévisible sur la géographie de la France à l'horizon 2025, 2050 et 2100. Paris : Office parlementaire d'évaluation des choix scientifiques et technologiques.

Desaint, B. (2004) Etude thermique du Rhône – Phase 2 – Rapport préliminaire. EDF, Branche énergie.

Duband, D. (2007) Personal communication.

Dugleux, E. (2002) Impact de la production de neige de culture sur la ressource en eau. Coll. "L'eau en montagne: gestion intégrée des hauts *bassins* versants." Megève.

Etchevers, P. and Martin, E. (2002) Impact d'un changement climatique sur le manteau neigeux et l'hydrologie des bassins versants de montagne. Coll. "L'eau en montagne: gestion intégrée des hauts bassins versants." Megève.

Etchevers, P., Golaz, C. and Habets, F. (2001) Simulation of the water budget and the river flows of the Rhône basin from 1981 to 1994. *Journal of Hydrology,* 244: 60–85.

Frangialli, F. Passaquin, F. (2003) Tourisme durable et changement climatique: l'exemple des Alpes françaises – Le cas de Morzine-Avoriaz (France). *1ère Conf. int. sur le Changement Climatique et le Tourisme.* Djerba, Tunisia.

Fruget J.-F. (2007) Personal communication.

Gerdeaux, D. (2005) Restoration of the whitefish fisheries in Lake Geneva. The roles of stocking, reoligotrophication, and climate change. *Annales Zoologici Fennici,* 41: 181–189.

Green, A., Broeker, W. S. and Rind, D. (1999) Swiss glacier recession since the little Ice Age: reconciliation with climate records. *Geophysical Research Letters,* 26: 1909–12.

Haeberli, W. (1990) Glacier and permafrost signals of 20th-century warming, *Annals of Glaciology,* 14: 99–101.

Haeberli, W. (1994) Accelerated glacier and permafrost changes in the Alps. In M. Beniston (ed.) *Mountain Environments in Changing Climates*, London and New York: Routledge. Ch. 5.

Haeberli, W. (1995) Glacier fluctuations and climate change direction. *Geografia Fisica e Dinamica Quaternaria,* 18: 191–199.

Haeberli, W. and Beniston, M. (1998) Climate change and its impacts on glaciers and permafrost in the Alps. *Ambio,* 27: 258–65.

Haeberli, W., Muller, P., Alean, J. and Bösch, A. (1990) Glacier changes following the Little Ice Age. A survey of the international data base and its perspectives. In J. Oerlemans (ed.) *Glacier Fluctuations and Climate.* Dordrecht: D. Reidel Publishing Company, pp. 77–101.

Horton, P. *et al.* (2005) Prediction of climate change impacts on Alpine discharge regimes under A2 and B2 SRES emissions scenarios for two future time periods. Bundesamt für Energie BFE (Berne), EPFLausanne.

Husting, P., Jouzel, J. and Le Treut, H. (ed.) (2005) *Changements Climatiques, Quels Impacts en France?* Paris: Greenpeace.

IPCC (1992) *Climate Change 1992. The Supplementary Report to the IPCC Scientific Assessment*, J. T. Houghton, B. A. Callander and S. K. Varney (eds) Cambridge:Cambridge University Press.

IPCC (2002) *Climate Change 2001, Synthesis Report.* Cambridge: Cambridge University Press.

IPCC (2007) *Climate Change 2007: The Physical Science Basis.* Contribution of Working Group I to the fourth assessment. Report of the Intergovernmental Panel on Climate Change [Solomon, S. *et al.* (eds)]. Cambridge and New York: Cambridge University Press.

Krasovskaia, I., Gottschalk, L. and Leblois, E. (2002) Signature of changing climate in river flow regimes of Rhône-Mediterranean-Corsica region. *La Houille Blanche*, 8: 25–30.

Leblois, E. (2002) Evaluation des possibles impacts du changement climatique par modélisation distribuée (projets Gewex-Rhône et GICC-Rhône. *La Houille Blanche,* 8: 78–83.

Leblois, E. and Grésillon, M. (2005) *Projet GICC-Rhône.* Short version of the revised report.

Lubès-Niel, H. and Giraud, L. (2003) Floods in France: is there a change? In *XVIe Conférence du Centre Jacques Cartier*, Lyon, France.

Maisch, M. (2000) The long-term signal of climate change in the Swiss Alps: glacier retreat since the end of the Little Ice Age and future ice decay scenarios. *Geografia Fisica e Dinamica Quaternaria,* 23: 139–51.

Martin, E. and Durand, Y. (1998) Precipitation and snow cover variability in the French Alps. In : Beniston M. and Ines J. L. (eds), *The Impacts of Climate Change on Forest*, Heidelberg/New York: Springer Verlag, pp. 8–92.

Mouthon, J. and Daufresne, M. (2006) Effects of the 2003 heatwave and climatic warming on mollusc communities of the Saône: a large lowland river and of its two main tributaries (France). *Global Change Biology,* 11: 1–9.

Noilhan, J., Boone, A. and Etchevers, P. (2000) *Application of Climate Change Scenarios to the Rhône Basin.* ECLAT-2 Toulouse Workshop, keynote paper 4.

OcCC (2003) *Evènements Extrêmes et Changements Climatiques.* Bern: Organe consultatif sur les Changements Climatiques.

Pardé, M. (1925) *Le Régime du Rhône. Etude Hydrologique.* Lyon : Etudes et Travaux de l'Institut des Etudes rhodaniennes, 2 vol.

Poirel, A. (2004) *Etude Thermique du Rhône – Phase 1 – Complément d'Étude. Extension des Résultats à la Période 2000–2003.* EDF, Branche énergie.

Pont, D. (coord.) (2003) Conséquences potentielles du changement climatique sur les biocénoses aquatiques et riveraines françaises. Rapport final. Programme GICC-AQUABIO.

Provansal, M. and Sabatier, F. (2000) Impacts de la montée du niveau de la mer sur la côte du delta du Rhône. In Paskoff R. (ed.): *Le Changement Climatique et les Espaces Côtiers*, Actes du colloque d'Arles, 12–13 October 2000, pp. 78–81.

Redaud, J.-L. *et al.* (2002) Changement climatique et impact sur le régime des eaux en France. MEDD, Mission Interministérielle sur l'effet de serre.

Sauquet, E. and Haond, M. (2003) Examen de la stationnarité des écoulements du Rhône en lien avec la variabilité climatique et les actions humaines. Coll. «Barrages et développement durable en France.» Paris: Comité Français des Grands Barrages et Ministère de l'Ecologie et du Développement Durable, pp. 261–70.

Schädler, B. (2003) Effets des changements climatiques sur les hydrosystèmes alpins. *EAWAG News*, 55, pp. 24–6.

Schäfli, B. (2005) *Quantification of Modelling Uncertainties in Climate Change Impact Studies on Water Resources: Application to a Glacier-fed Hydropower Production System in the Swiss Alps.* Doctoral Thesis, n° 3225. Lausanne: Ecole Polytechnique Fédérale de Lausanne.

Six, D., Reynaud L. and Letréguilly, A. (2002) Variations des bilans de masse des glaciers alpins et scandinaves sur les dernières décennies, leurs relations avec l'Oscillation du climat de l'Atlantique Nord. *La Houille Blanche*, 8, pp. 34–5.

Stoffel, M. *et al.* (2005) 400 years of debris-flow activity and triggering weather conditions, Ritigraben, Valais, Switzerland. *Artic, Antarctic, and Alpine Research*, vol. 37, n° 3: v387–95.

Vincent, C. (2002) Fluctuations des bilans de masse des glaciers des Alpes françaises depuis le début du 20 siècle au regard des variations climatiques. *La Houille Blanche*, 8: 2024.

Vivian, H. (1989) Hydrological changes of the Upper Rhône. In Petts *et al.* (eds) *Historical Changes of Large Alluvial Rivers. Western Europe.* Chichester: Wiley & Sons, pp. 57–77.

Warner, R. (2000) Gross channel changes along the Durance River, Southern France, over the last 100 years using cartographic data. *Regulated Rivers: Research and Management,* 16: 141–57.

Warner, R. (2001) Relevance of geomorphology in exploitive and sustainable management of water resources in the Durance River, France. Integrated Water Resources Management (Proc. Symp. held at Davis, California, IAHS Publ. n° 272:277–284).

Zierl, B. and Bugmann, H. (2005) Global change impacts on hydrological processes in Alpine catchments. *Water Resources Research*, 41: W02028, doi: 10.1029/2004WR003447.

Part II

Managing opportunities in the face of global challenges

6 Adaptive management of upland rivers facing global change

General insights and specific considerations for the Rhône

Claudia Pahl-Wostl, Ger Bergkamp, and Katharine Cross

Water management was successful in the past in securing the availability of water-related services and protecting society from water-related hazards through technical means, based on a control approach. Prospects of climate and global change leading to increases in extreme weather events have increased the awareness of complexities and uncertainties and triggered critical reflection about prevailing water management paradigms. There are now calls for more robust, flexible, and adaptive strategies. Drivers and barriers for the implementation of new management approaches and the importance of processes of social learning are exemplified by the Rhône.

6.1 Challenges for water management

Water management has been successful in the past in securing the availability of water-related services and in protecting society from water-related hazards through technical means. Rather than adapting to periodic variability in water levels (i.e. flooding), the approach has been to control rivers to provide for hydropower production or navigation. The control approach can reach its limits in upland rivers that experience extreme weather events. For example, channeled rivers with high rainfall can have severe floods, some of which increasingly result in damage since people began settling in vulnerable areas such as floodplains. However, once high-risk areas are settled, economic investments and assets need to be protected from natural disasters, despite the fact that land use should have been restricted originally. Reliance on infrastructure for protection against water-related hazards means that societies have become more vulnerable when this infrastructure fails.

Water quality has been the preliminary focus of improving the ecological integrity of riverine ecosystems. Consequently, there has been a lack of attention to the structural changes in riverbeds and changes in the spatio-temporal variability of water flows which have a strong influence on habitat diversity and ecological function. The building of reservoirs and the use of hydropower have altered the flow regimes of many rivers resulting in detrimental effects on stream ecology (Ward 1998; Pahl-Wostl 1998; Bergkamp *et al.* 2000). Efforts are being increasingly undertaken to restore the ecological integrity and functions of river basin ecosystems by focusing on the structural properties of river and ecosystem flow requirements (Tockner and Stanford 2002). Prospects of climate and global change leading to possible increases in extreme weather events and fast-changing socioeconomic boundary conditions mean that more attention needs to be focused on water flows and river structure. The growing awareness of complexities, unexpected consequences of management strategies and an increase in uncertainties have triggered critical reflection about prevailing water management paradigms (Pahl-Wostl 2007a). There are now calls for more robust, flexible and adaptive strategies (Gleick 2003; Moench *et al.* 2003; Kabat and van Scheick 2003; Pahl-Wostl 2007b).

6.2 Adaptive management

Adaptive management in relation to ecosystem management has been discussed for several years (Holling 1978; Walters 1986; Pahl-Wostl 1995; Lee 1999). It is based on the insight that the ability to predict future key drivers influencing an ecosystem, as well as system behavior and responses, is inherently limited. Therefore, management must be adaptive and have the ability to change depending on environmental events.

Adaptive management can more generally be defined as a systemic and systematic process for improving management policies and practices by learning from the outcomes of implemented management strategies. One form of adaptive management employs management programs that are designed to experimentally compare selected policies or practices, by evaluating alternative hypotheses about the system being managed (e.g., Gunderson 1999; Kiker *et al.* 2001: Richter *et al.* 2003). This implies that hypotheses can be generated and that the outcomes of experiments can distinguish which of the different hypotheses is more appropriate to explain system behavior and to guide management. However, an experimental approach may also structure dialogue and, in the spirit of reflexive governance, support processes of social learning and develop the capacity of actors to deal with uncertainties and to learn from experience.

- Capacity in adaptive management is needed to deal with different kinds of uncertainties.
- There are ambiguities and conflicts of interest in defining operational targets for different management goals, thus participatory goal setting based on different kinds of knowledge is needed.
- Outcomes of management measures are uncertain due to the complexity of the managed system; furthermore, there are uncertainties in environmental and socioeconomic developments that influence the performance of implemented management strategies.
- New knowledge about system behavior may suggest options for change in management strategies.
- Changes in environmental and/or in socioeconomic boundary conditions may demand change in management strategies.

Overall, a clear need for a more coherent and comprehensive approach can be identified, based on sound conceptual foundations that deal with uncertainties in integrated water resource management (IWRM). Uncertainty has often been perceived as an impediment for effective and efficient resource management, and the main goal has always been to reduce and control uncertainties. However, such a strategy may be counterproductive when uncertainties cannot be reduced. Acknowledging uncertainties along with open negotiation processes may help move entrenched positions and start constructive dialogue as different actors may perceive opportunities in collaborative efforts, rather than continuing to defend their rigid positions.

The requirements for implementing adaptive management in river basins include:

1   New information that is available and/or consciously collected (e.g. indicators of performance of management regimes, indicators for change that may lead to desirable or undesirable effects) and monitored over appropriate time scales (longer than those mandated by short-term political objectives).
2   Actors in the management system must be able to process new information and draw meaningful conclusions. This can be best achieved if the learning process is open and transparent by uniting actors in all phases of assessment, policy implementation and monitoring.
3   Management must have the ability to implement change, based on the availability of new information. Implementation of changes in adaptive river basin management is part of a learning process where it must be made clear who decides how and when to change management practices, based on available evidence.

It can be argued that current water management regimes are not adaptive (Pahl-Wostl 2002; Tillman *et al.* 2005). Large infrastructure and investment costs prevent change. Rigid legal regulation prescribes technical standards and practices and leaves little room for innovation. Infrastructure (flood protection, water supply, waste-water treatment) is designed to cope with extremes, which is a strategy very sensitive to errors in the prediction of extremes. Water supply and waste-water infrastructure have, for example, been designed to meet peak loads rather than trying to break demand peaks by introducing flexible pricing schemes (Tillman *et al.* 2005). In addition, the professional culture in the water sector tends to be risk averse and does not reward innovative thinking. Such attitudes are partly understandable, given the task of the water sector is to protect the public from water-related hazards and guarantee water-related services. Processes of social learning are needed to develop structural conditions, as well as to implement and to sustain adaptive and integrated water management regimes. The following section critically explores the situation in the Swiss Rhône basin using the background and arguments already presented.

6.3 Rhône – Analysis of current management regime and suggestions for improvement

The major implications of climate change for Switzerland, in general, and the Rhône basin, in particular, are (Frei and Schär 2001; OcCC 2002; Schmidt et al. 2002):

- Temperature: increase of 3–5 degrees by 2100.
- Temperature extremes: increasing a maximum of +5 degrees, increasing a minimum of + 1–4 degrees.
- Precipitation: heavy rains and higher precipitation during winter seasons will become more frequent
- Snow: rise of the snow line to approximately 200–300 meters
- Floods: more frequent winter floods
- Drought: southern part drier, low-flow conditions more frequent
- Glaciers will largely disappear
- Permafrost: Rise of the altitude of permafrost
- Landslides: increased likelihood due to melting of permafrost soil.

Climate change will have pronounced impacts on the hydrological regime of many Alpine watersheds. The increase in temperature will result in a decrease in the amount of precipitation in the form of snow in winter. Glaciers will disappear, resulting in reduced natural water storage capacity. Changes in the seasonal distribution of precipitation, with more rain in winter and less rain in summer, and an increased probability of extreme precipitation events will result in a greater likelihood of extreme floods in winter and spring and a higher chance of drought and low-flow conditions in summer. Due to temperature increases, the altitude of the permafrost zone will be higher which, in combination with increased extreme precipitation events, will likely lead to more frequent landslides. Overall, the Alpine region will be more vulnerable to extreme weather events.

Consequently, the water sector has serious challenges ahead, in particular the management of extreme climate conditions (Schädler 2002). In summer, water shortages are expected due to decreasing precipitation, the increased likelihood of drought periods, an increase in the probability of low-flow conditions (decline of natural buffering capacity due to retreat of glaciers and snow fields), and an intensification of water demand for irrigation. This will have undesirable consequences for water temperature and quality. Due to the increased likelihood of winter and spring floods, there will be increasing demand to use reservoir storage for flood prevention. Overall, a request from downstream areas for balancing water flows to buffer extremes (floods and droughts) is expected. Such requests will require negotiations about changing use priorities and potential trade-offs in reservoir and flood management. Given the considerable uncertainties in climate change predictions, it will be important to develop appropriate adaptation strategies. This has been clearly acknowledged at the ministerial level in Switzerland, and pleas for new integrated and flexible strategies have been made (Willi 2006).

To determine whether management practice can respond to these challenges, a major construction effort to improve flood protection in the Rhône basin will be investigated more closely. The first coordinated attempt to protect the Swiss portion of the Rhône valley against floods was undertaken in the nineteenth century, after a series of heavy flooding events. Following the catastrophic floods that took place in 1860, federal funds were attributed in 1863 by the Cantonal Administration to undertake a first major construction of the River Rhône. After being completed in 1894, the first phase provided the conditions for the drainage and reclamation of the plain area (Colenco 2005).

The second major construction phase began in 1937, after a dike broke during a flood event in 1935. The purpose of the second correction project was to complete the works that began during the first phase, and to improve the solid and bed load transport capacity of the river (Département Fédéral des Affaires Intérieurs 1964). Another dike broke in 1948, so work continued until 1960, which improved the surface drainage of regularly flooded land.

A change in the control paradigm began in the 1990s, due to extreme floods occurring in 1987 and in 1993, in which observed changes indicated an imminent rupture of the protection dikes. In addition, accretion of the riverbed was still occurring in places and could not be fully controlled. Thus, doubts emerged whether dikes constituted a safe control against floods. In addition, it became progressively evident that the systematic embankment of the river initiated at the end of the nineteenth century had modified the river's morphology by reducing the area of the natural channel, thus diminishing most of the river's natural ecological functions. Furthermore, retention reservoirs for hydropower production constructed in the twentieth century have changed the flow of Alpine tributaries and the embankments of the Rhône, resulting in reduced surface areas of pristine floodplains. Today, floodplains are a remnant of the original biodiversity in the nineteenth century, occupying six percent of the original floodplain area. As a consequence, more than 170 flora and fauna species are endangered. In spite of intensive aquaculture, the fish population of the river remains low. The geometric straightness of the river embankment is also a factor, limiting both biodiversity and alluvial dynamics.

In recognition of the detrimental effects outlined above on ecosystem functions, the third Rhône River Correction (R3) Project, officially approved by the provincial government in 2002, has three main objectives:

i   safety, to ensure the protection against floods;
ii   environmental, to re-establish and even strengthen the biological functions of the river;
iii socioeconomic, to re-establish the social and economic legacies that normally take place along the river.

The R3 project aims to control potential flood damage within the plain area of the upper catchment of the Rhône River, particularly between Brig and the mouth of the river in Lake Geneva in the Canton du Valais. The project will be implemented over a period of approximately 30 years with an anticipated start of the construction work in 2008.

6.3.1 Analysis of the participatory process

Among the leading stakeholders (the implementing entities) there is a tendency to identify participation with consultation (Colenco 2005). As a result, the public, invited to express an opinion on an already planned concept, might use its right to opposition. This might not occur in a scenario with public representatives participating in the early stages of the planning. Further, consultation processes are insufficient when profound changes in management strategies and the role of different actors are envisaged (Pahl-Wostl 2002; Pahl-Wostl *et al.* 2007). Construction plans for the third correction of the Rhône have been published for consultation for all affected stakeholder groups (Rhoneprojekt 2005). The implementation plans reveal that economic considerations, technical considerations, and the avoidance of any use conflicts dominate the overall planning process. A widening of the riverbed of up to twice the current size is foreseen, whereas a three- to four-fold widening would be desirable from an ecological point of view. An accompanying research project (*EAWAG News* 2006; www.rhone-thur.eawag. ch) has provided empirical evidence that the planned construction measures and the flow regime will not lead to a significant improvement of the ecological situation, despite the rhetoric in official documents conveying the impression that a balance between the competing interests of flood protection, hydropower generation, and ecosystem restoration have been found. Given the dual objective of the project of flood protection and ecosystem restoration, the trade-off between both objectives could be reduced by explicitly taking into account the function of ecosystem services in floodplains. To realize such an approach would, however, require major changes in current and future land use in the floodplain. The consultation report mentions uncertainties and climate change only once – in parentheses. If they have been taken into account, it seems information on climate change and associated uncertainties are not a high priority to communicate to the public. Dimensions of flood protection measures are still derived from the expected magnitude of a century flood. Uncertainties are taken into account only by an increase in the safety margins. However, as shown by Aerts *et al.* (in press) a strategy combining a portfolio of measures with different damage to discharge characteristics may be a more robust strategy than relying on measures that are designed to provide complete safety but lead to disaster in the case of failure.

Despite the stated policy goals by government to foster innovation in flood management, the suggested strategies are conservative. The situation observed in the Rhône basin is quite characteristic for many river basins, as has been shown by first results from the European project NeWater (New Approaches to Adaptive Water Management Under Uncertainty), exploring the need for a transition towards adaptive water management in a number of river basins in Europe, Central Asia, and Africa. A reluctance to change at the operational level, similar to that in the Rhône basin, can for example be observed in the Netherlands. On the one hand, the Dutch government asks for a radical rethinking of water management – more space for rivers and living with water rather than control. On the other hand, management practice is very slow in adopting new strategies. Such inertia can be explained by the radical changes in the management regime that would be needed for more integrative flood management practices.

6.4 Radical change in management regimes and the importance of processes of social learning

The implementation of integrated and adaptive management strategies and the reduction of the trade-off between flood protection and floodplain restoration can be achieved by taking into account ecosystem services of floodplains and by moving towards multi-functional dynamic landscapes. As highlighted by Pahl-Wostl (2006), efficient integration requires processes of social learning, since fundamental changes are needed in the governance structure as summarized in Table 6.1. This table also incorporates classifications according to the water management hierarchies for adaptive management as described in section 6.5. This classification outlines how decisions and management of water resources are interrelated between different political levels (context, network, and game levels).

6.4.1 What is social learning?

Social learning in river basin management refers to developing and sustaining the capacity of different authorities, experts, interest groups, and the public to manage river basins effectively. Collective action and the resolution of conflicts require that people recognize their interdependence and their differences, and learn to deal with them constructively. The different groups need to learn and increase their awareness about their biophysical environment and about the complexity of social interactions.

6.4.2 Why is social learning needed to move towards and to sustain integrated, adaptive water management?

As previously mentioned, technical infrastructure (e.g. large technical infrastructure for flood protection), citizen behavior (expectations regarding safety in floodplains, risk perception), and engineering rules of good practice are often mutually dependent and stabilize each other, resulting in the blockage of new and improved resource management schemes (Pahl-Wostl 2002). Social learning is assumed to be crucial to break through such "lock-in" situations. It is also required to implement change to sustain adaptive management practices.

A new concept for social learning in river basin management has been developed in the context of the European project, HarmoniCOP. Figure 6.1 shows the framework for social learning, developed to account for learning processes in water resources management (Craps *et al.* 2003; Pahl-Wostl 2002). The framework is structured into context, process and outcomes, and has a feedback loop to account for change in cyclic and iterative processes. The context refers to the governance structure and the natural environment in a river basin. To improve the state of the environment in practice most often implies a change in governance structure.

Table 6.1 The current management regimes in regulated and controlled rivers, compared with a future state that has multi-functional and dynamic landscapes

	Current state with regulated and controlled rivers	Potential future state with a multi-functional dynamic landscape
Important stakeholder groups and their (changing) roles (Roles of actors at the game level – Switching)	authorities as regulators in a highly regulated environment engineers constructing and operating dams, reservoirs environmental protection groups fighting for floodplain restoration house owners living in floodplains agriculture using land in the vicinity of rivers shipping industry interested in well functioning waterways	authorities as contributors to an adaptive management process with shared responsibilities neutral third parties as facilitators of the decision making process engineers with skills in systems design house owners with property in a floodplain at a higher risk of being flooded tourism industry and tourists using the floodplains for recreation
Stakeholder participation (Roles of actors at the network level – Activating)	Little stakeholder participation – occasional consultation where different stakeholder groups and the public at large are asked to give their opinion on a management plan prepared by experts	Stakeholders and the public are actively involved in river basin management in a kind of co-production of knowledge and co-decision making.
Management Paradigm (Perceptions at the network level – Reframing)	Management as control. Technology driven. Risk can be quantified and optimal strategies can be chosen. Zero-sum-games in closed decision space.	Adaptive and integrated water management. "Living with water". Acceptable decisions are negotiated.
Institutional setting and governance (Institutions at the network and game level – Reforming and Arranging)	Institutional fragmentation: flood protection, nature conservation, regional planning and water management located in different authorities.	Polycentric governance and better institutional interplay Horizontal and vertical integration of formal institutional settings to overcome fragmentation Stronger role of informal institutions and participatory approaches.
Adaptive capacity (Tools at the Network and Game levels – Selecting and Using)	"Hard" approach to systems design aiming at implementing long-lasting optimal solutions. Adaptive capacity in general quite low due to high investment in infrastructure and often inflexible legal regulations.	"Soft" approach to systems design allows new insights to be taken into account, including responses to changing environmental and socio-economic boundary conditions.

Source: Pahl-Wostl 2006.

The concept referring to multi-party interactions in actor networks has two pillars (Figure 6.1). The pillars refer to the processing of factual information on a problem (content management) and to engaging in processes of social exchange (social involvement), respectively. Social involvement refers to essential elements of social processes, such as the framing of the problem, the management of the boundaries between different stakeholder groups, the type of ground rules and negotiation strategies chosen, or the role of leadership in the process. As one example, the role of framing is explained in more detail.

During the initial stages of dealing with a problem, framing and reframing of a problem domain determines the direction of the overall process. Frames may be derived from culture, social roles, and scientific disciplines. Actors have frames that determine how they make sense and meaning of information and their physical and social environment. Differences in the framing of an issue are among the key reasons for problems in communication and entrenched conflicts among actors. The framing of an issue includes, for example, what is at stake, who should be included and in which role. Processes of framing and reframing are essential elements of social dynamics in a group during the negotiation of meaning of key issues, such as goals to be achieved, or how to measure success of management. It is important to be aware that powerful actors often impose their frames or interpretation of an issue onto a process. A relational practice may be a role-playing game or policy exercise in which actors are willing to reflect and discuss their own perspectives

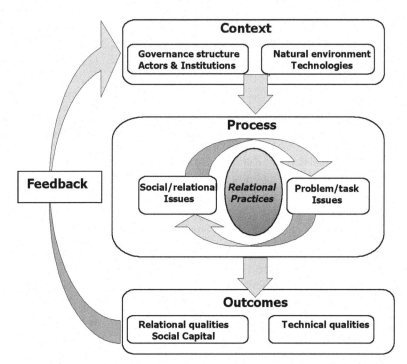

Figure 6.1 Conceptual framework for social learning in resources management.

as well as listen to others. This type of social learning, which does not necessarily lead to consensus, develops the ability to deal with differences constructively.

The overall social learning process in a group leads to input on how to move the state of the environment towards desired properties (technical qualities), and to social capital, such as an increase in the capacity of a stakeholder group to manage a problem.

Table 6.2 summarizes results from the case studies in HarmoniCOP, regarding factors that constrain and support social learning (Tippett *et al.* 2005; Mostert *et al.* 2007).

There is a recognized need for social learning processes in the transition towards integrated and adaptive management approaches, and a requirement for the insights on the nature of such processes and factors that constrain and support social learning. This gives rise to the question – what are the appropriate approaches to facilitate change?

6.5 How to promote change

Decisions related to, and management of, water resources do not take place in isolation but are rather complex political processes that take shape at different political levels (Figure 6.1).

Table 6.2 Factors that constrain and support social learning

Factors constraining Social Learning	*Factors supporting Social Learning*
STRUCTURE – CONTEXT	*STRUCTURE – CONTEXT*
Centralised political and economic systems Privatisation and commercialisation of environment Bureaucratic systems political secrecy and poor public access to information.	Increased decentralisation of power Move away from overregulated bureaucracy Political recognition of the positive value of the public voice Greater environmental awareness by members of the public developing a more consensus based culture.
PROCESS	*PROCESS*
Lack of clear objectives and process for involvement Lack of time and effort taken to build trust Lack of process to explore common ground rules and manage conflicts constructively Lack of process to link planning at different levels of scale Ineffective communication of technical issues Non-communication of supposedly shared or common knowledge or premises.	Provision of sufficient time and resources Opportunities for participation early enough in process Use of facilitators and process management Definition of commonly accepted ground rules Explicit recognition of different perspectives C\clear formulation of interests/illustrate the framing of the respective issue.

- The **Context** level, which incorporates the wider political and institutional environment, determines the governance structure.
- **Networks** (policy arenas) determine actors and institutions, who is in and who is out of the process, as well as the boundaries and framing of the problems and solutions taken into account.
- **Games**, the level of rules, are institutions that shape individual behavior and collective negotiation, learning, and decision-making processes.

Understanding how at the level of context, networks and games, actors, and institutions create perceptions and make use of tools is critical for an adaptive management of water resources. The coupling between the various levels shapes the outcome of water decisions and investments and hence determines the adaptive capacity of the water sector or of a specific river basin. Table 6.1 shows how perceptions, tools, actors, and institutions can be used and applied at the network and game levels in relation to managing rivers in the current state, which focuses on regulated and controlled rivers. This was then compared to a potential future state with more multi-functional and dynamic management of rivers that incorporates adaptation to change.

These ideas are worked into a coherent framework for analyzing the political context within which an adaptive capacity needs to be developed for river basin management. In Table 6.3 12 political actions (PA) are described that actors need to consider if they wish to develop adaptive capacity for the management of a river basin. The case of the upper Rhône River is used to provide tangible examples for each of the 12 PAs. Examining the R3 project through the lens of the water management hierarchies framework demonstrates that elements of adaptive management are being used, but there is considerable potential to do more through reframing and social learning. The challenge is to build further on each of the described political actions. Efficient application of adaptive management can ensure that a river basin such as the Rhône can respond to pressures such as climate change. If a river is widened sufficiently to take into account changes in flow due to climate change, then the significant investment into watersheds will be worthwhile and have an effective impact.

6.5.1 The context level

The context level refers to the wider context within which river basin management takes shape. It refers to societal views, cultural norms, (national) constitutions and laws, the approaches and tools used for management, and the existing landscape of actors and organizations. The context level has been formed over long periods of time: decades or even centuries. It typically affects the management of several river basins as it constrains and determines practices at larger spatial scales – countries or (economic) regions.

Table 6.3 Water management hierarchies for adaptive management

Hierarachical Levels	Perceptions	Tools	Actors	Institutions
Level 1: Context level	*Shaping*	*Developing*	*Grouping*	*Creating*
Description applies to the national policy level on a slow time scale of decades.	→changing society-wide views and ideas that shape the context within which networks are created and are functioning.	→emergence of new tools relevant for policy networks and games can shift the tool options networks have at their disposal.	→new groups of actors are created from which actors for the network can be selected.	→setting up new (groups of) institutions that that can be a driver of reforms.
Level 2: Network level	*Reframing*	*Selecting*	*Activating*	*Reforming*
Description at a provincial or Canton level decisions are made over years.	→changing actor's perceptions of the network, its role, goal, structure and functions.	→choosing the tools or changing the tools with which the network can alter the functioning of the network.	→bringing new actors or changing (network) positions of existing actors.	→changing rules and resources in networks that change fundamentally the network's structure and functioning.
Level 3: Game level	*Convenanting*	*Using*	*Switching*	*Arranging*
Description individuals and organizations decisions are made over months	→exploring similar-ities and differences in actor's perceptions and the opportunities that exist for goal convergence using the 'rules of the game'.	→changing the access to and ability of actors to use tools.	→(de)mobilising actors possessing resources to (un)block the game.	→creating, sustaining and changing ad hoc provisions which suit groups of institutions.

6.5.1.1 Shaping and developing

Actors at the context level sometimes have the possibility of changing, or can create the opportunity to change, societal views that determine how a problem can be framed. They also might have the opportunity to change existing water policies at national or regional levels in such a way that water problems can be framed differently. As such, actors and organizations can *shape* the context and discourse within which networks are managed and games are conducted.

For the management of the upper Rhône basin, the context is, amongst others, defined by the Swiss and French constitutions and the water management organizations in both countries. Increasingly, though, this context is changing through the implementation of the EU Water Framework Directive, Nature 2000 directive, and other EU directives. In France, for example, the established water organizations are challenged by the obligation to allow for much wider public participation in decision making (Pflieger 2006). Furthermore, societal perceptions are (slowly) changing in both Switzerland and France. In Switzerland, rivers are increasingly viewed as important recreational and nature areas and not only as conduits of irrigation water or drains of storm water (ProNatura 2006). However, at the same time the opening of the European energy markets has generated interest from Swiss electricity companies to generate hydropower to service peak power demands (e.g. on Monday mornings). The generation of this power results in significant fluctuations in river levels throughout the upper Rhône River system at short time intervals, impacting negatively on the Rhône River's ecology (Romande Energie 2005).

New tools or mechanisms can be developed that can change the way networks and policy actors find solutions for water allocation problems. For example, the 'green power tool' allows Swiss electricity companies to generate 'green hydropower' that can be sold for a premium price. In the upper Rhône valley, the hydropower plant Pont-de-la-Tine is currently operating using the 'NatureMade' certification label (Romande Energie 2005). The plant generates electricity but also leaves residual water in the river to maintain the downstream river ecology. Though the capacity of this plant is small, it is still significant as it demonstrates that hydropower generation can be combined with ecological objectives. It also shows that a new tool can change the way water is managed and even create a win-win situation – in this case at the local level.

6.5.1.2 Grouping and creating

Stakeholders in river basins and at national levels often cluster in different groups that hold similar views or interests. Creating or (re-)grouping actors, either at national levels or within a river basin, can help to change the way a policy network is managed or functions. This type of grouping has been done to an extent in the Rhône River basin, in which stakeholders are at the internal and external levels. At the internal level, the heads of government departments are grouped into the steering council (described further below) and are in charge of strategy and project implementation. At the external level, there are thematic and local/regional groups. The thematic group consists of various subgroups of actors who represent different sectors of interest (tourism and leisure, the environment, the economy, agriculture, land and safety). The local/regional groups represent local/regional interests of communities or municipalities, which are represented by regional steering committees (Colenco 2005).

While different actors can cluster in different ways, another option is to create new (groups of) institutions. This often happens at the national level when a new water policy is developed and the existing institutional set-up needs to be brought in line with the policy. A typical mechanism in water management is the creation of a national-level coordinating body. This body then includes representatives from different ministries and each has responsibilities for some aspects of water management, such as water quality monitoring, operation and maintenance of river infrastructure, hydropower generation, irrigation and drainage development, and maintenance. The state council of the Canton du Valais created a number of institutional bodies to direct the implementation of R3. The steering council, or the Conseil de Pilotage (COPIL), consists of representatives from various federal offices including the Office of Water and Geology, the Department of Transport, Infrastructure and the Environment, as well as external stakeholders in the form of associations of municipalities and organizations (Canton du Valais 2005; Colenco 2005). Although this group was specifically created for the R3 project, it could be useful in creating more dynamic groups that fully incorporate external stakeholders from the very beginning of the planning process.

6.5.2 The network level

The network level refers to the provincial context of river basin management. It includes interactions between actors across organizations at the basin level, and is influenced by the context level. The network level refers to the relationships established between interdependent organizations, and how they cooperate (or do not cooperate). The context level determines how the network level will be formed and how it will function, and in turn the network level will determine how organizations will play the game (i.e., their approach to decision making, their attitudes to new tools for river basin management). The network level is formed over years and usually applies to the management of a regional river basin.

6.5.2.1 Reframing and selecting

As previously mentioned, social learning includes reframing of problems to make sense of available information and how it can be used in adaptive river basin management. Reframing changes the perception of the network's role, goal, structure, and functions. Problems can be redefined and possibly solved using different approaches derived from reframing. However, reframing can be a long process, as perceptions are rooted in mental constructs derived from past experiences (Kickert *et al.* 1999). Often actors within a network will need to go through a learning process to understand how reframing occurred and why. In addition, the network also can be used as a tool to bring forward ideas and redefine river management problems into a more manageable form. In the case of the R3 project, reframing should occur around the main project goals (ensuring safety from floods), changes in the river landscape and its use to change the view from flood management to watershed management. The impacts of climate change and uncertainties need to be incorporated so that the management plan is adaptive and flexible to changing events.

Traditional instruments such as existing regulations used for river basin management may not be very effective within a network; instead instruments must be selected and altered to fit the frame of reference of the network. Legal, economic, and communicative tools within a network must be able to be deployed at a horizontal level across the network as opposed to the vertical top-down approach. Although tools are what enable networks to function, they need to fit into the network structure within which they are used. The tools selected and adapted for the network depend on the actors that make up the network and the relationships that exist between the actors (Kickert *et al.* 1999). Tools introduced to the R3 project, such as the www.rhone.vs site, were implemented to facilitate social learning in the general public but had limited outreach to stakeholders (HarmoniCOP 2005; Canton du Valais 2005). The use of geographical information systems and other computer graphic displays such as AutoCad and PowerPoint were found to have some success in facilitating dialogue and understanding of the R3 project (Luyet 2005). The Canton of Valais has produced a report on the structural plan for the third correction, as well as maps for each commune displaying land use and flood-prone areas along the Rhône (Canton du Valais 2005). These types of visual tools can aid in understanding the problems and help stakeholders in the network with reframing their understanding of the extent of the ecological and social issues to be tackled in the Rhône floodplain.

6.5.2.2 Activating and reforming

Sometimes new actors are activated, created, or brought into a network to carry out functions needed to manage the network. The introduction of new actors can occur by setting up or reorganizing a commission, recruitment, and bringing in an advisor (Kickert *et al.* 1999). For example, an association of business owners could be created to take part in public participation discussions on floodplain management in order to ensure the interests of the business community are represented. Introducing a new party into a network does not automatically solve problems and create new ideas; rather problems are solved and ideas develop through the course of interaction. Including organizations in public discussions is only useful and representative if they are actively involved in the network and their input is considered important to the decision-making process. In the Rhône example, new actors were brought into thematic working groups within the R3 project by the State Council of the Canton du Valais to ensure representation of interests outside government. The stakeholders include five municipalities, the Sierre region association and six different regional associations representing agriculture, ecology, environment and nature protection (HarmoniCOP 2005). It would be useful also to bring in new actors with specific knowledge on climate change and ideas on adaptation within the river basin.

Reframing problems in discussions will lead to actual reformation through action. For example, institutions that are created or activated can be part of the reforming process in a network. Policy processes in networks can be unpredictable and complex. There are often a variety of actors whose preferences can change during the course of interactions. Consequently, rules and resources within networks can change, leading to structural and functional shifts. However, networks do not function without management, which can be seen as promoting the mutual adjustment of the diverse objectives of actors, and ensuring a cooperative strategy with regard to tackling problems (Kickert *et al.* 1999). Network management steers the process of reforming as perceptions shift and actors enter and leave the network. In the R3 project, new actors brought into the river basin network in the

Canton du Valais can be a mechanism to reform project organization and ensure the participation and perspective of external stakeholders.

6.5.3 The game level

Networks, which are the relation patterns between actors, are the context in which games take place. At the same time, the games change and influence the shape of networks. Actors within networks choose game strategies (i.e. policy-making processes) that seem rational according to the network they interact with, their individual goals, and the overall context of the policy-making process. Furthermore, actors driving river basin management at the game level are influenced by other forms of management (e.g. agricultural management) and the relationships developed in the network through present and past interactions. A characteristic feature of a game is that the result derives from the interaction between the strategies of all actors involved (Kickert *et al.* 1999). The rules of the game put constraints on actors, but are at the same time the product of their interactions (Kickert *et al.* 1999).

The game level includes individuals and organizations that are making decisions over periods of several months. These decisions are steered by context and network structure, but also have an upward impact that can shape interactions within the network level, leading to shifts in the context level. Actors' perceptions undergo incremental change during games due to interaction or confrontation with other actors' perceptions (Kickert *et al.* 1999).

6.5.3.1 Convenanting and using

Convenanting refers to a management strategy aimed at improving the consistency of decisions made in the game by exploring and consolidating perceptions of actors (Klijn and Teisman 1997). Consistency is improved through social knowledge and learning, which involves changes in norms, practices and behavior, as well as changes in perception and understanding among stakeholders. This management strategy uses the informal rules that exist in a meeting, committee or organization to manage the participants. The convenanting concept is used to emphasize that specialized actors (i.e. network managers) have potential for enriching new initiatives. An effective network manager will interlink specialized initiatives in order to improve the policy initiative around which a game is constructed (Klijn and Teisman 1997). Convenanting in the R3 project occurred to an extent as the Regional Steering Committee was involved in workshops during which actors representing various interests learned and discussed the advantages, disadvantages, and consequences of implementing the plans of the third correction, as well as ensuring that participants understood the rules of the game (i.e. the boundaries in which they have to make decisions). Workshops and discussions promote social learning, allow actors to make informed decisions, and work towards goal convergence using the rules of the game.

For a management strategy to achieve its goals, a process of social knowledge and learning progression is undertaken by actors involved in a game. Actors may need to be trained to use the tools they need to be effective in playing a game. For example, a toolkit for environmental flows can be developed to guide river basin management, but it may be of little use unless the actors are trained in how to apply the knowledge from the toolkit. This learning can evolve over time through interactions with other actors or through active training courses. The result is that the actors can shift the balance of the game as their perceptions change. As previously mentioned, a few visual tools were selected to help stakeholders in facilitating constructive dialogue. Taking photographs was a tool employed to help stakeholders identify their objectives in the participatory process in the R3 project. Participants were asked to take pictures of what they thought was beautiful, ugly, unsustainable and attractive to tourists in the river basin, and then elaborate why they took each picture. This approach was used to get stakeholders to think about how to transform their theoretical knowledge into concrete pictures (Luyet *et al*. 2004). This approach is a good start, but application of tools and training should be taken further and incorporate adaptive management to climate change and uncertainties.

6.5.3.2 Switching and arranging

Policy-making processes can be improved by switching on specific participants. Selective activation demands that managers assess which actors are essential at given moments in a policy process, whether and how to involve them. The success of activating and deactivating depends on choosing the appropriate actors, as well as the willingness of actors to invest time and resources in a policy process. The R3 project involves internal and external actors at the federal, canton, and municipal levels, as well as independent organizations concerned with ecology, agriculture, business, and land ownership. R3 depends on activating or deactivating the different stakeholders at the appropriate levels to determine solutions to problems such as water allocation. There is no point in engaging actors in a game if they do not possess the necessary resources to actively participate. If the input of a set of actors is considered essential to the policy process then tools must be used to ensure that they have the needed capacity to participate.

'Arranging' refers to the capacity of the participants involved to develop platforms on which games can be played and to the capability of the participants to develop or use rules for interaction (Kickert *et al*. 1999). Arranging includes creating, sustaining, and changing ad hoc provisions to suit various situations or games (Klijn and Teisman 1997). Arrangement as a management activity is the art of linking interdependent actors in such a way that the arrangement costs are low and do not result in high transaction costs (Kickert *et al*. 1999). Arrangement in the R3 project can refer to the evolution of the structure of the project and relationships between stakeholders. Different actors may be brought in or new relationships forged in order to change the status quo and move forward on an issue.

6.6 Conclusions and policy implementation: requirements and challenges for the implementation of adaptive management in upland watersheds

The analysis in the previous section provides evidence that there have been opportunities to engage in a dialogue that could influence a change in management practices in the Rhône case, but further development in all political actions is needed to implement effective adaptive management practices. Undergoing reframing and the process of social learning can open up discussions to alternative perspectives, solutions and other stakeholders. Social learning leading to change requires leadership and clear commitment from those designing and coordinating the process. Developing adaptive capacity with a long-term vision would be a wise strategy, rather than responding to disaster and escalating conflicts.

Currently, adaptive management in relation to climate change is limited in prevailing designs, practices, and ideas surrounding river basin management. Therefore, reframing issues of river basin management to include climate change scenarios may aid in shifting the focus from flood management to a wider basin management view that includes storage and buffering of flow and capacity upstream (Dyson *et al.* 2003). Another example of the importance of adaptive management pertains to ecological restoration. If ecological restoration of a watershed is narrowly defined (i.e. one section of a river), then the results are unlikely to be sufficient to significantly justify investment, as other sections of the river will not be restored and benefits will be minimal.

Drawing on conceptual and empirical analyses, it is possible to make a number of recommendations for policy making to develop, implement, and sustain adaptive management practices in upland watersheds facing increased uncertainty due to global and climate change.

- The complex socio-ecological nature of river basin environments and the inherent uncertainties associated with their management have to be taken into account in policy development and implementation.
- Selected management strategies should be robust and perform well under a range of possible, but initially uncertain, future developments.
- The design of transparent and open social learning processes is a key requirement of sustainable water management regimes.
- Effort has to be devoted to building trust and social capital for problem solving and collaborative governance.
- An increase in, and maintenance of, the flexibility and adaptive capacity of water management regimes should be a primary management goal.
- Trust in a collaborative process is a more robust strategy in conditions of uncertainty then any belief in prediction and control.
- Entrenched perceptions and beliefs block innovation and change. Space has to be provided for creative and out-of-the-box thinking.
- There is a significant need to train a new generation of water management practitioners skilled in participatory system design and implementation.

References

Aerts, J. *et al.* (in press) Dealing with uncertainty in flood management through diversification. *Ecology and Society.*

Bergkamp, G. *et al.* (2000) *Dams, ecosystem functions and environmental restoration.* Prepared for the World Commission on Dams (WCD). Cape Town, South Africa.

Canton du Valais (2005) *Plan sectoriel 3ème correction du Rhône. Version pour consultation.* May 2005.

Colenco (2005) *Public participation in the Upper Rhône Basin, Switzerland.* Case Study Report for WP5 of the HarmoniCOP Project. Available online at http://www.harmonicop.info.

Craps, M. (ed.) 2003 *Social learning in river basin management.* Report of workpackage 2 of the HarmoniCOP project. Available online at http://www.harmonicop.uni-osnabrueck. de/_files/_down/SocialLearning.pdf.

Département Fédéral des Affaires Intérieurs (1964) *La correction du Rhône en amont du lac Léman.* Bern : Office Fédéral des Imprimés.

Dyson, M., Bergkamp, G. and Scanlon, J. (eds) (2003) *Flow: the essentials of environmental flows.* Gland, Switzerland : IUCN. 2nd Edition.

EAWAGNews (2006) *Hochwasserschutz und revitalisierung – neue wege für unsere flüsse. EAWAG News,* 61, März, 2006. Available online at http://www.eawag.ch.

Frei, C. and Schär, C. (2001) Detection probabilities of trends in rare events: theory and application to heavy precipitation in the Alpine region. *Journal of Climate,* 14: 1564–84.

Gleick, P.H. (2003) Global freshwater resources: soft-path solutions for the 21st century. *Science,* 302: 524–8.

Gunderson, L. (1999) Resilience, flexibility and adaptive management – antidotes for spurious certitude? *Conservation Ecology,* 3(1): 7. Available online at http://www. consecol.org/vol3/iss1/art7.

Holling, C. S. (ed.) (1978) *Adaptive environmental assessment and management.* New York: John Wiley & Sons.

Kabat, P. and van Schaik, H. (coordinating lead authors) (2003) *Climate changes the water rules: how water managers can cope with today's climate variability and tomorrow's climate change.* Netherlands: Dialogue on Water and Climate.

Kickert, W. J. M., Klijn, E.-H. and Koppenjan, J. F. M. (1999) *Managing complex networks: strategies for the public sector.* London: Sage.

Kiker, C. F., Milon, J. W., and Hodges, A. W. (2001) Adaptive learning for science-based policy: the Everglades restoration. *Ecological Economics,* 37: 403–16.

Klijn, E.-H. and Teisman, G. R. (1997) Strategies and games in networks. In Kickert, W. J. M., Klijn, E.-H. and Koppenjan, J. F. M. (eds.) *Managing complex networks: strategies for the public sector.* London: Sage, pp. 98–118.

Lee, K. N. (1999) Appraising adaptive management. *Conservation Ecology,* 3: 3–16.

Luyet. V. (2005) *Bases méthodologiques de la participation lors de grands projets ayant des impacts sur le paysage. Cas d'application: la plaine du Rhône valaisanne.* Thèse No 3342. Lausanne : Ecole Polytechnique Fédérale de Lausanne (EPFL).

Luyet, V., Iorgulescu, I. and Schlaepfer, R. (2004) *Taking pictures: a tool that can help stakeholders to identify their objectives in a participative process. Case study: the third Rhône correction project (R3) in Switzerland.* International Commission on Irrigation and Drainage (ICID) 2004. Tools for Public Participation, Conflict Resolution and Decision-Making in Water Resources Management, Seminar held on 14 October, 2004. ICID British Section, London.

Moench *et al.* (2003) *The fluid mosaic: water governance in the context of variability, uncertainty and change*. Nepal Water Conservation Foundation, Kathmandu, Nepal and the Institute for Social and Environmental Transition, Boulder Colorado, USA.

Mostert, E. *et al.* (2007) Social learning in European river basin management: barriers and fostering mechanisms from 10 river basins. *Ecology and Society*, 12(1): 19. Available online at http://www.ecologyandsociety.org/vol12/iss1/art19/.

NeWater (2008) *New Approaches to Adaptive Water Management Under Uncertainty.* Available online at http://www.newater.com.

OcCC (2002) *Das Klima ändert – auch in der Schweiz. Die wichtigsten Ergebnisse des dritten Wissensstandberichts des IPCC aus Sicht der Schweiz*, Bern.

Pahl-Wostl, C. (1995) *The dynamic nature of ecosystems: chaos and order entwined.* Chichester: Wiley.

Pahl-Wostl, C. (1998) Ecosystem organization across a continuum of scales: a comparative analysis of lakes and rivers. In Peterson, D. and Parker, T. *(eds.) Scale Issues in Ecology.* New York: Columbia University Press, pp. 141–70.

Pahl-Wostl, C. (2002) Towards sustainability in the water sector – the importance of human actors and processes of social learning. *Aquatic Sciences*, 64: 394–411.

Pahl-Wostl, C. (2006) The importance of social learning in restoring the multifunctionality of rivers and floodplains. *Ecology and Society,* 11(1): 10. Available online at http://www.ecologyandsociety.org/vol11/iss1/art10/.

Pahl-Wostl, C. (2007a) The implications of complexity for integrated resources management. *Environmental Modelling and Software*, 22: 561–9.

Pahl-Wostl, C. (2007b) Transition towards adaptive management of water facing climate and global change. *Water Resources Management*, 21: 49–62.

Pahl-Wostl, C. *et al.* (2007) Social learning and water resources management, *Ecology and Society,* 12(2): 5. Available online at http://www.ecologyandsociety.org/vol12/iss2/art5/.

Pfleiger, G. (2006) The French model of water supply management challenges by users' empowerment. *Water Policy*, 8: 211–29.

ProNatura (2006). Available online at http://www.pronatura.ch.

Rhoneprojekt (2005) Sachplan 3. Rhonekorrektur: Version für die Vernehmlassung. Departement für Verkehr, Bau und Umwelt. Diensstelle für Strassen- und Flussbau.

Richter,B. D., Mathews,R., Harrison,D. L., and Wigington,R. (2003) Ecologically sustainable water management: managing river flows for ecological integrity. *Ecological Applications*, 13: 206–24.

Romande Energie (2005) *L'Esprit Bien-Être*. No1/05.

Schädler, B. (2002) Auswirkungen der klimaveränderungen auf Alpine gewässersystems. *EAWAG News*, 55: 24–6.

Schmidt, J. *et al.* (2002) Mesoscale precipitation variability in the region of the European Alps during the 20th century. *Journal of Climatology,* 22: 1049–72.

Tillman, D. E., Larsen, T., Pahl-Wostl, C. and Gujer, W. (2005) Simulation for strategy development in water supply systems. *Hydroinformatics*, 7/1.

Tippet, J., Searle, B., Pahl-Wostl, C. and Rees, Y. (2005) Social learning in public participation in river basin management. *Environmental Science & Policy*, 8(3): 287-99.

Tockner, K. and Stanford, J.A. (2002) Riverine flood plains: present state and future trends. *Environmental Conservation*, 29: 308–30.

Walters, C. J. (1986) *Adaptive management of renewable resources.* New York: McGraw Hill.

Ward, J. V. (1998) Riverine landscapes: biodiversity patterns, disturbance regimes, and aquatic conservation. *Biological Conservation*, 83: 269–78.

Willi, H.-P. (2006) Hochwasserschutz – eine herausforderung. *EAWAG, News*, 61: 9–11.

7 Effects of climate change on drought frequency

Potential impacts and mitigation opportunities

Richard M. Adams and Dannele E. Peck

Climate change is expected to affect the frequency and intensity of extreme weather events, including droughts. This chapter reviews the current understanding of possible impacts of climate change on water resources, with emphasis on the frequency and intensity of droughts. The chapter also reviews possible means to mitigate the effects of droughts. Results from recent research on drought effects are presented to examine the efficiency of alternative mitigation strategies. Findings indicate that use of long-term weather forecasts, coupled with improved management practices, may offset some of the adverse consequences of more frequent and/or more intense droughts.

7.1 Introduction

The recurring drought and heat observed over large portions of the western United States in the last decade have generated adverse and costly effects, including lost agricultural productivity in rain-fed regions of the Great Plains, record wildfires in Arizona, Montana, Idaho, Oregon, Colorado and California, and large fish kills in California's Klamath River, triggered by warm water temperatures. Drought has persisted for nearly a decade in some regions of the western United States, leading to severe stress on water users. The intensity and frequency of recent droughts, coupled with rising temperatures observed globally over the past decade, and increased frequency of other extreme weather events, such as hurricanes, has raised concerns that fundamental climate shifts may be occurring in North America and elsewhere.

This chapter reviews the current understanding of possible impacts of global climate change on water resources, with emphasis on the frequency and intensity of drought. The focus on drought, rather than long-term climate change more generally, is intended to provide managerial and policy relevance to what otherwise is an overwhelmingly complex topic. The chapter reviews the physical and economic consequences of drought, as well as the potential to mitigate the adverse consequences of these events by using long-term weather forecasts and other meteorological information in water resources management. Examples from empirical research are presented that examine the efficiency of selected strategies to mitigate drought effects in North America. These examples demonstrate the potential economic benefits arising from the use of drought forecast information in agriculture and fisheries management.

7.2 Global climate change, water resources and drought

The ability of the earth's atmosphere to trap solar radiation and increase global temperature (the so-called "greenhouse effect") has been recognized for at least 150 years. More recently, global climate change has been a topic of intense scientific and political debate. Certain evidence is unequivocal; carbon dioxide concentrations (the most abundant greenhouse gas in the earth's atmosphere) have been increasing steadily for over a century. Specifically, the atmospheric mixing ratio of CO_2 has increased by 36 percent over the past 250 years (Forster *et al.* 2007; Section 2.3.1), and are higher now than they have been in the last 400,000 years (National Assessment Synthesis Team (NAST) 2000). Average annual air temperature in the United States has risen almost 0.5°C over the twentieth century, due, in part, to increased CO_2 levels (Hansen *et al.* 2001). Additionally, 11 of the 12 warmest years on record since 1850 occurred during the years 1995 to 2006 (Trenberth *et al.* 2007). The role that humans have played in recent global warming, and whether it is possible to offset that effect in any meaningful time scale, is still debated. However, the belief that global warming will continue is becoming more widely accepted in the science and policy communities. Thus, it is prudent to consider both the impacts of such warming as well as mechanisms to adjust to those effects.

An ensemble of general circulation models (GCMs) predicts annual-mean temperatures in the United States will rise over the next 100 years by 2°C to 3°C along the western, southern, and eastern continental edges, by 5°C or more in northern regions, and by 10°C in northern Alaska (Christensen *et al.* 2007; Section 11.5.3.1). Atmospheric scientists anticipate numerous climatic effects to arise from these increasing temperatures. For example, precipitation, which has increased in the United States by 5 to 10 percent over the twentieth century (Intergovernmental Panel on Climate Change (IPCC) 2001a), is predicted to continue to increase in many regions, particularly those at higher latitudes, such as the Northeast (Christensen *et al.* 2007; Section 11.1.2 and 11.1.3). More specifically, two early generation GCMs projected 25 percent precipitation increases in the Northeast, 10 to 30 percent increases in the Midwest, 20 percent increases in the Pacific Northwest, 10 percent decreases in the southern coast of Alaska, and up to 25 percent declines in the Oklahoma panhandle, north Texas, eastern Colorado and western Kansas (NAST 2000).

More recent GCM analyses, as reported in the IPCC's Fourth Assessment, offer less detailed projections for individual regions of the United States. Large model-to-model differences in projected regional impacts indicate that GCMs are unable to consistently represent dynamic features that affect regional climates in North America; climate scientists therefore place little confidence in most of these regional projections (Christensen *et al.* 2007; Section 11.5). The following projections are sufficiently consistent, however, to be included in the IPCC's Fourth

Assessment Report. Specifically, an ensemble of GCMs predicts a 20 percent increase in precipitation for northern regions of North America, a 15 percent increase in winter precipitation for northwestern regions, and a 20 percent decrease in summer precipitation for southwestern regions. Predictions for the central and eastern regions are more general, including an expected increase in winter precipitation for northern areas, and a decrease in summer precipitation for southern areas (Christensen *et al.* 2007; Section 11.5.3.2).

7.2.1 Consequences of drought

As noted above, GCM results suggest a range of potential effects of global climate change on water resources and agriculture (see IPCC 1998, 2001a, 2007 for details). These include increased surface temperatures and evaporation rates, increased global precipitation, increased proportions of precipitation received as rain, rather than snow, earlier and shorter runoff seasons, increased water temperatures, and decreased water quality. Precipitation patterns also are expected to become more variable, resulting in increased risk of extreme precipitation events, including drought, which is the focus of this chapter (Meehl *et al.* 2007; Sections 10.3.5.1 and 10.3.6.1; also see Adams, Hurd and Reilly 1999 for a review of the economic effects of such climatic changes on agriculture and agricultural resources). More frequent and intense droughts arising from climate change would have serious management implications for water resource users.

The economic consequences of drought are well documented. On average, annual costs in the United States due to drought are estimated at $6 to $8 billion (Knutson 2001). Flooding and hurricanes, though more publicized than drought, are reported to be responsible for only $3.6 to $7.2 billion in combined annual damages (Knutson 2001), although this estimate will likely be higher when damages from the 2005 hurricane season (e.g. Katrina) are included. The economic costs of drought largely arise from direct physical impacts, such as crop failure, municipal water shortages, wildfires, fish and wildlife mortality, and water deficits that reduce hydroelectric power generation and increase electricity prices. The National Oceanographic and Atmospheric Administration (NOAA, 2002) and Claussen (2001) provide comprehensive discussions of the physical and socioeconomic impacts of drought in the United States. Most economic effects occur during the time period of the drought event. However, other delayed or lagged effects can occur subsequent to the drought, as a result of decisions made during the drought event (see Peck and Adams 2006, for a discussion of the "persistent effects" of drought on economic outcomes in an irrigated agricultural setting). It is important to recognize and account for both the direct and delayed effects in assessments of the costs of droughts.

Water resource managers, agricultural producers, timber managers, and policy makers can reduce the negative effects of drought through a number of strategies. These include revising water storage and release programs for reservoirs, adopting drought-tolerant cropping practices, adjusting crop insurance programs, pre-positioning fire suppression equipment, and supporting water transfer opportunities. However, the ability to anticipate and efficiently prepare for future drought conditions is currently limited by imprecise long-term weather forecasts and climate models, among other reasons. Improvements in some forms of climate forecasts, such as those associated with the El Niño-Southern Oscillation (ENSO) phenomenon, offer potential for reducing the impacts of both drought and flooding. Economic costs associated with drought could be reduced further with improvement in the ability to detect drought farther in advance, to more precisely forecast drought location and intensity, and to use such forecasts to refine basic drought management strategies.

7.2.2 Water quantity, timing, and quality

Increases in precipitation, given warmer atmospheric conditions, will not necessarily mean more available water at the state or regional level. The higher evaporation rates that accompany rising surface temperatures are expected to result in less water being available in many regions (Frederick and Gleick 1999; Christensen *et al.* 2007; Section 11.5.3; Field *et al.* 2007: p.627). For example, some early generation GCMs projected global average evaporation to increase 3 to 15 percent with doubled CO_2 levels (Gleick 2000). Simulation studies suggest that precipitation must increase by at least 10 percent to balance evaporative losses resulting from a 4°C temperature increase (Gleick 2000). Projections of rising evaporation rates indicate they will outpace precipitation increases, on a seasonal basis, in many regions (IPCC 1998; Gleick 2000). The greatest deficits are expected to occur in the summer, leading to decreased soil moisture levels and more frequent and severe agricultural drought (IPCC 1998; Gleick 2000; Miller, Bashford, and Strem 2006).

Shifts in the form and timing of precipitation and runoff, specifically in snow-fed basins, are also likely to cause more frequent summer droughts (Kundzewicz *et al.* 2007: p.187). More precisely, rising temperatures are expected to increase the proportion of winter precipitation received as rain, with a declining proportion arriving in the form of snow (Christensen *et al.* 2007; Section 11.4.3; Field *et al.* 2007: p.622; Frederick and Gleick 1999). Knowles *et al.* (2006) shows that these changes are already taking place in the western United States. It is also expected that snow pack levels will form much later in the winter, accumulate in much smaller quantities, and melt earlier in the season, leading to reduced summer flows (IPCC 2001b; Kundzewicz *et al.* 2007; Section 3.4.1).

These changes in snow pack and runoff are of particular concern to water managers in a number of settings, including hydropower generation, irrigated agriculture, urban water supply, flood protection and to commercial and recreational fishing. For example, if the runoff season occurs primarily in winter and early spring, rather than late spring and summer, water availability for summer-irrigated crops will decline during crucial spring and summer months, causing water shortages to occur earlier in the growing season, particularly in watersheds that lack large reservoirs. Timing of runoff will affect the value of hydropower potential in some basins if peak water runoff occurs during periods of non-peak electricity demand. Shifts in runoff, precipitation, and evaporation patterns may also intensify interstate and international water allocation conflicts, as water managers struggle to meet obligations of contracts and court decrees, given more variable water availability and timing in headwater areas.

A shift in stream hydrographs to more winter flow in the western United States and Canada may also disrupt the life cycle of anadromous fish species, such as salmon, which depend on late spring flows to "flush" young salmon (smolts) to the ocean, and on summer flows to moderate stream water temperatures. Unless some mechanisms are in place to capture and store winter runoff for late spring or summer use, fewer salmon smolt will survive their migration to the ocean and more frequent fish kills from lethal stream water temperatures, such as those observed recently in the Klamath River of northern California, could occur. Similar effects have been reported for the Rhône River in France (Bravard, Chapter 5).

Water quality impairment is also predicted to increase under climate change (Field *et al.* 2007: p.629; Gleick 2000; Kundzewicz *et al.* 2007; Section 3.4.4; Bravard, Chapter 5). Specifically, precipitation is expected to occur more frequently via high-intensity rainfall events, causing increased runoff and erosion. More sediments and pollutants, such as fertilizer, will be transported into streams and groundwater systems, decreasing water quality (Field *et al.* 2007: p.629). Water quality also will be impaired in watersheds that experience a net decrease in water supply as nutrients and contaminants become more concentrated (IPCC 2001b). Such a net decrease in water supply is possible even with more precipitation, due to higher evaporation rates expected to accompany increased surface temperatures. Reductions in surface water supplies also can increase reliance on groundwater, a response to prolonged drought already observed in many coastal areas.

In addition to increased groundwater pumping arising from reduced surface water supplies, rising sea levels could also cause saltwater intrusion in coastal areas. As global temperatures increase, seawater warms, causing ocean density to decrease and sea levels to rise. (Frederick and Gleick 1999; Nicholls *et al.* 2007; Section 6.4.2.1). Sea levels are also rising in response to the melting of land ice, which includes glaciers, and the Greenland and Antarctica ice sheets (Lemke *et al.* 2007: p.339; Solow 1993). Global sea levels rose 1.7 ± 0.5 mm/year through the twentieth century (Nicholls *et al.* 2007; Section 6.2.5). Recent projections of sea-level rise by the end of the twenty-first century range from 19cm to 58cm, relative to 1980–99 (Nicholls *et al.* 2007; Section 6.3.2). A more dramatic increase in sea level, on the order of meters rather than centimeters, is possible, but most scientists consider it a low probability risk (Nicholls *et al.* 2007: p.346). For example, complete melting of the Greenland Ice Sheet or West Antarctic Ice Sheet would be required to trigger such a large rise (Lemke *et al.* 2007; Section 4.6.1). It is expected that it would take several hundred years for such melting to occur, even under much warmer conditions than are currently forecast (Meehl *et al.* 2007: p.819). Rising sea levels may also affect water availability in coastal areas indirectly by causing water tables in groundwater aquifers to rise. Higher water tables cause surface runoff to increase at the expense of aquifer recharge. As noted above, groundwater quality and recharge are impaired by rising sea levels and saltwater intrusion. Radical changes to the freshwater hydrology of coastal areas, caused by saltwater intrusion, threaten many coastal regions' freshwater supplies.

Rising air and water temperatures also will impact water quality by increasing primary production, organic matter decomposition, and nutrient cycling rates in lakes and streams, resulting in lower dissolved oxygen levels (Field *et al.* 2007: p. 629; IPCC 2001b). Increased evaporation rates from open water bodies threaten to increase the salinity of surface water. Increased groundwater pumping in coastal areas also leads to increased salinity levels in groundwater, due to saline seawater intrusion. Lakes and wetlands associated with return flows from irrigated agriculture are of particular concern (IPCC 2001b). Water quality impairment is thus a threat to agricultural water supplies, as well as to fish and wildlife (Adams *et al.* 1988).

7.2.3 El Niño-Southern Oscillation and seasonal to inter-annual climate variability

The El Niño-Southern Oscillation (ENSO) is a natural weather phenomenon resulting from interactions between the atmosphere and ocean in the tropical Pacific Ocean (Trenberth 1996). Concurrent weakening and strengthening of ocean and air currents causes warm and cold ocean currents to mix, with one covering the other (warm water over cold during an El Niño; cold water over warm during a La Niña) (IPCC 2001a). Changes in the thermal profile of ocean currents alter wind, sea surface temperature, and precipitation patterns in the tropical Pacific, and drive climatic effects throughout much of the world (IPCC 2001a; Trenberth *et al.* 2007; Section 3.6.2.1).

El Niño and La Niña events are associated with both droughts and floods in many regions of the world (Trenberth *et al.* 2007: p.288). For example, El Niño events cause drier winters in the northwestern United States, the Great Lakes region, southwestern Mexico, and parts of South America, but cause increased precipitation in southern California (IPCC 1998). The effects of global warming on the behavior of ENSO events are uncertain. No consensus exists at this time about the expected effects on ENSO amplitude (Meehl *et al.* 2007; Section 10.3.5.4). There is some scientific evidence that global warming could decrease the periodicity of ENSO events, that is, increase ENSO frequency (Timmermann *et al.* 1999; Merryfield 2006), although this conclusion could also change as more is learned about the linkages between ENSO and global warming. If the prediction of decreased ENSO periodicity is realized, the variability of precipitation and streamflow in many ENSO-sensitive regions of North and South America could also increase (IPCC 1998), leading to greater risk of droughts and floods (IPCC 2001a; Trenberth *et al.* 2007: p.288).

The negative economic consequences of ENSO events in North America have been estimated in several studies (e.g., Adams *et al.* 1995, and Chen *et al.* 2001, for the U.S.; Adams *et al.* 2003, for Mexico). ENSO-related droughts have historically generated billions of dollars in damage annually in the United States (NOAA 2002), as have ENSO-related floods. Increased drought frequency and intensity under global warming scenarios threaten to increase these damages, unless adaptive measures are taken.

7.3 Examples of water resource challenges in the uplands

Upland areas in much of North America are largely in agriculture or forest uses. In addition to timber, forested areas produce a range of marketed and non-marketed ecosystem services, such as recreational activities, habitat for fish and wildlife, watershed and source water protection, and the sequestration of carbon. In regions where agriculture is the dominant land use, agriculture not only provides food and fiber, but also may result in positive and negative externalities, ranging from open space and carbon sequestration potential, to air and water pollution. Earlier discussions in the chapter highlighted some possible effects of climate change, primarily drought, on these various resource uses and services. This section provides a more detailed examination of the effect of prolonged droughts on agriculture in Oregon and southwestern Mexico, and the impacts of rising water temperatures on salmonid production in the Pacific Northwest.

7.3.1 Agriculture and water resources

Numerous studies have estimated the effects of climate change on agriculture and agricultural resources (see IPCC 2007, for the latest review of effects of climate change on agriculture). Most early studies focused on changes in "average" climate over relatively large regions. More recently, attention has been focused on changes in climatic variability that may arise from the general warming of the earth's atmosphere. As noted earlier, this variability is expected to manifest itself as more extreme weather events, such as droughts or floods, or more systematic climate anomalies, such as the El Niño-Southern Oscillation phenomenon.

Two recent studies address the consequences and mitigation possibilities for agriculturalists in dealing with two aspects of changes in weather variability. The first (Peck and Adams 2006) estimates the effects of more frequent and severe drought on irrigated agriculture in Oregon. The other (Adams *et al.* 2003) assesses the impacts and adjustment possibilities for rain-fed agriculture in southwestern Mexico. Each is described briefly below.

In the first study, Peck and Adams developed a multi-year farm model within a dynamic and stochastic decision environment to examine the effects of increased drought frequency and intensity on irrigated agriculture. The model is parameterized for a representative mixed-crop farm in eastern Oregon. The farm receives water from the irrigation district's reservoirs, which store spring snowmelt from the mountains. The water allotment for the upcoming growing season is uncertain (known only in probability) at the time the producer makes fall and preliminary spring decisions. The producer therefore chooses fall activities that maximize expected profit over the planning horizon. The water supply is revealed in early spring, after which final spring decisions are made. Fall decisions constrain spring decisions, thereby creating intra-year dynamics. The farm system also includes agronomic constraints that generate inter-year dynamics, the source of the persistent drought effects. The model is solved for the following four climate scenarios: historical drought frequency and intensity (base case), increased drought frequency (case 1), increased drought intensity (case 2), and increased drought frequency and intensity (case 3). The three climate change scenarios' relative impact on expected farm profit and cropping patterns, as compared to the base case, are analyzed.

Table 7.1 summarizes the impact of the alternative climate change scenarios, when responded to optimally, on the following characteristics of profit: expected profit for the six-year planning period, standard deviation of profit (profit varies depending on which scenario materializes), minimum profit (which occurs when six years of drought are experienced), and maximum profit (which occurs when zero years of drought are experienced). Note that the probability of a six-year drought increases from 0.4 percent to 1.6 percent when the frequency of drought increases from 4 out of 10 years to 5 out of 10 years.

The impact of increased drought intensity (case 2) on expected profit, standard deviation, and minimum and maximum profit is more severe than that of increased drought frequency (case 1). An adaptation to increased drought frequency includes a reduction in the number of fields allocated to high-value, fall-prepared crops in any particular year of the planning horizon, which reduces the risk of crop failure in the event of a dry year. An adaptation to increased drought intensity is a decrease in

Table 7.1 Impact of increased drought frequency and/or intensity on the distributional characteristics of profit, when responded to optimally by an agricultural producer

Case scenarios[1]	Drought frequency (x out of 10 yrs)	Drought intensity (annual water supply in ac-in./ ac.)	E(profit) for a 6-year period (US$1,000) [% change from Base]	Std Dev of E(profit) (US$1,000) [% change from Base]	Min profit[2] (US$1,000) [% change from Base]	Max profit[3] (US$1,000) [% change from Base]
Base	4	24	$1,328 [0%]	19 [0%]	$1,297 [0%]	$1,349 [0%]
1	5	24	1,324 [−0.3]	14 [−25]	1,303 [+0.5]	1,345 [−0.3]
2	4	18	1,257 [−5.4]	77 [+310]	1,126 [−13.2]	1,331 [−1.3]
3	5	18	1,248 [−6.0]	15 [−21]	1,224 [−5.6]	1,272 [−5.7]

Source: Peck and Adams, 2006

Notes

1   The four scenarios include the Base Case (historical drought frequency and intensity, Case 1 (increased drought frequency, from historical), Case 2 (increased drought intensity, from historical) and Case 3 (combined increase in frequency and intensity)

2   Minimum profit is associated with six years of drought (during a six-year period).

3   Maximum profit is associated with zero years of drought (during a six-year period).

the acres of low-value, fall-planted crops, and the acres of crops with low profit per acre-inch of water. These adaptations provide more flexibility in the spring plan, after the water allotment is revealed, and save more water for high-value crops in the event of a dry year. In both cases, producers also shift irrigation technology for some crops from furrow to furrow with tail-water reuse. When both drought frequency and intensity increases (case 3), expected profit is only slightly less than when drought intensity alone increases. Standard deviation and minimum profit are actually better for case 3 than case 2, although maximum profit is not. Adaptations in response to case 3 reflect a combination of the adaptations seen for cases 1 and 2. Results of the model solutions indicate that the producer is better able to adapt to a drought that occurs at historical intensity but with increased frequency than to drought that occurs with increased intensity but at historical frequency. The implication of climate change for agriculture depends on which distributional characteristics of the water supply are affected.

In the second study, Adams *et al.* (2003) developed a profit maximizing mathematical model of crop production in five southwestern states of Mexico to assess the economic consequences of ENSO events and to identify possible actions by which negative impacts can be minimized. The model encompasses the large number of crops found in the region and is representative of current cultural and agronomic practices in the area. The effects of weather associated with three ENSO states (El Niño, La Niña, and Normal) on crop yields are modeled with plant biophysical simulation models. The main behavioral response of producers is to change crop mixes in anticipation of various ENSO states. The advantage of such behavior is reflected in the difference in profits between decisions based on events' historical probability of occurrence and those based on a long-range forecast of such an event, as is now commonly available from NOAA and Mexican climate agencies.

The results indicate that the three ENSO events affect agriculture in different ways. Specifically, an El Niño results in economic losses across the region amounting to almost $1 billion pesos (approximately 90 million U.S dollars), whereas a La Niña slightly increases total production and profits. Thus, if El Niño events become more common as a result of climate change, the expectation is for increased economic losses in this region. The results also reveal that a strategy of using pre-season ENSO forecasts in planting decisions can offset some of the expected losses of an El Niño and increase some of the benefits that may follow from a La Niña event. In the case of an El Niño, use of forecasts to make crop mix decisions can offset 15 to 20 percent of the losses associated with the use of traditional crop mixes. These estimates assume that forecast accuracy is approximately 70 percent (Prob. 0.7); lower or higher levels of accuracy will affect the gains from using forecasts. The implication is that use of forecast information, coupled with flexibility in planting and other cultural decisions, will be increasingly important in dealing with a more variable climate.

7.3.2 Water quality and fisheries

The streams that drain upland areas in the western United States, western Canada, and Alaska provide critical breeding and rearing habitat for salmonids and other cold-water fish species. Salmon play an important commercial, recreational and cultural role in this region, and have been a religious icon for native peoples for thousands of years. Salmon populations are depressed in many parts of the region due to a number of factors, including over-harvesting, dams, logging, and water diversions. Some populations within the United States are sufficiently depressed to be listed as "endangered" or "threatened" under provisions of the Endangered Species Act. Increased water temperature in streams has recently been recognized as another threat to salmonids. Causes of this warming include mismanagement of riparian zones in the uplands, water diversions, and global warming.

Continued global warming is expected to exacerbate rising water temperatures. In anticipation of this effect, Oregon and other states have enacted temperature standards for the protection of salmonids under the Total Maximum Daily Load (TMDL) provisions of the Clean Water Act, as amended. Although the temperature standard may vary by location and season, the standard is approximately 17°C. The challenge to managers for achieving this standard is that most streams currently exceed it during at least part of the year. In some cases, temperatures exceeding lethal levels (24–25°C) are observed during critical summer and fall periods.

Several studies have examined least-cost ways to meet the TMDL standard for temperature. One study (Watanabe, Adams and Wu 2006) focuses on a higher-elevation, mid-size stream in eastern Oregon (the Grande Ronde River), while another (Seedang 2005) addresses temperature issues in a larger stream in western Oregon (the Willamette River). Both streams are home to several salmonid species and both contain stocks of these species that are listed as endangered or threatened. Although the studies' stream location and geomorphology differ, the studies are similar in that they combine input and models from hydrology, forestry, geomorphology, and economics to develop cost-effective management regimes that achieve the temperature standard.

Several findings are common to both studies. First, in some regions of each watershed, it is not possible to meet the standard under any management regime. This calls into question the nature of the standard, given that future global warming will increase the areas in violation. Failure to meet the standard, however, does not mean that some cooling will not be beneficial. Second, in areas that can reach compliance, a range of management actions are required to achieve the standard in a cost-effective manner, including riparian restoration, stream flow augmentation, and river channel restoration to increase hyporheic cooling. Third, targeting of key reaches or areas of the watershed is needed to achieve the standard cost-effectively. This implies that location matters in stream management, and that a "one size fits all" regulatory regime is not likely to be successful or cost-effective today, nor in a warming world with increased climate variability.

7.4 Coping with drought and other events: implications and conclusions

One step towards preparing for potential increased frequency and intensity of drought, ENSO, or other climate events is an improved understanding of potential shifts of regional precipitation and evaporation under a changed climate. The accuracy, precision, and timing of seasonal or longer-term forecasts are likely to affect their adoption by farmers and other resource managers. Providing reliable year-to-year forecasts of precipitation is difficult; decadal forecasts as provided by GCMs are even more problematic. However, as noted in previous sections, some types of forecasts, such as those associated with ENSO events, are becoming more reliable (NAST 2000; Trenberth 1996). Adaptation strategies to ENSO events, such as changing crop mixes, are currently being practiced in many parts of the western hemisphere.

More accurate, precise and timely forecasts can reduce the risk for decision makers and decrease economic losses due to drought (see NOAA 2002). Current drought management tools also can be reassessed and revised in light of more reliable forecasts. For example, drought insurance programs may need to revise coverage conditions and premiums in order to provide efficient coverage in a changed climate. Increased crop diversity on individual farms or in economic regions could also reduce losses during extreme weather events (IPCC 2001b; Wall and Smit 2005). Reservoir capacity, timing of water releases, and safety will need to be reconsidered and updated as well. Voluntary water transfers, with or without climate change, will become an increasingly important tool to mitigate water distribution problems. Municipalities are currently considering the vulnerability of their surface water and groundwater supplies to drought, pollution and saltwater intrusion, and may need to consider new protection programs and supplemental water sources. Improved confidence in regional forecasts of climate change impacts is, however, of primary importance in helping managers understand risk levels, identify management priorities, and define realistic adaptations.

In summary, global climate change is likely to increase the frequency and intensity of drought for many regions of the world. Although subject to substantial uncertainty, GCMs' regional forecasts of long-term climatic change do offer a glimpse into possible future climatic conditions. Predicted impacts vary by region, but include increased temperatures and evaporation rates; increased, but more variable, precipitation; higher proportions of winter precipitation arriving as rain, not snow; earlier and more severe summer drought, and decreased water quality.

Drought currently results in substantial economic losses in the United States annually. These losses, which occur across a range of sectors, from agriculture to energy and recreation, have profound effects on local communities. More frequent or intense drought implies increased costs to society, unless agricultural producers, water users and others are able to adapt. Improved forecasts concerning future drought conditions, particularly at the regional scale, are necessary for managers and policy makers to identify efficient adaptive strategies, and reduce the economic costs of drought.

References

Adams, R. *et al.* (1995) Value of improved long range weather information. *Contemporary Economic Policy,* 13(3): 10–19.

Adams, R. M. *et al.* (2003) The benefits to Mexican agriculture of an ENSO early warning system. *Journal of Agricultural and Forest Meteorology,* 115:183–94.

Adams, R. M., Glyer, J. D., McCarl, B. A. and Dudeck, D. J. (1988) The implications of global climate change for western agriculture. *Western Journal of Agricultural Economics,* 13: 348–56.

Adams, R. M., Hurd, B. H. and Reilly, J. M. (1999) *Agriculture and global climate change: a review of impacts to U.S. agricultural resources.* Arlington, VA: The Pew Center on Global Climate Change.

Claussen, E. (ed.) (2001) *Climate change: science, strategies, and solutions.* Arlington, VA: The Pew Center on Global Climate Change.

Chen, C., McCarl, B. A. and Adams, R. M. (2001) Economic implications of potential ENSO frequency and strength shifts. *Climatic Change,* 49: 147–59.

Christensen, J. H. *et al.* (2007) Regional climate projections., In Solomon, S. *et al.* (eds) *Climate change 2007: the physical science basis.* Contribution of Working Group I to the Fourth Assessment Report of the Intergovernmental Panel on Climate Change. Cambridge: Cambridge University Press, pp. 847–940.

Field, C. B. *et al.* (2007) North America.,In Parry, M.L. *et al.* (eds). *Climate change 2007: impacts, adaptation and vulnerability.* Contribution of Working Group II to the Fourth Assessment Report of the Intergovernmental Panel on Climate Change. Cambridge: Cambridge University Press, pp. 617–52.

Forster, P. *et al.* (2007) Changes in atmospheric constituents and in radiative forcing, In Solomon, S. *et al.* (eds) *Climate change 2007: the physical science basis.* Contribution of Working Group I to the Fourth Assessment Report of the Intergovernmental Panel on Climate Change. Cambridge: Cambridge University Press, pp. 129–234.

Frederick, K. D. and Gleick, P. H. (1999) *Water and global climate change: potential impacts on U.S. water resources.* Arlington, VA: The Pew Center on Global Climate Change.

Gleick, P. H. (2000) *Water: the potential consequences of climate variability and change for the water resources of the United States.* A report of the National Water Assessment Group for the U.S. Global Change Research Program. Oakland, CA: Pacific Institute for Studies in Development, Environment, and Security.

Hansen, J., Ruedy, R. and Sato, M. (2001) A closer look at United States and global surface temperature change. *Journal of Geophysical Research,* 106: 23947–63.

Intergovernmental Panel on Climate Change (1998) *The regional impacts of climate change: an assessment of vulnerability.* A special report of IPCC Working Group II [Watson, R. T., Zinyowera, M. C. and R. H. Moss (eds)]. New York: Cambridge University Press.

Intergovernmental Panel on Climate Change (2001a) *Climate change 2001: synthesis report.* A contribution of Working Groups I, II, and III to the Third Assessment Report of the Intergovernmental Panel on Climate Change [Watson, R. T. and the Core Writing Team (eds)]. New York: Cambridge University Press.

Intergovernmental Panel on Climate Change (2001b) *Climate change 2001: impacts, adaptation, and vulnerability.* A contribution of Working Group II to the Third Assessment Report of the Intergovernmental Panel on Climate Change [McCarthy, J. J. *et al.*(eds)]. New York: Cambridge University Press.

Intergovernmental Panel on Climate Change (2007) *Climate change 2007: synthesis report.* A contribution of Working Groups I, II and III to the Fourth Assessment Report of the

Intergovernmental Panel on Climate Change [Pachauri, R.K. and Reisinger, A. (eds.)] IPCC, Geneva, Switzerland, 104pp.

Knowles, N., Dettinger, M. D. and Cayan, D. R. (2006) Trends in snowfall versus rainfall in the western United States. *Journal of Climate,* 19: 4545–59.

Knutson, C. (2001) *A comparison of droughts, floods and hurricanes in the U.S.* Lincoln, NE: National Drought Mitigation Center. Online. URL: http://enso.unl.edu/ndmc/impacts/compare.htm.

Kundzewicz, Z.W. *et al.* (2007) Freshwater resources and their management. In Parry, M. L. *et al*(eds) *Climate change 2007: impacts, adaptation and vulnerability.* Contribution of Working Group II to the Fourth Assessment Report of the Intergovernmental Panel on Climate Change. Cambridge: Cambridge University Press, pp. 173–210.

Lemke, P. *et al.* (2007) Observations: changes in snow, ice and frozen ground, In Solomon, S. *et al.*(eds) *Climate change 2007: the physical science basis.* Contribution of Working Group I to the Fourth Assessment Report of the Intergovernmental Panel on Climate Change. Cambridge: Cambridge University Press, pp. 337–84.

Meehl, G.A. *et al.* (2007) Global climate projections. In Solomon, S. *et al.*(eds) *Climate change 2007: the physical science basis.* Contribution of Working Group I to the Fourth Assessment Report of the Intergovernmental Panel on Climate Change. Cambridge: Cambridge University Press, pp. 747–846.

Merryfield, W. J. (2006) Changes to ENSO under CO_2 doubling in a multimodel ensemble. *Journal of Climate,* 19: 4009–4027.

Miller, N. L., Bashford, K. E. and Strem, E. (2006) Changes in runoff. In Smith, J. B. and R. Mendelsohn (eds) *The impact of climate change on regional systems.* New Horizons in Environmental Economics, Cheltenham, UK: Edgar Elgar. Ch. 6.

National Assessment Synthesis Team (2000) *Climate change impacts on the United States: the potential consequences of climate variability and change.* U.S. Global Change Research Program. New York: Cambridge University Press.

National Oceanic and Atmospheric Administration (2002) Economic implications of drought and the potential benefits of improved drought forecasting. *NOAA Magazine*, 17 September 2002. Available online at http://www.noaanews.noaa.gov/magazine/stories/mag51.htm.

Nicholls, R. J. *et al.* (2007) Coastal systems and low-lying areas. In Parry, M. L. *et al.* (eds) *Climate change 2007: impacts, adaptation and vulnerability.* Contribution of Working Group II to the Fourth Assessment Report of the Intergovernmental Panel on Climate Change. Cambridge: Cambridge University Press, pp. 315–56.

Peck, D. E. and Adams, R. M. (2006) *Optimal response to drought in a stochastic and dynamic farm system.* Selected paper, Western Agricultural Economics Association Annual meeting, Anchorage, AK, 28–30 June 2006.

Seedang, S. (2005) *Economic Analyses of Temperature Reduction Practices in a Large River Flood Plain.* PhD dissertation. Corvallis, OR:. Oregon State University.

Solow, A. R. (1993) The response of sea level to global warming. In Bras, R. *The world at risk: natural hazards and climate change.* AIP Conference Readings 277, Cambridge, MA:, 1992. New York, NY: American Institute of Physics.

Timmermann, A. *et al.* (1999) Increased El Niño frequency in a climate model forced by future greenhouse warming. *Nature,* 398(22Apr): 694–97.

Trenberth, K. E. (1996) El Niño-Southern Oscillation. In Giambelluca, T. M. and Henderson-Sellers, A. (eds). *Climate change: developing Southern Hemisphere perspectives.* New York: John Wiley & Sons, pp. 145–173.

Trenberth, K. E. *et al.* (2007) Observations: surface and atmospheric climate change. In

Solomon, S. *et al.*(eds) *Climate change 2007: the physical science basis.* Contribution of Working Group I to the Fourth Assessment Report of the Intergovernmental Panel on Climate Change. Cambridge: Cambridge University Press, pp. 235–336.

Wall, E. and Smit, B. (2005) Climate change adaptation in light of sustainable agriculture. *Journal of Sustainable Agriculture,* 27: 113–23.

Watanabe, M., Adams, R. M. and Wu, J. (2006) The economics of environmental management in a spatially heterogeneous river basin. *American Journal of Agricultural Economics,* 88: 617–31.

8 Upland watershed management in the developing world

The case of Tunisia

Sihem Benabdallah

Managing upland watersheds in developing countries is a complex process involving soil conservation and natural resource preservation, water management policies, land use planning, legal and institutional framework development, regional economic development, and improvement of living conditions of rural communities. This chapter provides a review of Tunisian soil and water conservation policies. Other relevant issues and challenges also are addressed in order to highlight certain constraints and underline the need to focus on local social and environmental issues, while considering the effects of global climate change.

8.1. Introduction

The eight millennium development goals are devoted to reducing hunger by half by 2015 and increasing the global food production by 60 percent to close the gap in meeting nutrition requirements, coping with population growth, and accommodating changes in diets over the next three decades (United Nations 2007).

Mountain watersheds provide 30 to 60 percent of the freshwater flowing downstream in humid regions, while in semi-arid and arid areas they provide 70 to 95 percent (FAO 2004). Further, they provide home and life support to at least one-tenth of the world population and supply water for drinking, domestic use, agriculture, and industry to almost half of the world's human population. Thus, the fulfillment of the international commitment stated by the millennium development goals (MDGs) at the local level ought to be coupled with efforts to ensure effective upland water management, the real asset of the rural population. Such efforts could be based on ensuring profitability, enhancing the living environment and also considering the sustainable use of natural resources.

In response to these and other concerns, watershed protection and management has become a policy imperative in many developing countries and, more specifically, for most of the densely populated regions (Doolette and Mcgrath 1990). Watershed management policies necessarily focus on upper catchments because of their dynamic land-water interactions, the importance of human settlements in poor rural communities, their lack of infrastructures, and their remaining forest and natural resources.

Given the importance of upland natural resources, a wealth of literature pertaining to the review of upland watershed management dealing with approaches, tools, performances and evaluations has focused on developed countries. However, drawing lessons from those experiences is made more difficult by constraints specific to developing countries. Chief among these are rapidly growing populations, tropical and sub-tropical semi-arid climates with intensive and erratic precipitation; forest management services sometimes nonexistent or just starting; and unrelenting pressure on upland resources. Although watershed management investments are spread throughout Asia, Africa, and Latin America, there has been relatively little research about their impact (Kerr and Chung 2001).

In addition to the above difficulties, the possible impacts of climate change represent a veritable threat to the socioeconomic development of these countries and to their inhabitants, whose lives are very much linked to climate and its fluctuations. Thus, the need for long-term sustainable management for upper watersheds becomes an important challenge on top of the MDGs that have to be achieved.

The purpose of this chapter is to shed light on some key issues facing effective upland watershed management in some developing countries described in section 8.2. As an illustration, a detailed historical review is provided in section 8.3 for the Tunisian water and soil conservation approach. Efforts in dealing with scarce resources, and social and environmental measures are described for the new developed methodology in order to ensure a sustainable development and improve the well being of the rural population. This case study is used to identify the more pressing needs for upland watershed management in developing countries, as presented in section 8.4.

8.2 Upland water management status

The approach used to elicit the information needed for this study is based on literature review, policy document analysis, evaluation reports concerning watershed management projects and their impacts.

From a hydrologic perspective, upland watersheds are the principal source areas for freshwater supplies through streams, water storages, irrigation systems and groundwater aquifer recharges upon which agricultural development and many downstream communities depend. These upland areas provide a source of food, natural resources and energy for a growing number of rural inhabitants (Brooks *et al.* 2003). Even though this might be true for both developed and developing countries, the impact of degraded upland watersheds is more substantial for the poorest and most disadvantaged population in developing countries, who usually reside in the upland areas.

Local population impacts on upland watersheds in different regions bear striking similarities. In the Andes, South America (Colombia, Ecuador, Peru, Bolivia, and Chile), human occupation affected the delivery of water and sediments to river channels and caused the vulnerability of soils for the fluvial systems. In this tropical region, higher elevations have long been favored by humans for settlements where they had more subtle and unintentional geomorphic effects on the fluvial system (Harden 2006). The impacts reported by Harden include (1) alteration of the fluvial systems engineered to store water in dams and to withdraw water for irrigation, (2) destabilization of slopes from mining activities, tree removal for cultivation, and irrigation activities by reducing flow in rivers and by conveying water across steep slopes with high erosion potential, and (3) changes in land uses as population increased and the economy changed.

Tens of millions of people belonging to numerous ethnic and linguistic groups inhabit the mountains of East Africa that extend from the Ethiopian Highlands in the north through Tanzania to the south. This region provides the overwhelming rural and predominantly poor population with water for drinking and irrigation, land for grazing and farming (especially for growing coffee), and forest for fuel and some medicinal plants. As a result, the Ethiopian Highlands have been almost entirely stripped of their original forests.

Thus, high rates of hill erosion and downstream sedimentation are among the most important issues in the developing world (World Bank 1992). For instance, the reported soil loss for the Philippines is between 74 and 81 million tonnes annually, affecting between 63 and 77 percent of the country's total land area (Shively and Coxhead 2004). This phenomenon is particularly acute in China's Southwest, where major and minor rivers, diverse mountain landscapes, and chronic poverty are intertwined. Landslides alone are estimated to cost US $15 billion, and 150 deaths annually (Li 1996). In Nepal, landslides and flood hazards cause destruction of important infrastructure worth US $2.5 million and about 400 deaths annually (Chalise and Khanal 1996).

Other negative effects include the silting of streams and increases in the risk of flash floods (UNESCO 1982); the accumulation of silt in coastal habitats that could be located hundreds of kilometers downstream and the reduction of aquatic ecosystems productivity (OECD 1993); and accumulation of sediment in reservoirs reducing hydroelectric power generation capacity and the expected life of the structure. In addition, it impacts the water quality for water consumption.

These problems are more intense in arid and semi-arid regions where land degradation can induce desertification, wind erosion, saline water, and poor structure and nutrient content of soils. Morocco, for instance, belongs to the countries with strong specific land degradation exceeding 2,000 tons/km²/year in upland watersheds. This constitutes a permanent threat for hydraulic structures' regulation and storage and a high loss in soil fertility (Ministry of Agriculture, Rural Development, Water and Forestry 2001). More than 50 million cubic meters (Mcm) of sediments are deposited each year in dams, corresponding to a water loss that could be used to irrigate around 5,000 hectares (ha). This problem is attributed to fragile soils with low organic matter content and to conflicts between the administration and the local population. The diagnosis of the forest resources shows in fact an important state of degradation under combined effects of abusive cuts, forest fires, and clearing. Nearly 33,000 ha of Moroccan lands are lost each year.

Algeria, a semi-arid to arid country with scarce and irregular water resources located mainly on the northern part of the country, where the Atlas Mountains pass through, is facing tough challenges in managing water resources in general because of the absence of a clear water management strategy and effective water policy (Kettab 2001). Sediments deposited are estimated at an equivalent 20 Mcm of water loss in storage per annum over a follow-up period of five years. The Algerian population was estimated at 28 million in 1995 and will nearly double by the year 2010, putting more pressure on upland watersheds through the building of dams and hydraulic works for water transfer.

The current degradation of natural resources and their extreme fragility, coupled with the prospect of global climate change, introduces serious implications for upland areas. The general trend for North Africa's estimated temperature rise and marked increase in the frequency of droughts and floods has been accentuated by years with strong rainfall over short periods. Thus, further risks need to be addressed, including the decrease in water availability, managing extreme rainfall events and flooding, greater erosion and widespread soil degradation, altered water quality, and changes in forest and vegetation cover. These risks lead to further pressure on land, water, and forest resources.

Upland water management requires information about the availability of water in time and space, in order to assess water availability, quality of streams, flood risks and routing, and sediment transport. Yet, hydrological measurements are very scarce in many developing counties. The discrepancies in assessing the water balance in Lebanon is just one example in which weak to nonexistent infrastructure for gathering water data reflects negatively on the quality and accuracy of the available water resources (Amery 2000).

In addition, water scarcity, coping with uneven seasonal and annual water distribution, and impaired water quality pose serious challenges to economic development (Vorosmarty *et al.* 2000). For instance, India gets 90 percent of its rainfall during the summer monsoon season, which makes it difficult to manage it efficiently. Because of the seasonal nature of precipitation, many developing countries can use no more than 20 percent of their potentially available freshwater resources. A small country like Tunisia receives on average 36 billion cubic meters per year (Bcm/year). This volume is limited to 11 Bcm/year during a drought year and can reach 90 Bcm during a wet year. Nevertheless, the potentially available surface water is only 2.7 Bcm/year, representing only 8 percent of the country's rainfall.

From a technical perspective, examples exist throughout the world in which upland resource conservation activities have been successful on the micro and macro scales; e.g. in Honduras, the Philippines, China, Thailand, Burundi, Nepal, Pakistan, Sri Lanka, India, Bolivia, Peru, and in Brazil (Tennyson 2002).

Lebanon, Morocco, Syria, and Tunisia were engaged in a program of constructing small uphill dams as water harvesting systems by providing water storage facilities containing a few hundred cubic meters. These structures are used for irrigation, water consumption for animals, domestic uses, and sometimes for aquaculture. They protect the downstream villages against flooding and erosion, and contribute to groundwater recharge.

In Tunisia, this experience was useful for improving the livelihood of the rural people and played a major role in the protecting the large downstream dams from siltation (Albergel *et al.* 2004). Case examples of water harvesting systems also are found in Mexico, India, Iran, and Pakistan (Ahmad 2000; Scott and Silva-Ochoa 2000; Agarwal and Sunita 1997).

Yet, putting in place the means to ensure sustainable land management and protection of soil and water resources is far from being accomplished in developing countries. This is because of the interrelationships between a wide spectrum of issues related to social, cultural and environmental matters, economic development, and involvment of government and non-governmental organizations. The Tunisian case study, presented hereafter, is an illustration of such interlinks and the way they were addressed.

8.3 Case study: Tunisian struggle with upland watershed management

Tunisia is located in Northern Africa at the eastern extremity of the Maghreb. The water and soil there are very vulnerable to degradation due to physical, geomorphological, hydroclimatical, and socioeconomic conditions. In fact, about 3 million hectares, out of 9 million hectares useful for agriculture and grazing, are threatened by erosion, with 1.5 million hectares critically affected (Tunisian Ministry of Agriculture 1993).

Faced with these problems, the Tunisian government has put considerable efforts into soil and water conservation through physical, institutional, and legislative measures for the past three decades. The Ministry of Agriculture enacted a national strategy for soil and water conservation for the decade 1991–2000, based on managing slope stability, gradients and shapes, and transferring surface water for agricultural development. Nevertheless, the problems of erosion and water degradation and their consequences continue to be present-day challenges. In this section, we shall discuss major problems and achievements, as well as challenges and continuing problems.

Several historical sites in Tunisia testify that the local population was seldom indifferent to erosion problems. The origin of this upland erosion can be attributed to its geographical situation, the succession of several civilizations [Roman (146 BC), Arab, Ottoman, French], its climatic conditions, and to the rural population's lifestyle. Even though land erosion is not a new phenomenon, its intensity has worsened. In fact, the area of land used for agriculture grew from 1.2 million hectares early in the previous century to more than 5 million hectares nowadays. At the same time, the Tunisian population growth rate has increased fivefold. The rural population density became more important, especially in areas with excessive erosion and low productivity. This demographic increase induced a considerable clearing of the natural vegetation, lands were put under cultivation, and uplands became overgrazed, exacerbating their degradation.

The mountain areas of Tunisia are made up of the final section of the two Atlas ranges that extend for about 2,400 kilometers (1,500 miles) through Morocco, Algeria, and Tunisia; where most of the forest and endemic plants are located. The

Tunisian mountains are diverse in geology and landscapes; from the Mediterranean cliffs to the canyons in the high plateau of Tunisia, to the southern sand dunes and the Sahara Desert.

The Khroumirie-Mogod mountain chains, which run along the north, are the wettest part of the country, containing forests of cork oak, zen oak, and the rare *Quercus afares*. They are characterized by brown-dark soils developed on sandstone and on non-calcareous clays. The Khroumirie-Mogod chain has steep and irregular slopes. The High Tell or the Tunisian Dorsal Mountain, in the center, which is the continuation of the Saharian Atlas, is home for *Pinus halipensi* and *Quercus ilex* forests and *Stipa tenacissima* (alfa). At the base of the large mountains are calcimagnesic soils, which are crusted, limestone, brown and degraded on hardpan. Mountains in the high steppes of central Tunisia and the Douirat mountains of southern Tunisia are mainly dominated by *Juniperus*.

In the last decade, the Tunisian Ministry of Environment and Sustainable Development initiated a program to protect what is left of the forests and the natural resources by the foundation of four national parks and seven natural reserves situated in mountainous areas. Any activity, or use of forest resources, is subject to permission from the Ministry of Agriculture under the National Forestry Law, which defines rights and benefits for forest management, planning and allocation.

The mountains of Tunisia are important sources of water, providing about 80 percent of the nation's water through dams and water transfer infrastructure, agricultural land, and forests exceptionally rich in biodiversity and home to rare and diverse ecosystems. However, the mountain forests are degraded by cattle and human activity, a phenomenon that is particularly serious in the Dorsal Mountain, and in the Khroumirie-Mogod forests. In addition, these areas are fragile, with soft rocks such as argillite and marl alternating with limestone and sandstone.

The climatic conditions, influenced by the mountain setups shown in Table 8.1, play an important factor in the erosion problems in the north and the center of the country. These areas are characterized by hot, dry summers and cool, moist winters; precipitation is very irregular and the rainfall varies considerably from the north to south and from year to year. Rainfall is torrential and event-based, and can reach

Table 8.1 Average annual rainfall distribution in mm

Natural Region	Average Annual Rainfall (mm/year)
North West	512
North East	480
Central West	282
Central East	264
South West	97
South East	137

Source: Ministry of Environment and Sustainable Development for Tunisia, 2005.

70 mm per hour in the mountains. High intensities up to 200 mm/hr have been measured in some exceptional years.

From the 1960s to the 1980s, significant efforts were deployed, resulting in several physical, institutional, and legal achievements. More than 1 million hectares were treated by measurements of soil and by water conservation techniques that varied from the north to the center, depending on suitable techniques: benches, cords, biological fixing and agro-pastoral management. In fact, this work was established based on targeting specific areas in need of urgent intervention for specific land use or for a degraded upland area. The measures were also designed to keep the rural population in the interior regions of the country, often through costly development projects, usually without considering the economic aspects. The evaluation of two decades of considerable effort showed that the engineering approach was not successful in winning the struggle against erosion. Further, the infrastructure implemented by the technicians was rarely maintained or protected by the farmers, which represents a part of the failure to of this approach (Bachta 1995). The concern of the farmers was for their survival, as they experienced a great deal of year-to-year variability in production and income, and had no alternate sources of irrigation in the area. In addition, the conservation techniques were considered to be the property of the administration.

In the early 1990s, new orientations were founded on an integrated watershed management approach. A national water and soil conservation strategy was put in place with key objectives to meet on the long run by the year 2000. Based on a progressive process for rural population involvement to take charge of the conservation and management of infrastructures, the strategy took into account capacity building both for the administrative needs and for the farmers through technical training, the encouragement of private companies to build services and the development of new cooperative institutions (Achouri 1995).

The main strategy was meant to achieve the following goals:

- reduction of arable land loss,
- improvement of soil fertility in order to avoid the decline of the outputs of production,
- storage of an additional volume of 500 million m3 of water by conservation measures,
- protecting the lifespan of dams,
- attenuation of flood damage caused downstream, and
- enhancement of groundwater recharge.

A program was then initiated to construct 1000 hill dams, 4000 structures for flood control and groundwater recharge, to protect 600 000 hectares by implementing conservation measures, and protect 400 000 hectares with the potential to grow cereal crops by soft conservation techniques, along with the maintenance of a million hectares already treated. The implementation of these actions was coupled with regional planning covering a number of governorates. Table 8.2 summarizes the rate of achievement with respect to the planned program for the period

Table 8.2 Water and soil conservation program

Program	Strategy objective	Accomplished Actions 1990–2001	Rate of achievement	Planned Actions 2002–2011
Landscape protection (hectares)	672,500	892,573	133%	550,000
Maintenance of existing water and soil conservation works (hectares)	858,000	338,496	39%	550,000
Construction of hill dams (unit)	1,000	580	58%	500
Structures for flood control and groundwater recharge (unit)	4,290	3,556	83%	3,000

Source: Ministry of Environment and Sustainable Development for Tunisia, 2002.

1990 to 2001 and presents the programmed actions for the period from 2002 to 2011.

At the institutional level, an administrative unit under the authority of the hydraulics and rural equipments department was established in 1960. It was in charge of planning, execution and control of the soil and water conservation activities. This unit became a sub-directorate under the Forest Management department in the 1980s, and it was transformed lately to a national directorate of Land Conservation and Management, with the following missions.

- Elaboration of plans and orientations to safeguard natural resources (soils, vegetation, and water).
- Promotion of technical measures in order to ensure a better use of natural resources.
- Evaluation of soils' aptitudes and follow-up soil behavior under the various modes of exploitation.
- Monitoring soil and water through analyses.
- Planning and elaboration of needed uphill catchment's studies, adjustment of anti-erosive work and follow-up of projects' implementation launched by the soil and water conservation programs.

On the legal level, soil and water conservation was governed by several texts, the most important of which are the declaration that water and soil conservation structures are public utilities, and the law for water and soil conservation enacted in 1995.

It was noted that observed failures were not due to the techniques used but mainly to the approach used. In fact, the most modern technology in the world can be useless if it is not understood, accepted and implemented by the local population. A number of socioeconomic studies in different parts of the world show clearly that each area has its individual set of interrelationships between people and the land they are living on (Weber 1989).

Other constraints were due to the social and economic characteristics of the affected areas. In fact, these areas are the most populated areas within the watershed. Consequently, land ownership is cut into small to medium parcels, which makes anti-erosive actions sometimes impossible to carry out.

Several years were taken to develop the methodology needed to apply the water and soil conservation strategy. Initiated in 1997, the new approach, called Integrated Agriculture and Rural Development Projects (PDARI), was based on encouraging production and the revenue potential of small agricultural holdings, as well as improving basic infrastructure available to poor populations. The major project components address soil and water conservation, forestry and pasture development (pasture plantings on private and collective land and agro-forestry activities), agricultural development for small holdings (promotion of fruit tree cultivation in some areas and rehabilitation of irrigated perimeters), upgrading of basic drinking water infrastructure, and support for women's and community-based development by targeting small landholders and medium landholders practicing rainfed or irrigated agriculture, forest users' communities, and rural women and youth. Thus, the project activities related to soil and water conservation will affect, as well, small landholders making a living on and using the resources.

The participatory approach proposed for these projects is not based on the integrated development approach by micro-basin, as is the case in other countries. It is designed to achieve participation by several interest groups, not necessarily located at the drainage basin but within the administrative area.

Accordingly, programming instruments were developed to promote greater involvement by populations in the planning process for development actions through consultative councils at the "imada" (village) and "delegation" (several villages) level, which were to play a central role in mobilizing populations and in programming and monitoring results. The land occupation intervention unit is in charge of undertaking forestry and pasture development actions, soil and water conservation works, and productivity improvements for agriculture. The authorized user associations bring together landholders to manage and maintain small hydraulic structures and assets with assistance from the government in providing water, agriculture-related finances, equipment, land training, and market information.

In some areas of the country, non-governmental organizations (NGOs) can provide small loans in the context of local savings and loan committees within a village-type credit system. Women's issues are provided for through specific mechanisms (financial and training) to promote the economic and social role of women in rural areas.

The full impact of PDARI activities will be seen a few years from now. However, some of the observable impacts in areas threatened by erosion include improvement in the production potential of small landholdings, and the reduction of silting in small dams and hill reservoirs. In terms of the farmers' assets, land values will increase as land becomes better protected and covered with valuable tree plantings. In terms of community-based development, agricultural training, as well as art and craft training, has given rise to hundreds of micro-projects and several marketable products (rabbits, honey through beekeeping, carpets and rugs, pottery, and decoration).

8.4 Needs and challenges for the developing world

Several countries are in the process of reforming their water management policies and could benefit from other countries' success and failures in water policies, plans and programs in the context of their economic feasibility, environmental sustainability and equity, and gender impacts. Thus, a useful step would be the documentation of alternative models that put principles of water management and soil conservation into action used in developing countries.

It seems that there is a general acceptance of the need to consider social and environmental objectives in water planning in general, and more specifically for upland watershed management. However, continued work is needed on several fronts to meet this challenge. In connection to the above sections, this part of the chapter aims to underline some specific and potential needs on which to focus in order to achieve effective upland watershed management.

Potential impacts of climate change are expected to exacerbate poverty and undermine socioeconomic gains made in recent decades in these vulnerable mountain areas, which are characterized by sensitive ecosystems, and regions of conflicting interests between economic development and environmental conservation. This vulnerability has important implications on nature conservation, mountain streams, water management, agriculture, and tourism.

Major effects of climate change affect water availability through changes in the hydrological cycle, the balance of temperature, and rainfall. Runoff could decrease even when precipitation increases, due to the large hydrological role played by evaporation. Seasonality of flow and persistent drought years can have devastating effects on groundwater, on water quality, and on storage capacity of reservoirs in relation to their ability to store excess and regulate water flows. Increased variability in rainfall and changes in temperature will likely disrupt key ecosystem processes, increase land degradation (including soil erosion, salinization, loss of soil organic matter and structure), amplify forest fires in places where summers become warmer and drier, and influence insect pests and diseases. Some climate change scenarios suggest that continued warming could cause vegetation zones to shift to higher elevations, resulting in the loss of some species and ecosystems. Those with limited climatic ranges could disappear. Thus, adaptive measures need to be built on assessments of past and projected climate change impacts on natural resources, agricultural systems, and local residents.

8.4.1. Technical issues

Some technical aspects in upland watershed management require further study. Research is required on leading topics related to the following issues.

Innovations in harvesting, storage, and management of water runoff in drought-prone areas would improve production of crops, trees, and rangeland species. This allows stakeholders to build on local capacity for adequate planning, efficient design, and sustainable implementation of water harvesting systems. The application of appropriate techniques for water yield and storage remain important issues (Roose 2006).

Techniques must be developed to quantify the extent and impact of erosion through simple measurement and monitoring at a small-scale of watersheds under arid and semi-arid conditions and low vegetation cover. It should be noted that although some sophisticated approaches to modeling hydrological processes and erosion are available, there is a shortage of appropriate hydrological data for watersheds in general and specifically for upland areas, which precludes a more complex assessment of erosion–sediment relationships in modeling. Adequate databases with extensive measurements and data collection programs will help to conduct further accurate assessments on both the scope and the impact of the problems and on the effectiveness of potential solutions.

The choice of native species (trees, plants, etc) best suited for eroded sites can make a significant contribution to creating micro-zones that can lead the way in economic and social change. Examples in the Maghreb region show that the transformation of landscape by tree planting (olive and peach) through government investments has strengthened production potential and created micro-zones for intensification of agricultural production and a local dynamic for agricultural development to bring in real socioeconomic change.

Methods should be developed for enhancing soil conservation and fertility, and farm income, through changes in land use activities that may result from combination of crops and inter-crop activities into crop rotations, different crop management techniques (irrigation and crop protection) and animal production.

Techniques must be developed to quantify relevant inputs and outputs of land use activities (i.e. balance of soil organic matter and nutrients, environmental impact of pesticides, labor and machinery requirements, and economic performance), using different quantitative methods. Special attention should be given to improving the current farming systems by means of intensifying their production systems, putting more pressure on already deteriorated soil, which may lead to further problems for river water quality.

Further research and studies should be conducted to better assess and evaluate the vulnerability of some regions of the developing world and to determine the most appropriate adaptive actions to face the effects of climate change. Even though several general circulation models converge to estimate global warming, they are not accurate enough at the regional or country level to allow the implementation of efficient and lasting adaptive strategies in key sectors, such as water management, upland conservation, and sustainable agriculture development. Development and possession of regional circulation models would help countries determine future climate forecasting and adjust to the local climate context.

8.4.2. Planning and policy

Planners and policymakers need better tools for understanding landscape-level effects of planning and policy. Sound scientific information is an essential ingredient to sound decisions (Santelmann *et al.* 2006).

Thus, modern tools for decision support purposes and spatial analysis, risk assessment, and the evaluation of effects of changes in water and land practices, including land suitability and land productivity assessment, are of substantial use for developing countries. Such tools contribute to better understanding the biophysical themes ranging from specific soil constraints and climatic parameters to land degradation status and population characteristics at national and sub-national levels. Undoubtedly, there will be problems such as data creation and the training of users. On the other hand, these tools present promises for enhancing information services for planners and engineers, giving greater insights, more objective analysis, more ease in data sharing among administrations, and more comprehensive studies. Chapter 7 by Adams and Peck provides examples from North America that address water-related problems in uplands using long-term forecasts and other meteorological information to solve the physical and economic consequences of drought under the overwhelmingly complex topic of global climate change.

From another perspective, it is noted that developing countries rush into drawing up national water management programs with a set of generic principals or goals. This is certainly not sufficient for upland watershed management. The methodology should allow for flexibility in planning, in designing the management process, development and review and evaluation processes, and should be adapted to the specific context and situation. Some of the important variables in successful upland watershed conservation plans are the contextual characteristics, even within the same country, in relation to conflicts, agreement on facts, culture, and social conditions.

Political awareness of the socioeconomic challenges linked to climate change becomes essential in determining its medium- and long-term repercussions.

8.4.3. Rural population involvement

The involvement and participation of local landholders should be integrated as a major component in the design and development of relevant upland watershed programs. The case study presented earlier testifies to such need. However, it seems that there is no single way to institute such procedures for rural areas. The promotion of local participation in water and soil conservation activities assumes the existence of a tradition of public participation in the administrative decision-making process on an institutional level, which is not necessarily the case in developing countries. Further, rural populations represent the lower-income group (and include issues related to poverty and illiteracy). These populations are resistant to new techniques and may lack confidence in the local administrations; there may be poor civic mobilization for local issues. Hence, participative actions need to be built progressively and may require educational steps and training for both technicians and the rural population to define new methods for making agreements, negotiating, and managing conflicts.

8.4.4. Social and economic aspects

Even if the ultimate objective is upland watershed protection, the designed projects should operate within the framework of a rural development approach that can reconcile the imperative of conserving natural resources with creating conditions for diversifying local monetary revenues (off-farm activities, promoting proximity services, etc). This framework could be a participatory local development. Means of investments involving the socioeconomic infrastructure, support for community-based organizations and the rapid development of certain revenue-generating activities have a positive impact on the dynamics of local economies and can improve the quality of life for the rural population, enabling them to remain in their villages. Attention must be paid to the context of growing off-farm employment opportunities that could result in capital and labor reallocation out of the agriculture sector to less productive sectors and to less skilled human capital.

Supported activities to create and strengthen management skills among women and, particularly, girls, can also generate new revenue sources and provide an important means to ensure family solidarity.

8.5 Conclusion and policy implications

This chapter focuses only on local upland watershed management in developing countries. Other important issues related to upstream-downstream planning and implementation, transboundary upland watersheds and intergovernment conflicts, adequate institutional and organizational arrangements, and an appropriate legislative framework to support watershed management policies would require further attention.

Overall, there has been general acceptance among developing countries of the need for considering social and environmental objectives in upland water resources management. However, effective planning is still a challenging process, depending on complex local social issues, environmental concerns, and economic and institutional factors.

Strengthening the organizational skills of rural populations and their ability to take charge of infrastructure upon completion can enhance soil and water conservation and forest development activities. Public awareness is of the utmost importance if people are to cooperate in facing water and soil conservation challenges.

Within the context of a development vision, further research in the field of hydrology, soil and water conservation, and upland watershed management is needed to consolidate the currently available information. Intensifying research on climate change forecasting and its consequences on upland management becomes highly relevant, given the economic and environmental constraints that developing countries face. In addition, there is a need for comprehensive monitoring programs,

144   *S. Benabdallah*

evaluation systems and processes to capitalize on local instruments and approaches from past experiences.

Acknowledgements

The author would like to thank all of the organizers of the Rosenberg International Forum on Water Policy.

References

Achouri, M. (1995) La conservation des eaux et du sol en Tunisie: bilan et perspectives. *Cahiers Options Méditerranéennes*, CIHEAM-IAMZ 9: 35–47.
Agarwal, A. and Sunita, N. (1997) *Dying wisdom: rise, fall and potential of India's traditional water harvesting systems.* New Delhi: Centre for Science and Environment.
Ahmad, S. (2000) *Indigenous water harvesting systems in Pakistan.* Food and Agriculture Organization discussion paper. Water Resources Research INstitute, National Agricultural Research Center, Islamabad (Pakistan). Available online at http://www.wca-infonet.org.
Albergel, J., Nasri, S. and Lamachère, J. M. (2004) Programme de recherche sur les lacs collinaires dans les zones semi-arides du pourtour méditerranéen. *Rev. Sci. Eau*,17 (2): 133–51.
Amery, H. A. (2000) *Water balances in the eastern Mediterranean*: Chapter 2: Assessing Lebanon's water balance. IDRC Publications, Canada.
Bachta, M.S. (1995) Conservation des eaux et du sol (CES) en Tunisie: intervention des pouvoirs publics et stratégies paysannes: un éclairage économique., *Cahiers Options Méditerranéennes,* CIHEAM-IAMZ 9: 49–59.
Brooks, K. N., Ffolliott, P. F., Gregersen, H. M. and DeBano, L. F. (2003) *Hydrology and the management of watersheds*, 3rd ed., Ames: Iowa State Press.
Chalise, S. R. and Khanal, N. R. (1996) *Assessment of natural hazards in Nepal.* International Centre for Integrated Mountain Development (Nepal), March 1996.
Doolette, J. B. and Mcgrath, W. B. (1990*) Strategic issues in watershed development: watershed development in Asia*, World Bank Technical Paper No. 127. Washington, D.C.: World Bank.
FAO (2004) *Twenty-seventh FAO Regional Conference for the Near East: forest and tree contribution to environment, water and food security*, 13–17 March 2004, Doha, Qatar.
Harden, C. P. (2006) Human impacts on headwater fluvial systems in the northern and central Andes. *Geomorphology,* 79: 249–263.
Kerr, J. and Chung, K. (2001) Evaluating watershed management projects. *Water Policy,* 3: 537–554.
Kettab, A. (2001) Les ressources en eau en Algérie: stratégies, enjeux et vision. *Desalination,* 136: 25–33.
Li, T. (1996) *Landslide hazard mapping and management in China*, ICIMOD.
Ministry of Agriculture (1993) *Stratégie national de la conservation des eaux et du sol (1990–2000).* Tunisian Ministry of Agriculture.
Ministry of Agriculture, Rural Development, Water and Forestry (2001) *Le programme d'action national de lutte contre la désertification et d'atténuation des effets de la sécheresse (PAN).* Report. Morocco.
Ministry of Environment and Sustainable Development (2002) Etat de l'Environnement 2002, Tunisian National Report, 246 pages.

Ministry of Environment and Sustainable Development (2005) Etat de l'Environnement 2005, Tunisian National Report, 246 pages.

OECD (1993) *Coastal zone management: integrated policies.*, OECD, Paris.

Roose, E. (2006) Evolution des techniques anti-érosives dans le monde. *14th International Soil Conservation Organization Conference: water management and soil conservation in semi-arid environments*, Marrakech, Morocco, May 2006.

Santelmann, M., Freemark, K., Sifneos, J. and White, D. (2006) Assessing effects of alternative agricultural practices on wildlife habitat in Iowa, USA. *Agriculture, Ecosystems and Environment*, 113: 243–53.

Scott, C. A. and Silva-Ochoa, P. (2000) *Collective action for harvesting irrigation in the Lerma Chapala Basin Mexico*, CAPRi Working Paper N°. 20. Washington, D.C.: International Food Policy Research Institute.

Shively, G. and Coxhead, I. (2004) Conducting economic policy analysis at a landscape scale: examples from a Philippine watershed, *Agriculture, Ecosystems and Environment*, 104: 159–70.

Tennyson, L. (2002) Review and assessment of watershed management strategies and approaches. *Proceedings of the European regional workshop on watershed management*, Megève, France.

UNESCO (1982) Sedimentation problems in river basins. Paris: UNESCO.

United Nations (2007) *The millennium development goals report*. New York: United Nations.

Vorosmarty, C.J., Green, P., Salisbury, J. and Lammers, R.B. (2000) Global water resources: vulnerability from climate change and population growth. *Science,* 238: 284–88.

Weber, F. R. (1989) Policy relating arid-zone forestry to rural development and desertification control. *Proceedings of the FAO on the role of forestry in combating desertification*, Saltillo, Mexico Rome: FAO.

World Bank (1992) *World development report 1992: development and the environment*. Washington, D.C.: World Bank.

9 Policy and adaptation in the Jordan Valley

Yousef Hasan Ayadi

The Hashemite Kingdom of Jordan is one of the 10 most water-stressed countries in the world. Less than five percent of the country's area contains most of the Jordan Valley's scarce water resources, including those shared with neighboring countries. The escalating demand on water for both irrigation and domestic purposes is a real challenge that needs to be met with good governance, wise and innovative management, and strong and determined will. The Jordan Valley Authority (JVA), which is in charge of water management and plays a comprehensive role in the socioeconomic development of the Valley, applies a combination of water supply and demand management to face this challenge.

9.1 Introduction

The Jordan Valley (JV) is part of the Great Rift Valley that extends from south Turkey to the horn of Africa. In the Hashemite Kingdom of Jordan (HKJ), it extends for about 400 kilometers from the Jordanian borders at the Yarmouk River in the north to the Gulf of Aqaba in the south.

According to the Jordan Valley Development Law, the JVA mandate extends westward to the western Jordanian borders and eastward to a level of 300 meters above sea level north of the Dead Sea, and 500 meters above sea level from the north shore of the Dead Sea to Aqaba Special Economic zone. The Valley is five to 10 kilometers wide, and its floor varies in elevation from –212 meters in the north to –418 meters at the Dead Sea; and rises to +250 meters in central Wadi Araba before it tapers down to sea level at Aqaba.

Variations in temperature, humidity, and rainfall produce distinct agro-climatic zones. Annual rainfall, most of which falls from December to February, starts in October and ends in May. The northern area receives about 400 mm/year, while the southern areas receive 100 mm/year. In dry years, precipitation drops to 200 mm in the northern area, and to 50 mm at the Dead Sea, while in wet years these same locations receive up to 650 mm and 250 mm, respectively.

The Jordan Valley can be considered a natural greenhouse with the relative advantage of producing off-season fruits and vegetables. Although its area represents less than five percent of the HKJ's area and its population less than six percent of the country's population, the Valley produces more than 60 percent of the kingdom's fruits and vegetables.

The salient variations between northern, central, and southern parts of the JV also are clear in terms of water availability, water quality, soil type, and cropping pattern. Water resources in the JV are scarce and deteriorating in quality, which severely constrains agricultural production. The annual available water resources in the Valley are estimated to be 300–350 million cubic meters (Mcm), while the annual demand exceeds 500 Mcm. The agricultural land that could be irrigated represents about 60 to 70 percent of the irrigable land in the valley due to the lack of water resources, and the gap between supply and demand is widening due to the increase in demand for municipal, industrial and agricultural uses of water.

The continuous decline of the available water resources, exacerbated by the extended drought cycles witnessed over the last decade, make it imperative for the water sector in Jordan, and for the JVA in particular, to use modern water management practices to cope with the situation. The national water strategy and policies, and the emerging action plans, are being implemented to face these challenges. Such actions include the reuse of unconventional water resources, the implementation of water-saving programs, including water scheduling according to the crops' real water needs, and the use of modern irrigation methods and techniques.

Figures 9.1 and 9.2 show the development areas in the Jordan Valley north and south of the Dead Sea.

9.2 Water resources in the Jordan Valley

9.2.1 Surface water resources

Water resources in the JV are characterized by scarcity, variability, and uncertainty. One of the main sources of water in the JV is the Jordan River. The lower Jordan River starts at the outlet of Lake Tiberias and discharges into the Dead Sea after a meandering course covering about 140 kilometers of aerial distance, with several tributaries flowing from the east and west of the river.

The Yarmouk River, joining the Jordan River shortly after it leaves Lake Tiberias, is the major Jordan River tributary. It is an international waterway with three direct riparian parties on it: Syria, Jordan, and Israel. As such, its waters are shared among the three riparian parties. The main remaining eastern tributaries of the lower Jordan River are the Zarqa River, and the side wadis of Arab, Ziglab, Jurum, Rayyan, Kufranja, Rajib, Shueib, Kafrein, and Hisban.

The East Dead Sea drainage area includes the wadis of Zarqa-Ma'aeen, Zara, Mujib, Wala, Karak, Hasa, Ibn Hammad and other inter-catchments. The South Dead Sea sub-basin includes the wadis of Feifa, Khneizerah, Ad Dahil, Fidan, Musa, Dana, and As Siq.

The total surface water resources currently available in the JV amounts to about 337 Mcm/ year, of which 217 Mcm/year is in the northern part of the Valley and 120 Mcm/year is in the south.

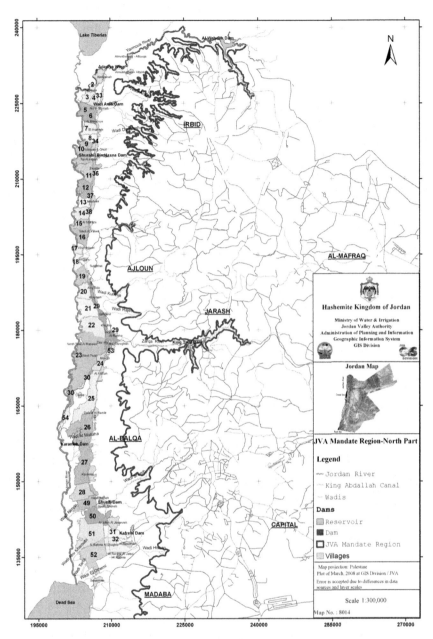

Figure 9.1 Development Areas North of the Dead Sea (Source: JVA – Planning Directorate – GIS Division).

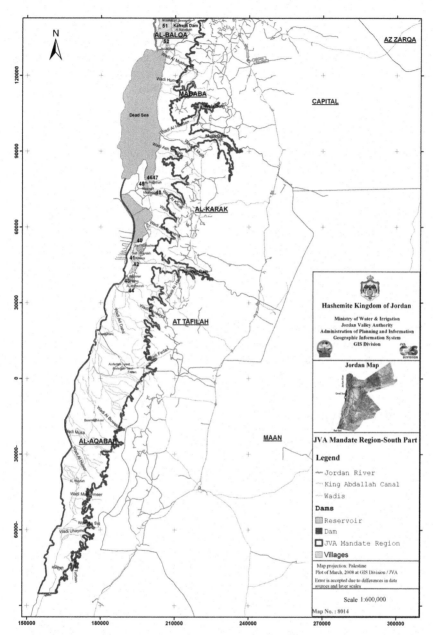

Figure 9.2 Development Areas South of the Dead Sea (Source: JVA – Planning
Directorate – GIS Division).

The extensive utilization of the Jordan River basin resources from the basin riparians has caused the sharp decline of the river discharge to the Dead Sea, which is estimated currently to be less than 10 percent of its historical flow, thus causing the decline of the Dead Sea level and damage to the whole eco-system in the area. Figure 9.3 shows the continuous decline in the Dead Sea's level.

9.2.2 Groundwater resources

Groundwater is not plentiful in the JV. There are a few aquifers producing freshwater. The more important are: the Mukheibeh well field (25 Mcm/yr), Wadi Arab well field (20 Mcm/yr including Zahar), Rajib well field producing some 6 Mcm/yr for domestic supply, South Shuna well field producing some 20 Mcm/yr to irrigate about 3,000 hectares, and Kafrein well field (8–12 Mcm/yr). South of the Dead Sea, the Safi aquifer produces about 14 Mcm/yr, most of which goes to meet industrial demand at the Arab Potash Company. In Wadi Araba, the aggregate amount of several small aquifers is in the order of 15 Mcm/yr.

9.2.3 Treated wastewater

There are 22 wastewater treatment plants (WWTP) in Jordan, producing about 80 Mcm/year, of which 60 Mcm flows down to the Jordan Valley, with Khirbet Al-Samra discharging to Zarqa River – the largest with an effluent of about 50 Mcm/yr.

9.3 Water sector challenges

The Hashemite Kingdom of Jordan is classified between the arid and semi-arid countries. With its annual 148 cubic meters of water resources per capita in the year 2006, it is considered one of the 10 most water-stressed countries in the world. Water resources depend on rainfall, which fluctuates in quantity and distribution from year to year, with less than 200mm annual precipitation over 90 percent of the kingdom.

Moreover, Jordan can be considered a residual downstream user, sharing water

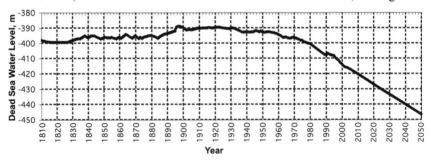

Figure 9.3 Dead Sea Level (Source: JVA – Planning Directorate).

resources with its neighbors. Its two main transboundary surface water resources are the Jordan River and its tributary the Yarmouk River. The overexploitation of these resources by the upstream users, and unilateral actions over the past decades left Jordan with almost negligible water quantities to use, if compared with the river's historical flows.

The water sector in Jordan and the Jordan Valley in particular faces immense challenges that can be summarized as follows:

- The gap between supply and demand is escalating in an unpredicted manner, due to the influx of newcomers to the country resulting from instability in the region, in addition to the increasing demand on water from urbanization and development needs. For example, the annual share of water resources decreased from around 3500 cubic meters per capita to less than 150 cubic meters in half a century.
- The intense use of the shared water resources by the upstream water users leaves Jordan with the residual declining flows.
- The lack of freshwater obliges farmers to use low-quality water from the treated wastewater effluent and the brackish underground water resources.
- Lack of funds hinder the rehabilitation of the aged irrigation projects and preventive and corrective maintenance to assure the sustainability of networks.
- There has been a loss of qualified staff from the public sector to private companies locally and abroad looking for better incentives.

9.4 Water sector strategy and policies[1]

The Ministry of Water and Irrigation (MWI) published in 1998 the Water Sector Strategy and developed a set of policies related to irrigation, groundwater, wastewater, and utilities. A Water Demand Policy is under preparation. The following sections discuss the main features of the water strategy and policies.

9.4.1 On resources development

- Water is a national resource and shall be valued as such at all times. A comprehensive national water data bank will be established and kept at the Ministry of Water and Irrigation, and shall be supported by a decision support unit. It will be supported by a program of monitoring and a system of data collection, entry, updating, processing and dissemination of information, and will be designed to become a component of a regional water databank.
- The full potential of surface water and groundwater shall be tapped to the extent permissible by economic feasibility, while addressing the social and environmental impacts. Investigation of deep aquifers shall be conducted to support development planning. The interactive use of ground and surface water with different qualities shall be considered. Assessment of the available and potential resources shall be conducted periodically.

- Wastewater shall not be managed as "waste." It shall be collected and treated to standards that allow its reuse in unrestricted agriculture and in other non-domestic purposes, including groundwater recharge. Appropriate wastewater treatment technologies shall be adopted with due considerations to economy in energy consumption, and quality assurance of the effluent for use in unrestricted agriculture. Consideration shall be given to blending of the treated effluent with fresh water for appropriate reuse.
- Marginal quality water and brackish water sources shall be enlisted to support irrigated agriculture. They shall be listed, along with sea water for desalination to produce additional water for municipal, industrial, and for commercial consumption. Technology transfer and the findings of advanced research in genetic engineering shall be introduced to the extent possible for this purpose.
- A long-term plan shall be formulated for the development of the resources, and a revolving five-year plan shall be derived from it and updated as necessary. The revolving plan shall be compatible with those formulated for other sectors of the economy. A parallel investment plan shall accompany the development plan.
- The priority criterion for project implementation, and for additional water allocation, shall be based on economic, social, and environmental considerations. A "critical path" shall be established for the allocation of each new source of water. Consideration shall be given to the sustainability of the allocation in light of the national water balance situation and the economic, social, and environmental opportunity cost of forgone alternative uses of water.
- First priority will be given to allocation of water to satisfy basic human needs; as such the first priority shall be given to the allocation of a modest share of 100 liters per capita per day for domestic water supplies. Expensive additional water shall be allocated for municipal purposes as a first priority, followed by tourism and for industrial purposes.

9.4.2 On resources management

- Priority shall be given to the sustainability of use of the previously developed resources, including resources mobilized for the irrigated agriculture in the Jordan Valley and for other established uses. Special care shall be given to the protection of water from pollution and from quality degradation and depletion.
- Mining of renewable groundwater aquifers shall be checked, controlled, and reduced to sustainable extraction rates. Mining of fossil aquifers shall be planned and carefully implemented.
- Resource management shall continually aim at achieving the highest possible efficiency in conveyance, distribution, application, and use. It shall adopt a dual approach of demand management and supply management. Tools of advanced technology shall be adopted to enhance the resource management capabilities.

- Interactive use of multiple resources shall be targeted to maximize the usable flows, and to maximize the net benefit from the use of a unit of water.
- Human resources development shall rank high in the priority scale. Continuous education, on-the-job training and overseas training programs shall be organized and implemented. Overemployment shall be trimmed to reach optimum employment levels compatible with efficient management entities elsewhere in the world.
- Management of wastewater shall receive attention with due regard to public health standards. Industrial wastewater shall be carefully monitored to avoid degrading the quality of the effluent of wastewater treatment plants destined for reuse.

9.4.3 On legislation and institutional set-up

- Periodically review institutional arrangements and legislation in effect to appraise adequacy of the status quo through the changing conditions and times. Institutional restructuring shall be made to match the changing needs.
- Assure cooperation and co-ordination among public and private entities involved in water development and management.

9.4.4 On shared water resources

- The rightful shares of the kingdom shall be defended and protected through bilateral and multilateral contacts, negotiations, and agreements. Peace water and wastewater projects, including the scheme for the development of the Jordan Rift Valley, shall be accorded special attention for construction, operation, and maintenance.
- Due respect will be given to the provisions of international law as applicable to water sharing, protection and conservation, and those applicable to territorial waters.
- Bilateral and multi-lateral cooperation with neighboring states shall be pursued, and regional cooperation shall be advocated, preferably within the provisions of a regional water charter.

9.4.5 On public awareness

- The public shall be educated through various means about the value of water for them and the well-being of the country for the sustainability of life, and for economic and social development.
- Challenges in the water sector are to be faced not only by the water administration, but also equally, if not more, by the public. The roles to be played in water conservation by the different sectors of society shall be defined and assigned.
- Facts about water in Jordan shall be disseminated along with the cost incurred to provide the service, and the mounting pressure of population on the water

resources. Introduction, adoption, and use of water-saving and recycling systems and devices shall be promoted.

- Economic measures shall be adopted to reinforce public awareness. Such measures as demand management, and efficiency improvements within supply management techniques shall be employed.

9.4.6 On performance

- Performance efficiency of the water and wastewater systems and the management thereof shall be monitored and rated, and improvements on performance shall be introduced with due consideration to resource economics.
- Human resources' performance shall be continually appraised to upgrade capabilities and sustain excellence. Incentives for excellence shall be introduced in compliance with the needs for dedication.

9.4.7 On health standards

- Setting and enforcing national health standards shall be enhanced and sustained, especially in regards to municipal water supply.
- Concerns for public health and the health of workers shall be a focus in the programs of reuse of treated wastewater.
- Laboratories for controls shall be maintained and properly equipped.

9.4.8 On private sector participation

- The role of the private sector shall be expanded. Management contracts, concessions and other forms of private sector participation in water utilities shall be considered and adopted as appropriate.
- The concepts of build, own and operate (BOO) and build, own and transfer (BOT) shall be entertained, and the impact of such concepts on the consumers shall be continually assessed, and negative impacts mitigated.
- The private sector role in irrigated agriculture shall also be encouraged and expanded. Emphasis shall be placed on the social benefits in conjunction with the private investments.

9.4.9 On financing

- Recovery of the cost of utilities and the provision of services shall be targeted. Recovery of operation and maintenance cost shall be a standard practice. Capital cost recovery shall be carefully approached. The role of water tariffs shall be considered as a tool to attract private investment in water projects.
- Cost recovery shall be linked to the average per capita share of the GDP and its level. It shall also be connected to the cost of living and the family basket of consumption. However, profitable undertakings in industry, tourism, commerce, and agriculture shall be made to pay the fair water cost.

- Until the cost recovery is full, and the national savings are at levels capable of domestic financing of development projects, project financing will depend on concessionary loans, private borrowing and/or build, and BOO/BOT arrangements.

9.4.10 On research and development

- Efforts to encourage and enhance indigenous water research targeted at the improvement of resource management, enhancing the understanding of resource economics, and adapting the research findings in other environments to local conditions, including but not limited to crop water requirements, minimizing evaporation and controlling evapotranspiration and the like.
- Emphasis will be placed on liaison with international institutions to stay abreast with modern technological advances, and to facilitate technology transfer and adaptation.

9.5 Legislation and institutional set-up

9.5.1 JVA mandate[2]

The Jordan Valley Authority (JVA) was established in 1977 with a broad mandate for the integrated development of the Jordan Valley, encompassing all aspects of life in the valley. In 1988, the JVA became part of the MWI. Its mandate includes:

A The development and use of water resources of the Jordan Valley for purposes of irrigated agriculture, domestic and municipal uses, industry, hydropower generation and other beneficial uses, for the protection and conservation of these resources, and the implementation of all works related to the development, utilization, protection and conservation thereof, including:

1 Conducting studies required for evaluation of water resources, including hydrological, hydro-geological and geological studies, drilling of exploratory wells and installation of observation wells.

2 Planning, design, construction, operation, and maintenance of irrigation projects and related structures and works of all types and purposes, including dams and appurtenant works, pumping stations, reservoirs and water conveyance and distribution networks, surface and subsurface drainage works, flood protection works, and roads and building needs for operation and maintenance.

3 Soil surveys and classification, and the identification and reclamation of lands for use in irrigated agriculture, and dividing them into farm units.

4 Settlement of disputes arising from the use of water resources.

5 In coordination with the Water Authority of Jordan, organize and direct the construction of private and public wells.

     6   Development and improvement of the environment and living conditions in the Jordan Valley, and implementation of the related works including:

- Setting rules and regulations for areas of land outside town and village borders on which construction of buildings is permitted, setback lines, rights of way.
- Development of land zoning to define land use: residential, industrial, agricultural.

B   Planning, design and construction of farm roads.
C   Development of tourism in the Jordan Valley, including construction of touristic and recreational facilities.
D   Social development of the valley inhabitants, including the establishment of private institutions in order to help them contribute to the improvement of the valley and to the achievement of development objectives.
E   Additional development activities as requested by the cabinet.

The Jordan Valley is divided administratively into four operation and maintenance directorates as shown in Figure 9.4, each responsible for a number of stage offices to serve the nearby farmers and citizens. This decentralized administrative structure, with the delegation of authorities from the headquarters to the directorates and stage offices, allows flexibility of the operation and maintenance activities and eases the life of farmers who can apply for their irrigation requests and pay their water charges at the office nearest to their farms.

9.5.2 JVA strategic plan 2003–2008

After completing the initial integrated development work in the valley, JVA's responsibilities became focused on bulk and retail water management and distribution, as well as land development and management. The Jordan Valley Development Law was amended in 2001, Law No. 30, to more accurately reflect the transformation in JVA's role. A five-year strategic plan was developed to reflect the new role and provide quality services to citizens with the following four goals:

1   Water resources management:
    Meet the needs of current and future water users by managing, developing, protecting and sustaining both existing and new water resources, taking into account economic, social, and environmental considerations and involving the private sector where appropriate.
2   Water supply and distribution:
    Manage JVA's existing water delivery and distribution infrastructure, systems and facilities in an efficient, transparent and equitable manner, and involve the private sector where appropriate.
3   Land development and management:
    Develop, manage, regulate, and protect land and related resources in the Jordan

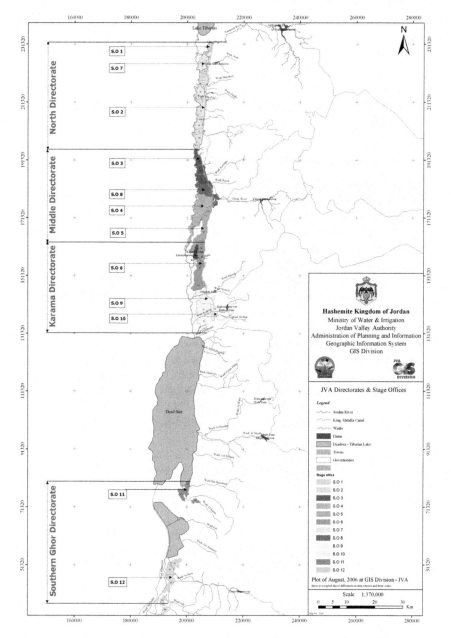

Figure 9.4 Jordan Valley Operation and Maintenance Administration (Source: JVA Planning Directorate – GIS Division).

Valley in order to maximize their economic usefulness while taking into account environmental considerations, and involve the private sector where appropriate.

4   Organizational performance improvement and development:
Develop and reorganize JVA to enable it to better achieve its new mission and improve its performance and effectiveness in providing quality service to its stakeholders.

9.6 Development activities in the Jordan Valley

The Jordanian government, through the JVA and its predecessor organizations, started since the early 1950s to implement infrastructure and irrigation project development in the Jordan Valley.

In 1959, the construction of the East Ghor Canal (now King Abdullah Canal) commenced. It allowed the conveyance of water from the Yarmouk River to irrigate lands in the JV. The first phase was 70 kilometers long, ending at the Zarqa River and irrigating 11,400 hectares financed with grants from the United States through USAID. The canal was later extended by 8 kilometers and financed by the Kuwait fund to irrigate 800 hectares. It was then extended by 18 kilometers, which was financed by USAID, to irrigate 3,600 hectares, and finally by 14.5 kilometers in 1989, with finance from the Federal Republic of Germany through Kreditanstalt für Wiederaufbau to irrigate 6,000 hectares. Other areas irrigated directly from side wadis amount to 1,750 hectares irrigated from Wadi Arab, Ziglab, and Jurum with finance from IDA of the World Bank Group; 1,500 hectares from the Zarqa River, financed by USAID; and 1,500 hectaares from Hisban and Kafrein, financed by Kreditanstalt für Wiederaufbau. The total length of the canal is now 110.5 kilometers.

These projects increased the total area served with irrigation infrastructure to about 31,000 hectares. South of the Dead Sea, stage I of the Southern Ghors irrigation scheme was constructed in the period 1983–85, to bring about 4,750 hectares under modern drip irrigation. Recently, other 900 hectares were developed in Ghor Mazraa, Feifa, and Khneizerah.

In parallel with irrigation projects, the developed agricultural land in the JV was divided into farm units of 3–4 hectares each, which were distributed to farmers/owners and to farmers/operators in the JV.

Dam construction started in 1962 by building the Sharhabil (Ziglab) Dam (4 Mcm), the Shueib Dam (1.5 Mcm) in 1965, and the Kafrein Dam in 1968 (8.4 Mcm after raising in 1994). In 1977, the King Talal Dam was completed at 56 Mcm total capacity and raised in 1987 to a new capacity of 85 Mcm. Silting and bed load have decreased its live storage capacity since to about 75 Mcm. The Wadi Arab Dam, with 20 Mcm, was completed in 1986. In 1994, the construction of the Karameh Dam (53 Mcm) started and was completed in 1997.

In addition to the dams in the north, three dams were built on tributaries to the Dead Sea in Southern Ghors: the Mujib (35 Mcm), the Wala (9.3 Mcm) and the Tannour (16.8 Mcm). Two conveyors from Mujib Diversion also were recently completed to convey water northwards (48 Mcm) to the city of Amman, and southwards (12 Mcm) to the Dead Sea industrial complexes, and to the agricultural areas in the Southern Ghors. Al-Wehda Dam (110 Mcm) has been recently installed on the Yarmouk River, which raised the total storage capacity of the existing 10 main dams to 327 Mcm.

Figures 9.5 and 9.6 show the schematic representation of the hydraulic structures and the irrigation projects north and south of the Dead Sea.

9.7 Adaptation activities

The following adaptive activities are performed by JVA and the water sector to face the challenges and look to the future.

9.7.1 Resources development

First, a continuous water-harvesting program is being implemented to capture winter floods and regulate the base flow of the side wadis. Three medium dams are planned with 16 Mcm storage capacity: Kufrenja, Ibn Hammad, and Karak. Five other small dams with a storage capacity of 5 Mcm also are planned: Whadi, Zarqa-Maein, Lajjoun, Shaizam and Dlaga. Other desert dams, lagoons and ponds are being implemented for irrigation, livestock and artificial recharge, according to the availability of funds.

Secondly, non-conventional water resources are increasingly used, including brackish and treated wastewater. Guidelines[3] were issued to help farmers in using the best practices to irrigate the dominant crops in the valley with brackish water, which is available mostly in the shallow aquifer north of the Dead Sea.

The crops were categorized according to their resistance to salinity, and production curves were developed to indicate the threshold point at which crop production starts to decline. The brackish water is used directly to irrigate salt-tolerant crops, or blended or alternately used with fresh water, according to the crop-growing status, or was even desalinated using small reverse osmosis (RO) units by some farmers (23 private desalination units were already installed in the JV). Alsio, desalination of brackish water for drinking purposes, by both the public and the private sectors, is increasing.

Thirdly, the quality of treated wastewater effluent is being improved by upgrading the old plants and designing new ones to meet the local and international standards for unrestricted use in irrigated agriculture. Al-Samara water treatment plant, the largest in Jordan, is being upgraded through a BOT contract.

Guidelines[4] for the use of reclaimed water in an environmentally safe and economically viable manner were prepared by JVA to help farmers in applying best practices in using the reclaimed water, which is increasingly used for irrigation in the JV, due to the lack of fresh water and its diversion for municipal purposes. Programs are being conducted to monitor surface water, groundwater soil and crops. The results of these monitoring programs are analyzed and used to take mitigation measures to remedy any negative effects from using reclaimed water.

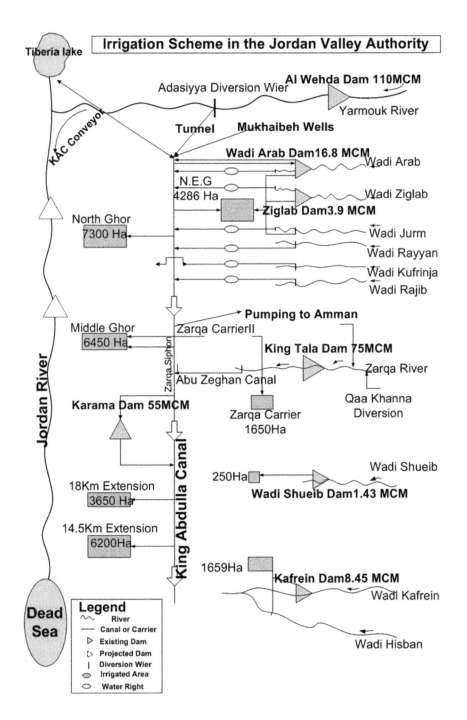

Figure 9.5 Hydraulic Schematic north of the Dead Sea (Source: JVA Planning Directorate – WMIS Project).

Integrated Water Supply System in the Southern Ghors

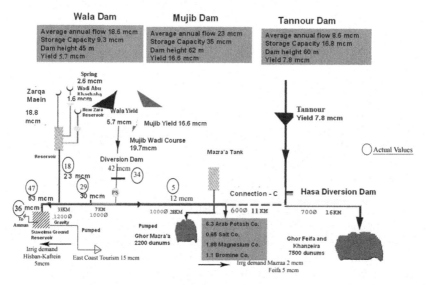

Figure 9.6 Hydraulic Schematic south of the Dead Sea (Source: JVA Irrigation Directorate).

9.7.2 Shared water resources

The Jordanian-Syrian Committee for the utilization of the Yarmouk River Basin Water meets regularly to coordinate the utilization of the basin water according to the agreement signed between the two countries in 1987.

The Joint Water Committee (JWC), which was formed after the signature of the Peace Treaty between Jordan and Israel in 1994, meets regularly to follow up the implementation of the Water Annex (Annex II).

A water conduit was built from Dajania Gates, at the southern outlet of Lake Tiberias, to King Abdullah Canal to convey water allocated to Jordan in accordance with the Water Annex.

A diversion weir was constructed on the Yarmouk River in Adasiyeh to control and regulate the flows of the Yarmouk to both sides as per the same Water Annex to the Peace Treaty with Israel.

Al Wehda Dam has been constructed on the Yarmouk River in the Maqarin area at the borders between Jordan and Syria to store the floods and to regulate the base flow of the river.

Several studies were conducted to supply Jordan with the additional 50 Mcm/year of water of drinkable standards as stipulated in the agreement between Jordan and Israel, and the issue is still under investigation.

Finally, competent joint ventures of engineering and environmental firms have been pre-qualified to participate in a bidding process to conduct the feasibility of the Red Sea – Dead Sea linkage[5]. The Terms of Reference document has been issued, and awards for the feasibility study and environmental and social study contracts were expected during the first quarter of 2008. When implemented, the project is expected to induce a rebound in the Dead Sea level, which has been decreasing dramatically due to the diversion of freshwater resources used to feed it. The difference in levels between the two seas will be exploited to generate electricity and to desalinate sea water.

9.7.3 Resources management

Surface irrigation channels are converted to pressurized pipe networks. Each farm unit was equipped with a farm turnout assembly (FTA), including a pressure regulator and a flow-limiting device. It should be noted that the flow at the standard farm gate was 20 liters/second when the open channels networks were used before the conversion into pressurized systems. This flow is limited to six to nine liters/second, which saved a considerable amount of irrigation water. The number of the gravity lateral turnouts along King Abdullah Canal (KAC) was reduced from 140 at the open channel system to 28 when converted to the pressurized system.

A hydraulic simulation model (EPANET)[6] is used to stabilize pressure and flow in each irrigation line from the water source to the FTAs. As a result, the pressure was stabilized to three bars throughout the irrigation network, and the flow at the FTAs was adjusted to six liters/second, thereby increasing equity and farmers' satisfaction in addition to raising the efficiency of irrigation water use.

Rehabilitation of KAC included fixing damaged slabs to reduce losses, re-designing its siphons, which were the bottleneck hindering excess flow between the canal sections, and doubling some of them to allow more flood flow through KAC to the storage reservoirs in the winter season. A water measurement network was installed along KAC, and a SCADA system was used to monitor and automatically control water flow in the canal from a control center located in the JV.

The system allows the automatic control of 28 out of the 38 check gates across KAC from the control center, in addition to the sluice gates at the tunnel inlet. It is a tool which enables the absorption of water inflows into KAC, and adjusting water levels at KAC sections, allowing discharges for irrigation and domestic uses according to a pre-defined schedule.

The system performs the following three associated actions at the check gates: anticipatory action, corrective action and coordination action. Accordingly, the discharge at each check gate and at each regulation time step is calculated. The system predicts the volume that will be stored in KAC at the end of the day, the flow for each outlet and inlet for the next hour, and the target volume for each reach of the canal. These forecasts are updated every 15 minutes. The system consists of 36 remote transmission units (RTUs), gate-opening sensors and actuators, upstream and downstream water level sensors, flow meters, water salinity sensors, PLC cabinet, and 30 pairs of underground communication cables to exchange data and instructions with the control center.

A computerized water management information system (WMIS) was introduced to help in making decisions to balance water resources with demands and to optimize water distribution to farm units. The system allows for calculation of seasonal, monthly, and daily water balances, and assists in setting reservoirs' target volumes and operational efficiencies of the different sections of the hydraulic network.

The WMIS application modules are classified into three categories, according to the type of water management activities: water distribution, water supply, and water management strategy. These modules will become Web-enabled in the context of a modernization plan that will be implemented in the near future.

The farm water quotas are computed on a seasonal basis, according to the water availability and the planting register. Irrigation orders are produced on a daily basis for each irrigation line, according to a pre-fixed schedule and irrigation requests from farmers. At the end of each month, water consumption is calculated for each farm unit and water bills are issued.

9.7.4 On-farm management

Pilot projects were introduced with the help of donors to illustrate how to optimize water use inside the farm units by the use of tensio-meters to help identify the exact time of irrigation according to crops' needs. An irrigation advisory service (IAS) also was instituted to help farmers use these devices and schedule their irrigation frequency. Universities, research centers, and non-governmental organizations (NGOs) are involved in the activities at the pilot areas.

Farmers also were encouraged to change their irrigation systems at the farm unit level from surface to micro-irrigation (drip and mini sprinklers), and to introduce advanced technologies to maximize irrigation water use efficiency (more crop per drop).

Good agricultural practices (GAP)[7] are introduced, and many farmers are certifying their products for export to external markets. Cash crops such as Charentais melons[8], strawberries, early grapes and other cash crops are being planted to maximize the benefits from irrigation water, and contract farming is being introduced to protect farmers against price fluctuations.

9.7.5 Stakeholders' participation

Farmers are encouraged to form water-user groups[9]. These groups started by forming water committees at the irrigation lines level and local water councils at a larger scale, and ended up by becoming officially registered water-user associations in accordance with the geographic zones and the social structure. Around 40 percent of Jordan Valley farmers participate in one way or another in these groups at 16 locations along the valley.

The main function of these groups is their participation in irrigation water distribution activities. Farmers now open and close their FTAs according to the irrigation schedule, thereby alleviating this burden on the JVA. In addition, there has been a significant reduction in water losses and illegal water use, due to this self-controlled water distribution. The farmers are satisfied because of the transparency and the share of responsibility with JVA. The next step is to transfer the water distribution responsibility of certain distribution networks to the water user associations, which necessitates legislative amendments.

9.7.6 Water tariff

A water tariff program was introduced and increased gradually to cover part of the operation and maintenance costs since the installation of KAC in the early1960s. An escalating tariff structure of four categories is applied now that encourages farmers to reduce consumption and save irrigation water. The bills for low-income vegetable growing farmers are normally in the lower tariff category, while those for large water consumers are in the higher categories.

A fixed rate is charged on the monthly water bill to cover the cost of FTA maintenance. Water sales for agriculture and industry covers most of the operation and maintenance costs of JVA.

9.7.7 Drought management

In case of severe droughts, farmlands are rented from farmers by JVA to save water, and farmers are compensated for losing their planting season. Irrigation water rationing became a general practice in the summer season, and summer vegetables are banned in some areas during drought seasons to save water for the permanent trees.

Licenses for planting banana and citrus trees are no longer issued to farmers, as these are high water consumers. Farmers with old licenses are given the water requirements when water is available but, in case of drought, a minimum amount of water is given to these trees to keep them alive.

9.8 Conclusion and policy implications

Some of the lessons learned from the Jordan Valley experience can be summarized as follows.

There is no perfect solution that fits all situations. New technologies and methods should be adapted to local conditions by experimenting with them on a small pilot scale in combination with applied research programs that take all parameters into consideration and utilize locally proven solutions that can be then carefully expanded on a larger scale.

The human factor is the pillar of success or failure. The more investments in human resources development, the better results we can get in adapting the new technologies and methods. Continuous on-the-job training programs should be conducted for the technical and administrative staff, including communication skills, with more focus on the field staff who have direct contact with end users.

Stakeholders' participation is a crucial factor in the successful operation and sustainability of the irrigation projects. State bureaucracy can lead nowhere, without the full and active involvement of water users. Forms of participation should take into consideration the social structure of local communities and should be supported by a legislative umbrella. Again, there is no fit-for-all solution.

When the water shortage is chronic, local measures, however efficient, cannot alleviate the situation, and basin-wide regional solutions must be sought. Such solutions require an integrated and sustainable basin management plan that takes into account the integrity and protection of the basin ecosystem, demographic and social needs, and geopolitical considerations.

Times of water abundance are beyond our control, and those who choose to work in the water sector should be aware of the seriousness of the path they have chosen and the challenges they have to face.

It is nice to look beyond the horizon, draw the best strategies and policies, and put together the best plans, but be sure to keep your feet on the ground and, when moving forward, watch your steps carefully – especially when the ground is shaky underneath.

Notes

1 Jordan's Water Strategy & Policies 2002. A publication of the Ministry of Water & irrigation.
2 Jordan Valley Development Law No.19 year 1988, modified by the law No. 30 year 2001.
3 Brackish Water Project – GTZ.
4 Reclaimed Water Project – GTZ.
5 www.worldbank.org/rds.
6 IoJV Project – MREA.
7 KAFAA Project – USAID.
8 IoJV Project – MREA.
9 Water Resources Management in Irrigated Agriculture – GTZ.

References

GTZ (Deutsche Gesellshaft fur Technische Zusammenarbeit). 2003.
GTZ (Deutsche Gesellshaft fur Technische Zusammenarbeit). 2003. Water Resources Management in Irrigated Agriculture project. Second and final progress report of phase I, pp. 45. GTZ and JVA. Amman, Jordan.
GTZ (Deutsche Gesellshaft fur Technische Zusammenarbeit). 2006.
Guideline for brackish water irrigation in the Jordan Valley. Brackish water project, pp. 109. GTZ and JVA. Amman, Jordan.
Guideline for reclaimed water irrigation in the Jordan Valley. Reclaimed water project, pp. 80. GTZ and JVA. Amman, Jordan.
HKJ, JVA. 2006. Water management information system. WMIS Database, Deir Alla, Jordan: Jordan Valley Authority. Deir Alla, Jordan.
HKJ, JVA. 2006. Geographic information system. GIS Database. Jordan Valley Authority. Amman, Jordan.
HKJ, MWI. 2002. Jordan's water strategy & policies, pp. 101. Ministry of Water and Irrigation. Amman, Jordan.

HKJ, MWI/JVA. 2006. Jordan Valley development law, pp. 50.

Ministry of Water and Irrigation/Jordan Valley Authority. Amman, Jordan.

MREA (Regional Mission for Water Agriculture, French Embassy) and JVA (Jordan Valley Authority). 2006. Feasibility Study of Phase II: Extension to all North Conversion Project. MREA and JVA. Amman, Jordan.

MREA (Regional Mission for Water Agriculture, French Embassy) and JVA (Jordan Valley Authority). 2007, pp. 136. Water saving in the Middle East, Agriculture and Export Project. MREA and JVA. Amman, Jordan.

USAID. 205. Assessment of agricultural extension services in the Jordan Valley and Amman Zarqa basin, pp. 34. KAFA'A project. Amman, Jordan.

WB. The World Bank web site/Red Sea – Dead Sea water Conveyance Study: Available online at http://www.worldbank.org/rds. WB, Washington DC.

10 Challenges in upland watershed management

The green-blue water approach

Holger Hoff

Increasing water scarcity requires a widened integrated water resources management (IWRM) approach, which includes green water as an additional resource to be managed. Best practices and cross-sectoral adaptation, according to the new green-blue water approach, provide new degrees of freedom by increasing water productivity and enhancing water-related ecosystem services for higher overall benefits, compared to conventional infrastructure and blue water solutions. Payments for environmental services (PES) can reconcile upland poverty alleviation with improved downstream water availability, and bridge the gap between field-scale soil and water conservation and basin-scale IWRM. Applying green-blue water principles to clean development mechanism (CDM) afforestations can increase their sustainability and generate additional funding for IWRM activities.

10.1 Introduction

Water stress in many parts of the world is increasing in terms of water quantity as well as quality. Humans are at the same time causing this water stress and suffering from it. Human appropriation of surface and ground water, changes in land use, release of pollutants, and other direct and indirect pressures are all contributing to the growing water crisis. Degradation of water resources and lack of access to safe water threaten human well-being and are closely linked to food insecurity and poverty in many parts of the world. The Millenium Development Goals cannot be achieved without improving water management significantly (Soussan and Noel 2005, Rockström *et al.* 2005). Also, aquatic and terrestrial ecosystems and their services critically depend on availability of sufficient amounts of water and the appropriate temporal distribution.

Global and regional assessments are projecting an increasing number of people, ecosystems, and basins subject to water scarcity (Rockström *et al.* 2008, Smakthin *et al.* 2004, Vörösmarty *et al.* 2000). Many basins have come close to, or have even reached, the state of a "closed basin," in which all available surface and ground water is committed and any re-allocations or improvements for one group or in one part of the basin would come at a cost of another. Under such conditions, any increases in upstream water use, e.g. from agricultural intensification, would cause downstream shortfalls in water supply.

In response to these mounting pressures, IWRM has been introduced as a useful framework, primarily to address solutions at catchment to river basin scale. According to what is probably the most widely used IWRM definition by GWP (2000), IWRM is "a process, which promotes the coordinated development and management of water, land and related resources in order to maximize the resultant economic and social welfare in an equitable manner without compromising the sustainability of vital ecosystems." Despite the good intentions of this definition, coordinated water and land management is not yet practiced in most river basins around the world. The key role of land management in alleviating water scarcity is hardly recognized.

This chapter demonstrates through some examples the important links between upstream land use and downstream effects on water resources, and attempts to identify successful institutional adaptations that address these upstream-downstream links for improved water availability, productivity and allocation equity. While upland management also can have strong impacts on downstream water quality, this chapter is limited to water quantity effects.

10.2 Upstream–downstream links: the green-blue water approach

Generally, assessments of water scarcity, as well as implementations of the IWRM concept, are limited to the so-called "blue water" and fail to recognize that most of the water in the hydrological cycle that supports humans and ecosystems is, in fact, "green water."

10.2.1 Green and blue water

The concept of green water is not new. Only recently, however, possibly in response to the growing water crisis in many parts of the world, has this concept received the attention it is due. Blue water is water in rivers, lakes and ground water, for use in irrigation and municipal and industrial water supply. It also sustains aquatic ecosystems. Green water is the water infiltrated into the soil from precipitation, which returns to the atmosphere via evapotranspiration. It provides a large natural storage of water, similar to ground water but accessible to natural and agricultural vegetation only. This green water storage by far exceeds that of man-made reservoirs in magnitude. Human appropriation of green water is almost an order of magnitude bigger than the appropriation of blue water. Green water storage and the green water fluxes between soil, vegetation and the atmosphere depend largely on land cover and management. Effective land management can improve the productivity of green water (mostly by reducing unproductive losses), which can contribute significantly to alleviating water scarcity for cases in which renewable blue water is already fully exploited.

Recognition of green water as a resource to be managed within the IWRM framework opens new degrees of freedom in so-called drylands, many of which are not all that dry, given their relatively high annual precipitation which can be managed better.

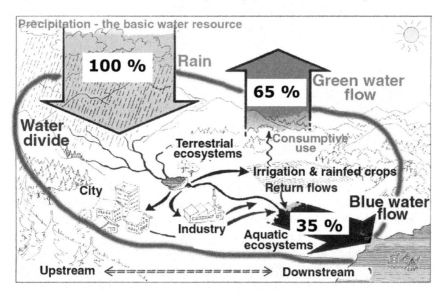

Figure 10.1 Partitioning of precipitation into blue water (surface runoff and groundwater recharge) and green (soil) water (Falkenmark 2003). (Source: Falkenmark and Rockström 2004).

Neglecting green water fluxes and their role in sustaining ecosystems and human livelihoods gives an incomplete view of the water situation in most regions of the world. In Africa, for example, more than 95 percent of agriculture is rainfed. The fluxes of green water that support agriculture and other terrestrial ecosystems and their services are generally not taken into account in IWRM planning in most countries and basins. Consequently, even in the driest places, under most pressing water scarcity, land use is generally not considered part of IWRM.

At the global scale, humans have significantly altered the partitioning of precipitation into green and blue water by changing land use. Initial assessments indicate that, cumulatively, deforestation and transformation into agricultural land have increased global discharge by about 1,700 km^3/yr, or by five percent, compared to the discharge from natural vegetation cover (Rost *et al.* 2008). In order to understand the magnitude of these anthropogenic changes, it is worthwhile comparing them to the total global blue water consumption for all municipal and industrial uses, which amounts to about 100 km^3/yr (Rost *et al.* 2008).

At local to regional scale, upland deforestation can significantly increase downstream water availability, often reducing evapotranspiration by 100 mm/yr or more (Gerten *et al.* 2005). The opposite is true for afforestation. In particular, larger afforestation schemes, such as the billion-tree campaign by the World Agroforestry Centre and the United Nations Environment Program (ICRAF/UNEP)[1] and also afforestations as part of the CDM or for biofuel production have to be evaluated for their hydrological consequences within the IWRM context.

The higher water losses to the atmosphere of forests compared to those of other vegetation types are explained by the fact that trees have:

1　higher leaf area indices, hence higher canopy interception losses and transpiration potentials, as well as higher surface roughness (thus greater evaporative losses);
2　deeper roots, which can tap additional layers of soil moisture; and
3　no fallow period as for agricultural vegetation (at least for evergreen trees that do not defoliate) during which transpiration is strongly reduced.

Despite these straightforward physical explanations backed up by experimental evidence of enhanced tree water use (Calder 2005), there is still a widespread misconception that afforestation would increase water availability (forests holding water in the landscape), upon which many watershed programs around the world have been built (Hayward 2005).

Besides changes in forest cover, a number of other upland changes generally affect downstream water availability. Upland irrigation water withdrawals from surface water reduce downstream runoff. Also, soil and water conservation measures often increase plant water uptake, reduce runoff, and contribute to lower flows downstream.

The green-blue water approach, which emphasizes precipitation as the key water resource to be managed, rather than blue water only, promotes a better understanding of land-water interactions and improved upland management, based on scientific evidence, rather than popular beliefs. A key component of this approach is the reduction of unproductive water fluxes (mostly evaporation) and associated increase in water productivity (mostly through enhancing beneficial transpiration), aiming at improved ecosystem services and multiple benefits for upstream and downstream water users.

There are numerous individual measures that can support these goals, summarized in the World Overview of Conservation Approaches and Technologies (WOCAT) database[2], including appropriately designed water harvesting and storage, supplementary irrigation, and conservation agriculture. Most of these interventions have been tested individually at field scale for their beneficial effects, in particular reduced runoff, more deep drainage, and less erosion and sediment yield, in various land and water conservation programs especially in Africa, such as the Regional Land Management Unit (RELMA)[3], the Smallholder System Innovations in Integrated Watershed Management (SSI)[4] and others.

However, the cumulative effects of upland interventions on downstream water availability have not been quantified systematically. The identification of these effects is difficult, because of the complex interplay of abiotic and biotic factors that determine water flows along the river course. Also, hydrological responses to these interventions, such as improved groundwater recharge or reduced siltation may be delayed in time. Upscaling from plot-scale experiments to the catchment and river basin requires integration over the cumulative primary and higher-order effects (Kabat *et al.* 2004). Separation of these effects from (increasing) climate variability may further complicate the analysis.

While there is no conclusive evidence, let alone guidelines on the overall effects of upland management on downstream water availability, initial applications of the key principles of integrated land and (green and blue) water management are found in various regions around the world, including the United States, South Africa, India, as well as in eastern Africa and the Middle East (see examples below).

The New York City Watershed agreement demonstrates how upland farmers – if paid for improved land management – can ensure good water quality downstream. New York City has agreed to provide $35 million for farmers in the upstream Catskills catchment to install pollution abatement devices, e.g. fencing to improve cattle feeding or riverside tree planting. Upstream benefits of this well-known scheme include increased farmers' incomes and higher farm productivity in nine out of 10 cases. Downstream benefits include the avoided costs of some $6 billion for a new water filtration system (CCCD 1997). From a basin-wide perspective, the protection of the upper watershed (at the source) is much more cost effective than downstream (end-of-pipe) rehabilitation measures.

The South African water legislation is another prominent example of applying the green-blue water principles (although not under this name). South Africa's National Water Act requires farmers to apply for permits before initiating so-called "streamflow reduction activities," in particular forest plantations (DWAF 1999). This "user-pays principle" has established a kind of water tax for owners of upland commercial tree plantations.

A related assessment of the different land uses in South Africa in regard to their water requirements concluded that all commercial tree plantations together reduce the nation's surface runoff by 1.4 billion m^3 per year, or 3.2 percent of total flows. Following the example of forest plantations, a designation of sugar cane plantations as streamflow reduction activities is now also under discussion in South Africa. While the legislative framework for integrated (green and blue) water and land management has been developed in South Africa, it is not yet clear to what degree it is now enforced through appropriate institutions.

These examples, as well as those of the Jordan and Tana Rivers described in subsequent sections of this chapter, indicate that integration of upstream land management into catchment-wide IWRM planning and accounting for all green and blue water uses, can increase overall productivity and benefits derived from limited water resources, while at the same time reducing costs, e.g. for maintaining water quality and ensuring sufficient water supply for humans and ecosystems. Economic incentives for adopting green-blue water principles and associated soil and water conservation techniques for promoting sustainable catchment management and eventually also for more equitable allocations of water between all users, will be described in the section of this chapter on payments for environmental services (PES). In order to move from scientifically established green-blue water principles to application, making land management integral part of IWRM, requires capacity building on many fronts and new cross-sectoral cooperation, e.g. between different ministries, water and land authorities and other institutions that are not commonly cooperating.

The new Green-Blue Water Initiative (Falkenmark and Rockström 2005) will establish pilot studies in several basins around the world, in order to demonstrate and promote the concept of integrated water and land management across scales, from a local, catchment, basin, national, and regional level up to the global scale. This concept is now receiving much attention, also under the impression of the latest climate change projections for increasing variability and water scarcity, and the need to increase resilience in many parts of the world.

10.3 Climate change impacts and adaptation

According to the Intergovernmental Panel on Climate Change (IPCC 2007), climate change is projected to add pressure to many water-scarce regions, resulting from increasing temperatures and evaporative demands, changing rainfall volumes and distribution, and increasing intra- and inter-annual variability and uncertainty in water management. With pressures from population and economic trends, these factors will increase the vulnerability of people and ecosystems to the vagaries of climate.

Upstream-downstream relationships also will be affected by climate change through hydrological and vegetation responses. Non-linear responses, even to relatively small temperature and precipitation changes, may produce large changes in runoff or groundwater recharge. De Wit and Stankiewicz (2006) showed that precipitation reductions of about 10 percent, as projected for parts of Africa over the twenty-first century, may translate into reductions in drainage of up to 50 percent and more. Döll and Flörke (2005) project reductions in ground water recharge of more than 70 percent by 2050 in parts of Africa and the southern Mediterranean for different emission scenarios.

The benefits of robust adaptation strategies to climate risks go beyond mitigating water scarcity: adaptive management of water and land can reduce vulnerability to other pressures and also mitigate upstream-downstream conflicts. In the case of transboundary basins, cooperative water management may foster political collaboration in other sectors, as in the Jordan River basin (see Jordan section of this chapter).

An integrated approach to water and land management also can support the coordination of climate change mitigation and adaptation. Environmental sustainability criteria for CDM-related afforestation projects, for example, should include impacts on hydrology and water resources. These need to be assessed also with respect to adaptive management under climate change. Benefits of afforestations in terms of carbon sequestration (or biofuel production) have to be balanced against downstream "water costs," particularly if there is competition for water for food production or other ecosystem services (see Tana section of this chapter).

In some regions, global warming will cause additional upstream-downstream effects from melting glaciers: the water draining from the Himalayan glaciers, for example, ensures continuous water supply in the dry-season to hundreds of millions of people living in the Indo-Gangetic plains. As much as 70 percent of the Ganges summer flow originates from these glaciers (Barnett *et al.* 2005; see also Messerli in Chapter 2). Melting of glaciers has already accelerated and, as a result of further warming, the Ganges runoff may increase by 30 to 40 percent over the coming decades, with more flooding projected for northern India and Pakistan. In the long run (after about 40 years), however, most glaciers will have disappeared and, subsequently, Indus and Ganges runoff is projected to decrease by more than 50 percent compared to the current situation, with severe consequences for water availability, food production, and livelihoods (Hasnain 2004). Similar downstream effects are expected or already observed for many mountain regions around the world. In this case, the responsibility is not with upland managers, but with greenhouse gas emitters around the world, who are ultimately responsible for melting glaciers in the headwaters and subsequent downstream water scarcity. Application of a "polluter-pays" principle would require compensation from major emitters to those being affected most. This could be in the form of adaptation funding from multilateral or bilateral donors.

The following two sections will focus on more direct upstream-downstream links in the Jordan and Tana Rivers, and the potential for institutional adaptation in view of the increasing scientific knowledge that supports integrated (green and blue) water and land management.

10.4 Jordan River basin management: addressing upstream-downstream links

The Jordan River is characterized by a strong climate gradient from its headwaters that receive more than 1000mm of precipitation per year, to the downstream section with less than 100mm/year. Most runoff is generated in the upper Jordan (and Yarmuk) basin(s), while water use primarily takes place in the lower part or outside of the basin via large-scale water transfers (see also the chapter by Rimmer in Chapter 4). Hence, contributions to and withdrawals from the Jordan River have very different national distributions, which is (among others) a cause for conflict between the different riparians, as shown in Table 10.1.

The strong degradation of the lower Jordan River, and the rapidly declining

Table 10.1 Contributions to Jordan River runoff and withdrawals from the basin (incl. groundwater)

	Contributions (million m³/yr)	*Withdrawals (million m³/yr)*
Jordan	530	320
Syria	435	260
Israel	160	<700
Palestinian Authority	155	60
Lebanon	120	10

Source: Phillips 2006a, b.

level of the Dead Sea – about one meter per year – are primarily caused by the enormous water withdrawals in the upper Jordan River, in particular the diversions through the National Water Carrier in Israel and King Abdullah Canal in Jordan, which together with other withdrawals reduce the Jordan River flow by more than 75 percent. Some of the ground water resources that extend beyond national boundaries also are overexploited. The transboundary nature of surface and ground water and the associated shared responsibility for the resource, seems to increase the risk of overexploitation.

Climate change is projected to aggravate this situation. Most global climate models agree on a decrease of precipitation in the eastern Mediterranean over the coming decades (IPCC 2007), in addition to the global trend towards higher temperatures and increasing climate variability. According to these projections, climate impacts will include:

- decreasing runoff, ground water recharge and water availability;
- increasing water demand for irrigated and non-irrigated agriculture and other vegetation;
- increasing frequency/intensity of droughts, and associated uncertainty in water management.

The GLOWA Jordan River project[5] assesses eco-hydrological and agro-economic impacts of climate change projections and has developed tools for evaluating different adaptation options and tradeoffs between them (Hoff *et al.* 2006a). Initial impact studies, based on downscaled regional climate scenarios, indicate severe reductions of surface and groundwater availability for all months, accompanied by strong increases in irrigation water demand – Figure 10.2a (Kunstmann *et al.* 2007) and Figure 10.2b (Menzel *et al.* 2007), and subsequent losses in yields and net returns on investment in agriculture – Figure 10.2c (Haim *et al.* 2008).

These climate-related pressures may intensify upstream-downstream imbalances and aggravate water-related conflicts, unless climate variability and change can be built into agreements on integrated and transboundary management of water resources. Unfortunately, the current political situation in the upper Jordan does not allow for any basin-wide agreements. Existing bi-lateral watersharing arrangements between Syria and Jordan, as well as between Jordan and Israel, are already disputed or are prone to fail in drought years.

Instead of developing sustainable upstream-downstream agreements including demand management, a new water transfer project is now planned in the lower Jordan. It is much larger than any previous infrastructure project: a conduit between the Red Sea and the Dead Sea, which could produce large amounts of desalinized water, utilizing the elevation gradient between the two seas. While this multi-billion-dollar project could also reverse the decline of the Dead Sea, the root causes of the problems that lie in the upper Jordan would not be addressed through such a conduit. Instead, this mega project would allow continued (unilateral) overexploitations of upstream resources, without any provisions for restoring the lower Jordan River.

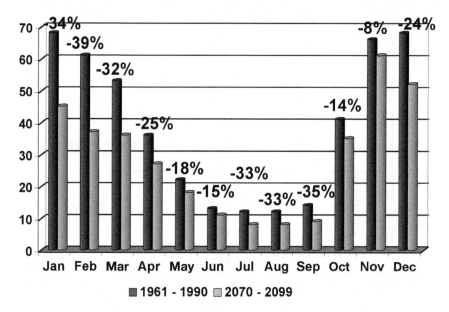

Figure 10.2a GLOWA scenario of changes in Jordan River discharge (ECHAM4 global climate model, SRES B2 scenario, MM5 regional climate model, WASIM hydrological model).

The Jordan basin is generally viewed as a so-called "closed basin" with fully exploited surface and ground water (blue water) resources. Politically, this is interpreted as a situation in which any re-allocations of water come with expensive tradeoffs, and the only significant improvement would require expensive schemes for generating "new water," such as the Red-Dead Conduit, or other desalination or other high-tech infrastructure projects.

In this situation, the green-blue water concept can provide a way forward, re-opening the basin, by identifying additional (green) water resources/soil water storage to be managed. Integrated land and water management offers a number of interventions, including small-scale affordable measures and win-win options within and between the riparian countries.

Currently unused potential for increasing water availability and productivity results mainly from the fact that 80 to 90 percent of rainfall in the drier parts of the basin neither becomes blue water, i.e. surface or ground water, which could be subject to water management, nor contributes to biomass production. Instead, most of the rainfall is lost uncontrolled and unproductively through evaporation. If only a fraction of this lost water were to be captured, e.g. through rainwater harvesting, water availability and productivity could be augmented significantly. Simple low-cost harvesting technologies, such as those tested successfully in the Negev and Badia drylands (i.e. adjacent to the Jordan basin) could become even more beneficial under climate change, when rainfall events are projected to become more sporadic but more intense with higher storm runoff losses.

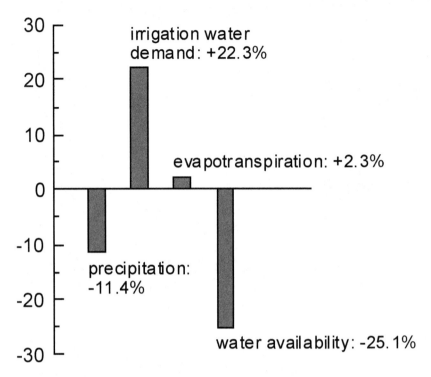

Figure 10.2b GLOWA scenario of changes in the different hydrological components
in the Jordan River basin (ECHAM4 global climate model, SRES B2
scenario, MM5 regional climate model, TRAIN hydrological model).

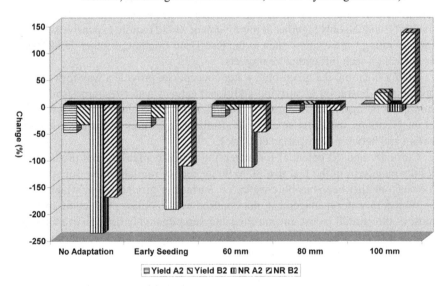

Figure 10.2c GLOWA scenarios of changes in yield and net return (NR) for cotton for
different climate scenarios (SRES A2 and B2) and adaptation options -
early seeding and different amounts of additional irrigation.

Another missed opportunity lies in agricultural practices in the Jordan region, which are generally assumed to depend primarily on blue water, i.e. irrigation. However, initial analyses by Haddadin (2006), indicate that at least half of the water supporting agriculture in the region is green water, either in rainfed agriculture or precipitation entering irrigated systems – plus much larger amounts of green water supporting grazing land. Improved co-management of green and blue water in agriculture, e.g. through rainwater harvesting, supplementary irrigation and conservation agriculture, can increase overall water productivity significantly by shifting water fluxes from unproductive evaporation to productive transpiration (Oweis and Hachum 2004) – see Figure 10.3. With that, pressure on blue water exploitation can be reduced, with positive effects on downstream water availability. Appropriate interventions, which improve green and blue water productivity, depend on the level of technologies available, which varies significantly across the Jordan River basin. Many green water management measures are affordable for the rural poor, so they can benefit directly from improved income and resilience to climate and other pressures – different from most large-scale blue water schemes, which do not necessarily yield direct benefits for the poor.

Further potential for improved land and water management is related to the rapid urban sprawl in the region, with urbanization often taking place on highly

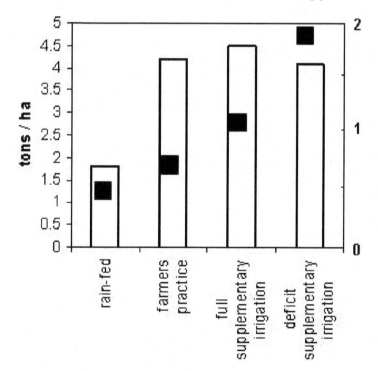

Figure 10.3 Grain yield (bars) in tons per ha (left y-axis), and water productivity (squares) in kg yield (right y-axis) per m³ water applied or per m³ evapotranspiration in rain-fed agriculture, after Oweis 2004.

productive agricultural land. Initial assessments of changes in blue and green water fluxes due to urbanization and associated surface sealing and losses of soil water storage, indicate that optimized land use and urban planning as part of IWRM could increase green and blue water productivity significantly.

Given the large gradients in climate, water availability (ranging from less than 150 m^3 per capita and year in Jordan to more than 1,300 m^3 in Syria (WRI 2008), technological capacity and water productivity across the basin, cooperative upstream-downstream allocations and management of green and blue water and land hold enormous potential for improving overall productivity, human welfare, and ecosystem integrity.

Examples of increased benefits from cooperation over scarce water resources, in particular integrated upstream-downstream management in the Jordan River basin, according to the categories by Sadoff and Grey (2002), include:

a   benefits to the river: restoration of environmental flows and aquatic ecosystem, improvements in water quality of the lower Jordan, and reduced shrinking of the Dead Sea;
b   benefits from the river: higher water productivity from re-allocating water to other sectors than agriculture such as tourism – which also depends on the river's water quality;
c   benefits of reduced costs: higher return on investment when addressing water problems at their source, i.e. in the upper catchment, rather than investing in downstream remediation projects;
d   benefits beyond the river: cooperation over water resources may have spill-over effects into other sectors, e.g. stimulating intra-regional virtual water trade, supporting economic integration, or increasing resilience against climate risks.

The second point was addressed by Becker and Katz (2006), who estimated that the market and non-market benefits from restoring and conserving the Dead Sea alone would be of the same order of magnitude as the economic value of the current water uses, i.e. agricultural yields from irrigation with Jordan River water. Potential gains from restoring the lower Jordan River would come on top of this. The third point is currently under investigation by assessing costs and benefits of different alternatives to the Red Sea – Dead Sea Canal. The last point, virtual water trade, i.e. the trade with agricultural commodities that require enormous amounts of water for their production (about 1,000–10,000 liters of water per kg of produce) is the single most important current water management measure practiced in the Jordan region. Net imports of virtual water (VW) to Israel, Jordan and the Palestinian Authority exceed renewable internal water resources by several hundred percent (Hoff *et al.* 2006b). While currently most of the agricultural commodities and embedded virtual water are imported from the United States or Europe, there is a large potential for intra-regional VW trade.

Each of the riparian countries in the Jordan basin has different comparitive advantages, e.g. in terms of water and land availability, labor cost, technological and economic capacity and buying power. Hence, coordinated land and water allocations and management by all riparians according to these comparative advantages, and subsequent virtual water trade, could yield significant gains in overall water productivity and welfare.

When taking into account climate change scenarios and their projections of increasing spatio-temporal variability of water availability, a cooperative approach to integrated land and water management becomes even more important, including "climate-proofing" of transboundary water sharing arrangements.

As in the case of South Africa (see green-blue water section of this chapter), science provides numerous suggestions for improved land and water management, but the political situation currently prevents the implementation of basin-wide green-blue water principles in the Jordan region. While some NGOs promote multilateral water projects, governmental institutions – in particular those in Israel – are generally not willing to share data and information with the other countries. Ideally a basin-wide management institution or commission, such as established in other transboundary river basins, would be made responsible for coordinated management and planning of land and water resources.

10.5 Tana River basin management: addressing upstream-downstream links

Kenya is a water-scarce country, with an average water availability of about 650 m^3/ cap year. The Tana basin is faced with acute water scarcity (WRMA 2006a). Just as is the case in the Jordan basin, high rainfalls are limited to the upper catchment, and precipitation declines towards the lower reaches of the river. The Tana headwaters ("water towers") receive more than 2000mm of annual rainfall, while downstream areas receive less than 600mm. Under increasing water scarcity, any changes in runoff generation in the uplands can have severe effects for downstream water users: hydropower production in the Tana basin, for example, provides more than half of Kenya's electricity. About 80 percent of the municipal water demand for Nairobi is met from transfers of Tana water. Irrigation in the Tana basin – also for export production – is growing rapidly. The Water Resources Management Authority of Kenya (WRMA) states that there is already "conflict due to over abstraction of water, especially in the upper zones of the catchment" (WRMA 2006b).

Ongoing land use changes in the headwaters, in particular deforestation, e.g. for marijuana cultivation, are associated with increasing runoff, but more importantly with increasing erosion and subsequent siltation of downstream reservoirs. These reservoirs, which are central for hydropower and municipal and irrigation water supply, are subject to rapid siltation and associated reduction in reservoir storage volume at a rate that is an order of magnitude higher than originally anticipated (Hoff *et al.* 2007). Any upland erosion reduction would have positive impacts on downstream water storage and availability in these reservoirs.

However, a thorough assessment is needed to quantify the overall effect from any upland intervention and possible tradeoffs between different ecosystem services affected, in terms of erosion reduction on one hand, and changes in runoff generation, ground water recharge[6] and water availability on the other hand. If, for example, UNEP's billion-tree-campaign leads to major afforestations in the upper Tana, severe losses in downstream runoff may result.

Again, as in the Jordan River basin, the green-blue water concept can provide a way forward, by adding green water to the supply of "manageable water." As in most parts of Africa, the Tana basin is dominated by rainfed agriculture with low green water productivity. If unproductive water losses are reduced and green water flows shifted to productive transpiration (vapor shift), food production can increase significantly, by a factor of two and more without compromising downstream water availability (Falkenmark and Rockström 2004).

The Green Water Credits (GWC) project demonstrates the potential for improved upland management to increase downstream water availability. In its pilot phase, the project has evaluated the downstream effects of different WOCAT-type interventions, e.g. conservation agriculture and rainwater harvesting and compared these "soft path" (Gleick 2003) solutions to the conventional "hard path" structural engineering approach, which in the Tana basin promotes additional reservoirs downstream of the existing ones. Like the Red Sea – Dead Sea conduit in the lower Jordan, additional reservoirs in the lower Tana will not tackle the root causes of water scarcity, many of which are located upstream.

Green water management in this case also can be interpreted as an attempt to conserve or rehabilitate ecosystems ("natural infrastructure") and their water-related services. In particular, the poor smallholder farmers in the uplands depend on these ecosystems and the services they provide. Also, like in the Jordan basin, these rural poor can benefit directly from improved land and water management. If this is promoted by Payments for Environmental Services, it can provide additional income and strengthen land rights (see PES section of this chapter).

The next step in the GWC project will be a combination of hydrological analysis of different soft-path and hard-path interventions with economic information for basin-wide cost-benefit and trade-off analyses, applying green-blue water principles. An initial example of such an analysis for the Tana basin was provided by Emerton and Bos (2004), who calculated the downstream costs of existing (newly planned) reservoirs to be in the order of $27 (additional $19) million, due to losses in floodplain agriculture, water for livestock, fisheries, mangroves, and other side effects of reservoir construction.

The water sector reform in Kenya, initiated through the Water Act in 2002, and new water management rules, under which water is increasingly viewed as an economic good, provide an appropriate legislative framework for a widened IWRM approach at basin level. As part of the decentralization process, a new Water Resource Management Authority (WRMA) has been established with regional branches for the six major catchments in Kenya (Tana being one of them). Each of these is currently developing a catchment management strategy, which provides the major avenue for entering green-blue water principles into basin management. The newly established water user associations, in which various stakeholder groups from all parts of the basin are represented, provide an opportunity for a participatory process when detailing the catchment management strategies. The

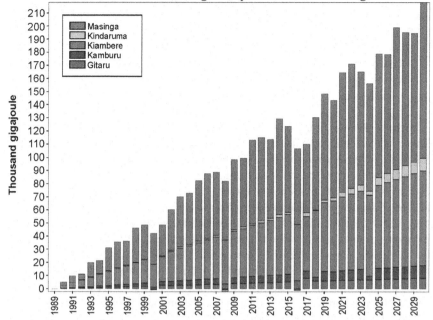

Figure 10.4 Initial results from the Water Evaluation and Planning (WEAP) tool in the Green Water Credits Project, projecting relative increase in hydropower production per reservoir, compared to Business-as-Usual, when assuming uniform reduction of erosion by 50 percent across the upper Tana catchment and associated reductions in reservoir storage losses (Hoff *et al.* 2007).

water user associations are expected to play an important role in the design and implementation of green-blue water measures and PES schemes by providing a bottom-up community perspective.

Surveys indicate that another pre-requisite for successful implementation of economic and cost-recovery principles may be present now in Kenya, i.e. the willingness to pay, expressed by major water users, e.g. large irrigators: MWI (2005) indicates that there is a positive trend for these groups to accept water use charges if accompanied by significant improvements in water resource management.

10.6 Payments for environmental services: how to make the green-blue water approach work

From the previous sections, the green-blue water approach emerges as a useful extension of the IWRM framework for various regional water scarcity situations. The green-blue water approach provides a starting point for assessing and eventually internalizing downstream costs and benefits of upland management, taking into account a range of water-dependent environmental services.

Such a basin-wide cost-benefit analysis can start from the classification of direct and indirect uses of green and blue water, provided by Falkenmark and Rockström (2004):

> If the provision of water for downstream users is interpreted as an environmental service controlled by upland farmers, compensations or rewards may provide incentives to improve or maintain this service.

The green-blue water approach helps us to understand the upstream-downstream links and to identify sustainable management practices from a basin perspective. Payments for environmental services (PES), based on this knowledge, can facilitate the adoption of best practices by upland farmers, if otherwise the return on investment is uncertain or delayed into the far future – see the analysis by Pagiola (1996) which suggests that in semi-arid regions of Kenya it would take almost 50 years to recover the costs of soil conservation structures. While currently payment schemes are often tied to public funding, ideally PES funds are generated by the downstream beneficiaries themselves. But this is only likely to happen if these are (convinced of the benefits and) economically strong, such as the national hydropower company (KenGen) and Nairobi Water in the case of the Tana River, or tourist operators in the national parks in the nearby Mara River basin, which critically depend on upstream water releases in the dry season for wildlife migration.

Other examples of strong downstream beneficiaries are found in South Africa, where large commercial farms are often located downstream in river basins, or in China where larger cities are often located in the lower part of river basins. Eventually, also the state of Israel can be seen as an economically strong downstream beneficiary in the Jordan River basin, with a per capita GDP 10 times higher than that of all upstream riparians. These types of upstream-downstream relationships provide a test bed for payment schemes related to water provision as an environmental service.

WATER FLOW, WATER USE	GREEN	BLUE
DIRECT	ECONOMIC USE Rainfed food, timber fibres, fuelwood, pastures, etc.	ECONOMIC USE irrigation, industry, domestic
INDIRECT	ECOSYSTEM SERVICES Wetlands, grasslands, forests, terrestrial biodiversity, climate regulation	ECOSYSTEM SERVICES aquatic freshwater habitats, biodiversity, resilience

Figure 10.5 Indirect and direct uses of green and blue water (after Falkenmark and Rockström 2004).

Payments for environmental services (PES) have been established for different types of services, such as carbon sequestration, biodiversity and landscape conservation, and also provision of water. Pagiola *et al.* (2007) and Börner *et al.* (2007) provide examples from Nicaragua (silvopastoral land use) and Brazil (forest and agricultural land use) for increasing carbon sequestration and biodiversity.

Water-related PES schemes until now have mostly been limited to Latin America, e.g. Costa Rica, Guatemala or Ecuador, mostly compensating upland farmers for the conservation and sustainable management of forests and for reforestation to sustain water provision for downstream uses (Emerton *et al.* 2003, Chomitz *et al.* 1998). While such schemes have often assumed improved and more regular water yield from maintaining or re-establishing forest, science has provided ample evidence (e.g. Calder 2005) that this image is misleading. While it may be true for cloud forest that trees intercept more atmospheric moisture than other vegetation, a more thorough analysis of the hydrological effects of forests or deforestation/afforestation is warranted in most cases (see green-blue water section of this chapter).

Only a few examples of water-related PES schemes are known from Africa, such as the Working for Water program[7] in South Africa, which pays and provides jobs for the poor, for eradicating water-intensive invasive alien vegetation. In principle, the poor can benefit in several ways from payments received, if PES schemes are designed well: payments enable them to invest and diversify their activities, to increase their productivity and to strengthen resilience to climate and other risks. Payments to farmers for improved upland management also may strengthen informal or formal land rights of the farmers, which in turn may promote further sustainable management that protects their very resource base.

In the Tana basin in Kenya, the Green Water Credits (GWC) project assesses eco-hydrological upland-downstream links and the costs and benefits of different management interventions as a basis for PES schemes that could simultaneously increase income for upland farmers and downstream water availability. The GWC approach will feed into the Tana Catchment Management Strategy, by allowing a comparison of marginal costs for a unit of water provided or saved, for different upland or downstream interventions. In the context of Kenya's ongoing water sector reform, that information can feed into the process of setting cost-recovery water use charges, by taking into account costs for catchment management and source protection. It also can support more stringent incentive schemes, such as the proposed 5 percent reduction in water charges for those irrigation farmers that adopt best conservation practice (Hoff *et al.* 2007).

10.6.1 The Green Water Credits project[8]

Green Water Credits (GWCs) are based upon the green-blue water concept as described above. GWCs are payments, rewards or compensations, in cash or kind, made to rural people in upland watersheds for specified management activities.

In the uplands, GWCs provide cash income, which can help to diversify livelihoods, increase productivity of farming and reduce vulnerability to external pressures such

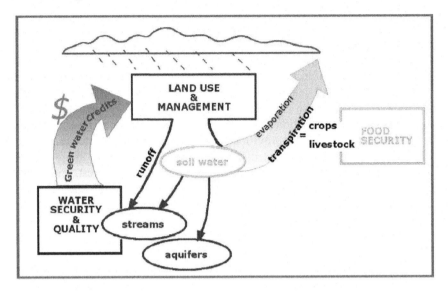

Figure 10.6 Green Water Credits scheme (Dent and Kauffman, 2007).

as climate change. Downstream, GWCs can contribute to water security, flood or drought mitigation, increased environmental flows, and improved water quality.

Goals of the GWC project in the Tana basin include:

- a quantitative understanding of upstream-downstream links and cumulative effects of different interventions, by using a set of hydrological and water management models and possibly also remote sensing applications;
- the identification and involvement of downstream beneficiaries, e.g. hydropower, municipal water users, irrigators, ecosystems;
- the identification and characterization of livelihoods, and involvement of "upland managers," in particular smallholder farmers;
- the assessment of different interventions for their costs and benefits from the local and catchment perspective;
- the participatory development of PES schemes (including intermediaries such as microfinance institutions) that provide income opportunities by compensating or rewarding upland farmers for implementing or continuing downstream-friendly measures; and;
- empowering and supporting local institutions in establishing and maintaining PES schemes.

(Source: Dent *et al.* 2007.)

With increasing recognition of the need for sustainable upland management as part of IWRM, additional funding will be required for these activities. The key water management institutions in Kenya, Ministry of Water and Irrigation (MWI) and Water Resource Management Authority (WRMA), concluded that "fees and water user charges are not seen as a mechanism to finance water resources infrastructure development or necessary catchment conservation activities." MWI (2005) suggests that the estimated costs for protecting catchment areas and building infrastructure, would amount to KSh 2–5 billion per year, which cannot be covered by the traditional type of revenue collection from water users.

Here again, the green-blue water approach can provide a way forward, through a more holistic approach, which goes beyond conventional user charges and taxes. In addition to sanctioning, or charging for, detrimental streamflow reduction activities, beneficial activities are rewarded through payments for environmental services, within the same green-blue water framework. This approach widens the potential funding base for catchment management activities. Going even one step further, also international funding for afforestations related to the clean development mechanism (CDM) could be directed towards sustainable land and water management: additional water demands from CDM-related afforestations could be quantified according to the green-blue water principles and become part of basin-wide financial schemes in support of improved management.

Eventually, such a comprehensive basin management approach that encompasses several environmental services could increase the overall benefits derived from scarce water resources by integrating land use, climate mitigation and adaptation activities with IWRM (or improve the environmental services index – see Pagiola *et al.* 2007).

10.7 Conclusions and policy implications

There is an increasing body of knowledge about the biophysical links between upland green water management and downstream water availability (and quality, which is not part of this chapter), as demonstrated in the previous sections for the Jordan and Tana River basins. The situation of these two rivers is typical for many so-called "dryland" basins around the world, in that most of the runoff is generated in the upland watershed which experiences increasing land and water use pressures, while downstream activities depend on stable blue water flows from the upper catchment. There is a large number of basins like the Jordan or Tana that are becoming closed basins, with all available blue water resources allocated, and any re-allocation perceived as a zero-sum-game.

Green-blue water science is beginning to address the cumulative downstream effects of the full range of upland interventions. By integrating eco-hydrological quantifications of green and blue water fluxes and productivities with socioeconomic assessments of the associated costs and benefits in terms of the different ecosystem services affected, the new emerging knowledge can support a widened IWRM approach in various "drylands." The practical implementation of this green-blue water knowledge requires a nested approach, scaling up from local pro-poor interventions that need to be embedded in meso-scale catchment management, all the way up to basin-scale planning.

In order to mainstream green-blue water knowledge into ongoing IWRM planning, a new level of cooperation between institutions will be required to overcome the traditional sectoral management approach, in particular the separation of land and water management in different ministries, authorities, and extension agencies. The strong interest of our institutional partners in the green-blue water approach, in the Green Water Credits Project (in East Africa), the GLOWA Jordan River Project and other initiatives, indicates an increasing awareness that more integrated management is required to meet the growing challenges of water scarcity, projected to be aggravated in many "drylands" by climate change.

However, while national policies begin to address integrated water and land management across scales, international cooperation remains difficult. In conflict situations, such as in the Jordan River basin, another level of water crisis or even more severe extreme events may be required before riparians may agree to coordinate their water and land management activities. Also in less critical transboundary contexts, such as in eastern Africa, green-blue water projects are likely to be limited to national contexts, avoiding the additional difficulties when involving institutions from several countries.

Adoption of the green-blue water approach and implementation of beneficial measures can be facilitated through financial or other rewards or compensations, following the experience with PES schemes from other sectors, such as carbon sequestration. Such payments acknowledge the fact that land and water managers, in particular smallholder farmers, are not guided by sustainability principles or abstract concepts such as improved water productivity, but rather need to maximize farm income. Intelligent designs of PES schemes also can strengthen land rights, another incentive for sustainable resource use by upland farmers. Eventually, PES as part of the green-blue water approach can contribute to poverty alleviation, allocation equity and increasing overall benefits for all water users in a basin.

Where economically strong downstream beneficiaries are identified, and provided with convincing scientific evidence about green-blue water links in the basin, they may join PES schemes and eliminate the need for continued public funding. There is in fact a better chance to identify and involve direct downstream beneficiaries from water-related ecosystem services, than for other more general (global) ecosystem services, such as carbon sequestration or biodiversity. Nevertheless, kick-starting water-related PES schemes will often require initial external funding, e.g. from international donors, such as in the Green Water Credits project. Longer term funding for sustainable green-blue water management as part of IWRM can possibly be generated by linking PES schemes to the CDM-related afforestations.

GWC-type integrated research needs to inform any potential PES-CDM or other upland-downstream schemes, in order to evaluate basin-wide bio-physical and socioeconomic costs, benefits and tradeoffs, and ensure that other ecosystem services supporting water and food security, livelihoods, and sustainability are not compromised.

Notes

1 www.unep.org/billiontreecampaign/.
2 www.wocat.org/databs.asp.

3 www.relma.org.
4 www.unesco-ihe.org/ssi/.
5 GLOWA: Global Change in the Water Cycle, www.glowa-jordan-river.de.
6 Knowledge about the sustainable yields of aquifers is limited, and not sufficiently addressed in water management plans.
7 www.dwaf.gov.za/wfw/.
8 www.isric.org/UK/About+ISRIC/Projects/Current+Projects/Green+Water+Credits.htm.

References

Barnett T. P., Adam, J. C. and Lettenmaier, D. P. (2005) Potential impacts of a warming climate on water availability in snow-dominated regions. *Nature,* 438: 303–9.

Becker, N. and Katz, D. (2006) Economic evaluation of resuscitating the Dead Sea. *Water Policy*, 8, 4, 351–70.

Börner, J., Mendoza, A., Vosti, S.A. (2007). Ecosystem services, agriculture, and rural poverty in the Eastern Brazilian Amazon: Interrelationships and policy prescriptions, *Ecological Economics*, 64, pp. 356–373.

Calder, I. R. (2005) *Blue Revolution*, London: Earthscan.

CCCD (1997) *Summary guide to the terms of the Watershed Agreement,* Arkville, NY: The Catskill Center for Conservation and Development.

Chomitz, K. M., Esteban, B. and Constantino, L. (1998) *Financing environmental services: the Costa Rica experience and its implications.* Environmentally and Socially Sustainable Development, Latin America and Caribbean Region, World Bank.

Dent, D. L.and Kauffman, J. H. (2007). *The spark has jumped the gap: green water credits proof-of-concept.* Green Water Credits Report 7, World Soil Information, Wageningen, The Netherlands: ISRIC.

DeWit, M. and Stankiewicz, J. (2006) Changes in surface water supply across Africa with predicted climate change. *Science Express*, 2 March 2006.

Döll, P. and Flörke, M. (2005) *Global-scale estimation of diffuse groundwater recharge – model tuning to local data for semi-arid and arid regions and assessment of climate change impact.* Germany: Frankfurt Hydrology Paper 03.

DWAF (1999) *Streamflow reduction allocations, combined licensing and authorisation guidelines.* Pretoria, South Africa: Department of Water Affairs and Forestry.

Emerton, L. (2003) *Tana River, Kenya – integrating downstream values into hydropower planning, case study in wetland valuation #6,* Gland, Switzerland: IUCN.

Emerton, L. and Bos, E. (2004) *Value – counting ecosystems as water infrastructure.* Gland, Switzerland: IUCN.

Falkenmark, M. and Rockström, J. (2004) *Balancing water for humans and nature.* London: Earthscan.

Falkenmark, M. and Rockström, J. (2005) *Rain: the neglected resource.* Swedish Water House Policy Brief Nr. 2. SIWI, Stockholm, Sweden.

Gerten, D., Hoff H. *et al.* (2005) Contemporary green water flows: simulations with a dynamic global vegetation and water balance model. *Physics and Chemistry of the Earth,* 30: 334–8.

Gleick, P. (2003) Global freshwater resources: soft-path solutions for the 21st century. *Science*, 302, 5650: 1524–8.

GWP (2000) *Integrated water resources management.* Global Water Partnership TAC background paper No 4, Stockholm, Sweden.

Haddadin, M. (2006) *Water resources in Jordan, evolving policies for development, the environment, and conflict resolution.* Washington, D.C.: RFF Press.

Haim, D., Shechter, M. and Berliner, P. (2008) Assessing the impact of climate change on representative field crops in Israeli agriculture: a case study of wheat and cotton. *Climatic Change,* 86: 425–440.

Hasnain, S. I. (2004) Glacier meltdown. *New Scientist,* 182: 2446

Hayward, B. (2005) *From the mountain to the tap: how land use and water management can work for the rural poor.*, Research Report, UK Department for International Development.

Hoff, H., El-Fadel, M. and Haddadin, M. (2006b) *Expert statement on political factors of virtual water trade.* Research Initiative on Virtual Water Trade. Bonn, Germany: German Development Institute.

Hoff, H., Küchmeister, H. and Tielbörger, K. (2006a) *The GLOWA Jordan River Project – integrated research for sustainable water management.* IWA Water Environment Management Series No 10.

Hoff, H., Noel, S. and Droogers, P. (2007) *Water use and demand in the Tana Basin: analysis using the water evaluation and planning tool (WEAP).* Green Water Credits Report 4. ISRIC – World Soil Information, Wageningen, The Netherlands.

IPCC (2007) *Impacts, adaptation and vulnerability.* Intergovernmental Panel on Climate Change, Fourth Assessment Report, Working Group II. Cambridge, UK: Cambridge University Press.

Kabat, P. *et al.* (2004) *Vegetation, water, humans and the climate.* Heidelberg, Germany: Springer Verlag.

Kunstmann, H., Suppan, P., Heckl, A. and Rimmer, A. (2007) Regional climate change in the Middle East and impact on hydrology in the Upper Jordan catchment. *Proceedings of Symposium HS2004 at IUGG2007,* July 2007, Perugia, Italy, IAHS Publ. 313, 141–9.

Menzel, L., Teichert, E. and Weiss, M. (2007) Climate change impact on the water resources of the semi-arid Jordan region, *Proceedings of the Third International Conference on Climate and Water,* 3–6 September 2007, Helsinki, Finland.

MWI (2005) *Report on operationalisation of the Water Act 2002 in water resources management.* Nairobi, Kenya: Ministry of Water and Irrigation.

Oweis, T. Y. and Hachum, A. Y. (2004) Improving water productivity in the dry areas of West Asia and North Africa. In Kijne, J. W., Barker, R.,and Molden. D. (eds), *Water productivity in agriculture: limits and opportunities for improvement.* Colombo, Sri Lanka: CABI.

Pagiola, S. (1996) Price policy and returns to soil conservation in semi-arid Kenya. *Environmental and Resource Economics,* 8: 255–71.

Pagiola, S. *et al.* (2007) Paying for the environmental services of silvopastoral practices. *Ecological Economics,* 64: 374–85.

Phillips, D. *et al.* (2006a) *Trans-boundary water cooperation as a tool for conflict prevention and broader benefit sharing,* Global Development Studies No. 4. Stockholm, Sweden: Ministry for Foreign Affairs.

Phillips, D., Attili, S., McCaffrey, S. and Murray, J. S. (2006b) The Jordan River Basin: potential future allocations to the co-riparians. *Water International,* 32, 1: 39–62.

Rockström, J. *et al.* (2005) *Sustainable pathways to attain the millennium development goals: assessing the key role of water, energy and sanitation.* SEI, Stockholm: SEI.

Rockström, J. *et al.* (2008) Future water availability for global food production: the potential of green water for increasing resilience to global change. *Water Resources Research,* in press.

Rost, S. *et al.* (2007) Agricultural green and blue water consumption and its influence on the global water system. *Water Resources Research*, in press.

Sadoff, C. W. and Grey, D. (2002) Beyond the river: the benefits of cooperation on international rivers. *Water Policy*, 4, 5: 389–403.

Smakthin, V., Revenga, C., and Döll, P. (2004) *Taking into account environmental water requirements in global-scale water resources assessments*, Comprehensive Assessment Research Report 2, Colombo, Sri Lanka.

Soussan, J. and Noel, S. (2005) *Poverty reduction and water management*. Joint Agency Paper for the Poverty Environment Partnership. New York: UNDP.

Vörösmarty, C. J., Green, P., Salisbury, J. and Lammers, R. B. (2000) Global water resources: vulnerability from climate change and population growth. *Science,* 289: 284–88.

WRI (2008) *Earthtrends*. Online. URL: http://earthtrends.wri.org.

WRMA (2006a) *Tana water catchment area*, Annual Report 2005–2006. Nairobi: Water Resources Management Authority.

WRMA (2006b) *Tana catchment management strategy* Nairobi: Water Resources Management Authority.

Part III

The view of practitioners and stakeholders

11 Factors for success

Public and private sector roles in securing a safe and reliable water supply

Donald J. Lowry

Canada's waters are being seriously challenged by growing populations, declining infrastructure, and inadequate watershed protection practices. To secure a safe and reliable water supply for the future, a significant shift in both public attitudes and policy must occur. An onus must be placed on improving current water use practices, empowering communities to meet their mounting challenges, and recovering the full cost of water supply and delivery from consumers. Increasingly, there is evidence that these outcomes can be achieved through well-structured public-private partnerships, as demonstrated in Western Canada by EPCOR Utilities Inc.

11.1 Introduction

With oceans on three sides, the Great Lakes in the middle and precipitation most of the year, it comes as a surprise to many that water quality and availability issues have come under close scrutiny in Canada.

In comparison to the citizens of many other countries, it would appear that Canadians have little to worry about when it comes to water management and supply. Indeed, the country is endowed with one of the greatest per-capita fresh water supplies on the planet. Canada's rivers annually discharge 7 percent of the world's renewable water supply.[1] Further, while water has historically been a source of transboundary conflict among nations, Canada shares a peaceful border with the United States with 40 percent of the border's distance running along waterways.[2]

But management of Canada's waters is being seriously challenged by growing populations, declining infrastructure, and inadequate watershed protection practices. This chapter will argue that Canadians should make significant changes to existing water system strategies in order to secure the future delivery of safe and reliable water, and that the Canadian experience can be used as a model for other jurisdictions.

These changes will be achieved only if there is a concerted effort to underscore the reality of the situation, and an effort is made to develop and implement new public policies that will improve water use practices.

Specifically, this chapter outlines how Canadians should seek to change the status quo in five ways:

1   Canadians should dispel the myth of a limitless abundance of water in southern Canada;
2   Consumers should pay the full cost of water supply and delivery, including return on capital, so jurisdictions can afford to build new infrastructure and maintain what currently exists, and because full-cost pricing provides an incentive for conservation;
3   Existing laws should be enforced to encourage water operators to invest in infrastructure, training, and innovative water quality systems;
4   Communities should be provided with the flexibility and appropriate tools to meet the mounting challenges they face. This requires re-inventing service delivery models, and building partnerships between governments and the private sector that – when structured well – can help deliver improved quality and lower costs to communities;
5   Multi-stakeholder watershed management strategies should be integrated with larger land-use policies and planning.

To make these changes, Canadians will need to confront and evaluate the negative claims made about the private operation of public water treatment and distribution systems. The evidence on this point is clear: well-structured partnerships have consistently delivered improved quality and cost. Partnerships that have failed to perform are often the result of a poor contract structure or inherited infrastructure gaps. Public and private partners can and should learn from these experiences to improve future performance.

11.2 The reality of the Canadian water supply condition

Canadians do not act upon issues relating to water until there is a crisis. A crisis, however, is looming that will force the country to consider how it manages its water supply. An increasing demand for water is overwhelming a rapidly aging and unreliable infrastructure. Adding further stress are the realities of geography: approximately 60 percent of Canada's fresh water drains north, while 85 percent of the population lives within 300 kilometers of its southern border with the United States.[3]

These challenges are not unique to Canada – they are faced by many nations. But having relied on an abundant supply of fresh water for most of their history, Canadians are unfamiliar with the coming challenge, and ill-equipped to confront the extent of the problem.

British environmental consultant Fred Pearce, who wrote *When Rivers Run Dry: Journeys into the Heart of the World's Water Crisis*, puts the Canadian situation in terms that most of its citizens would not recognize. "No country on Earth has such contrasts of drought and water plenty as Canada," he wrote. "Canada is learning that national statistics do not begin to portray the complexity of its relationship with its most vital resource. On the Mackenzie and the Rupert and the South Saskatchewan; in the leaking water mains of Montreal and the emptying reservoirs of Vancouver, down Canada's turbines and toilets, a new reality is emerging. It is a reality in which water is in increasingly short supply in some places at some times, where water suddenly has a real value rather than being an unlimited resource – and where rivers truly can run dry."

In Alberta, for example, one of the province's seven watersheds – the South Saskatchewan, which serves the communities of Calgary, Red Deer, Lethbridge and Medicine Hat – is believed to be at or near its water allocation limit[4] and is now subject to a moratorium on new water license applications. A significant tributary basin in central Alberta (Battle River) is already over-allocated. These shortages are leading to inter-government conflict and uncertainty for developers. For example, the Municipal District of Rockyview recently sought an allocation of water rights from neighboring Calgary, to support a proposed development within its jurisdiction. After the city of Calgary declined to provide water from within its license, the developer sought an inter-basin transfer, which also was unsuccessful. The project eventually proceeded on the basis of water rights acquired from agricultural producers for $15 million. Canadians are only now beginning to appreciate how water scarcity can lead to conflict.

The Alberta government's "Water for Life" strategy is clear about the extent of the current and future challenge: "The potential scarcity of water, especially in southern Alberta, is an ongoing issue. Climate change may make this a more pressing issue. As the climate changes, there will be a need to increase water management and conservation."[5]

There are serious concerns, then, about the security of Canadian water supplies. There also are serious concerns about its safety.

Repeated, tragic incidents have underscored the fact that North Americans – Canadians included – cannot take clean, safe drinking water for granted. The 1993 contamination of Milwaukee's water supply with *Cryptosporidium* sickened more than 400,000 residents, resulted in 4,000 hospitalizations, and 111 people died. It remains the largest outbreak of a waterborne disease in United States history.

Contemporary accounts make it clear that governments and water treatment operators were aware that Canadians were exposed to similar risks as the citizens of Milwaukee. Ontario's Ministry of Environment and Energy reported in 1992 that fewer than half the province's water treatment plants complied with provincial health guidelines. The next year, a *Cryptosporidium* outbreak occurred in Kitchener-Waterloo and, in 1996, an outbreak struck the community of Collingwood, Ontario. Another provincial report following the Collingwood outbreak found that 43 water treatment plants were at risk.

Despite these repeated warnings, the worst was yet to come. In 2000, seven people died and 2,300 fell seriously ill in Walkerton, Ontario, as a result of drinking water that was contaminated with *E. coli* and *Campylobacter jejuni*. In addition to the loss of life, and the permanent disabling injuries experienced by about 150 residents, the outbreak is estimated to have cost $150 million. A year later, a *Cryptosporidium* outbreak endangered the health of 7,000 residents in North Battleford, Saskatchewan.

In his forthcoming publication, "A Layperson's Guide to Western Canadian Drinking Water," Robert Sandford of the United Nations Water for Life Decade

Canadian Partnership Initiative paints a stark picture. Despite federal oversight, Walkerton is repeating itself on an annual basis on federal lands designated as First Nations reserves. In 2005, contaminated water forced the residents of a largely aboriginal community in Kashechewan, Ontario, to evacuate their homes. In the first eight months of 2006, 83 "boil water" advisories were issued on Indian reserves across Canada. Today, 59 percent of reserve drinking water systems are considered "at risk."

But it is not just on First Nations reserves that Canadians are beginning to confront serious drinking water quality issues. Each year, hundreds of Canadian municipalities have to issue "boil water" advisories because of the existence of or the threat of contaminated water. British Columbia issues some 500 boil water advisories a year, more than any other province. In Alberta, health authorities issued 123 advisories between 2002 and 2004. Poor water quality bears a high social and economic cost. Health problems related to water pollution in general cost Canadians an estimated $300 million per year. In April 2008, an early release article in the Canadian Medical Association Journal stated that at least 1766 boil water advisories were in place in Canadian communities and neighborhoods.[6]

This data demonstrates that there can be a huge gap in the quality of services that supply drinking water to rural and urban Canadians. It also points to significant problems in the future with respect to the infrastructure created in this country to ensure the reliable delivery of safe water supplies.

These conditions must be confronted by governments, operators, and the public alike. There must also be an acknowledgement that investment alone will not provide the answer: training and local community leadership are essential for ensuring that investments in water systems and infrastructure lead to sustained improvements in drinking water quality. Public, private and not-for-profit partners must work continuously to bring a public profile to the issue and help educate and inform their communities.

One community that has responded effectively to the challenge is Edmonton, Alberta. This north-central Alberta community draws its water from the North Saskatchewan River, a glacier-fed prairie river that is exposed to upstream agricultural run-off. In 1982 the city experienced a *Giardia* outbreak that was linked to 895 cases of illness.[7] The scare prompted a vigorous response – initially from the city's water department and, subsequently, from EPCOR, which became owner and operator of the city's water utility in 1996. Increased time for chlorine to be in contact with water, use of activated carbon particles to improve the water's taste, smell and color, in addition to the use of electric monitors on the system's clarifiers and filters were among the measures undertaken. Today, EPCOR performs 109 000 tests annually on the region's drinking water, monitoring 326 different physical, chemical, and microbiological parameters.

In 2002, EPCOR installed what was at the time the largest ultraviolet disinfection treatment system in the world. This earned Edmonton the distinction of being the first Canadian city of its size to have its drinking water protected by UV treatment. The company later installed UV technology in Canmore, a rapidly-growing Alberta community in the Rocky Mountains, and also advised on its application to the Greater Vancouver Regional District and New York City.

Edmonton and Canmore are but two cities within a vast country that is spread over a diverse geography dotted with urban metropolises, sprawling suburbs, and farming communities. But their examples demonstrate that communities of all sizes are capable of confronting the reality of the threats to their drinking water supplies and taking action.

11.3 Full-cost recovery model

Once communities have identified the scope of the challenge, one of the next steps is realizing the real cost of water. Water is not and should not be a free good – it is a precious resource that should be used responsibly and conserved. Canadians need to pay the full cost of water and water delivery in order to invest in necessary system improvements and new infrastructure.

Additionally, placing a monetary value on water has proven to be an effective means to achieve overarching conservation goals. The creation of a culture of conservation reduces demand on the watershed, and instills the attitude and behaviors necessary to mitigate human impact on the environment. If consumers manage their water consumption through individual action and the use of energy-efficient home appliances, they will take a collective step forward in addressing the issue of climate change.

According to the Organisation for Economic Co-operation and Development, Canadians pay some of the lowest water rates in the world.[8] In many communities, water rates remain low because they are subsidized by municipal governments through tax-supported allocations to water utilities in municipal budgets. A recent report by an expert panel reviewing Ontario's water system noted that municipalities in the province recovered only 65 percent of the total cost of providing water services.[9]

While low rates may create the illusion of affordability, they limit opportunities for reinvestment, as the burden of debt being placed on publicly owned utilities has a cumulative effect on economic growth and development. Low rates undermine overall system sustainability. Reflecting on the capital-intensive nature of water and wastewater services, the report noted, "utilities are starved for the funds they need to maintain their systems properly."[10] Ultimately, rates that do not reflect the full cost of producing and delivering the service lead to a gap between what the system is expected to deliver and what that system can deliver without on-going subsidies.

The scale of the accumulated gap is staggering. The Government of Canada recently reported that the nation's wastewater treatment facilities had exhausted 63 percent of their useful life by 2003.[11]

According to a provincially commissioned report, published in 2005, Ontario alone requires a $30 to $40 billion investment in water and wastewater facilities.[12] In Alberta, the initial estimates for the value of actions outlined in that province's Water for Life Strategy in February 2004 amounted to $916 million over 10 years.[13]

These gaps may persist because they are literally hidden below ground – out of sight and out of mind for both citizens and their governments.

Yet the recent catastrophic failures of transportation infrastructure in the United States and Canada – including collapses of bridge decks in Minnesota and Quebec – serve as reminders that governments can find it difficult to maintain their infrastructure investments even when the deterioration is visible to all.

Provincial governments in Canada use water license systems to control how much water is withdrawn, for what purpose, and by whom. But there are far too many instances in which the true cost of treating and distributing water is hidden by subsidies, or absorbed by the tax system, or left unfunded.

Customers of water and wastewater services should fund the full cost of building, operating, and maintaining the system for two reasons. First, it creates a pool of funding that is sufficient for the ongoing maintenance of the system – as long as the contributions remain dedicated to the system, and not diverted to other uses. Second, it sends an appropriate price signal – one that reminds people to conserve and make more prudent use of natural resources. If water is perceived as being free, the security of supply suffers.

In Canada, only 61 percent of urban water consumption is metered. Estimates show that consumption in unmetered areas is almost double: 474 liters per person per day, compared to 272 liters per person in a metered home.[14]

In addition, many jurisdictions do not yet price for large-scale raw water extraction as is done for most other resources withdrawn from the environment. For every square cubic meter of timber logged in Canada, governments charge the logger anywhere from $8 in Ontario to more than $20 on the British Columbia coast.[15] In oil-producing provinces such as Alberta, the government charges a royalty rate* based on the amount of oil or gas and the market price for oil, which generally varies between five percent and 40 percent of production at the current day barrel price.[16] For minerals, the Alberta government charges 55 cents per tonne for coal used for electricity purposes, and 37 cents per tonne for silica sand. [17]

However, for raw water in Alberta, users are charged an annual one-time fee – often as little as $150 annually for the rights to 125,000 cubic meters of water.[18] Irrigation water fees are paid only according to land area irrigated, not according to the volume of water applied to irrigated acres. Typically, license fees for water merely serve to cover license administration costs.

The question one would pose to anyone concerned with the future of water resources is this: does charging more for sand than for water really reflect the values of Canadians, and is it the best way to manage the resource? If governments mandate that pricing regimes transition toward full cost-recovery, then public and private water utilities will be able to properly maintain existing facilities and build new ones, while succeeding in conserving water resources.

Political realities pose a significant challenge – no one wants to pay more for

---

* Royalty rates decrease with lower rates of well production and increase at higher rates of production.

basic services, and many consider water a free good, on principle. Customers are accustomed to paying rates well below the real cost of water, and so the process of transition will require time, and it will require public education.

The transition period is important. The community of Windsor, Ontario, for example, announced in 2007 that water and sewer rates would increase 60 percent in one year to pay for "crumbling pipes, years of maintenance neglect and the rehabilitation of the ... Wastewater Treatment plant."[19]

Some residents responded with a protest, including demands to "flush in solidarity" in an attempt to overwhelm the system. While the protest was of little risk to the system, it demonstrated an obvious truth: that sudden significant rate increases are never popular, and therefore governments may avoid both the rate increases and the required investments for fear of the political consequences.

It's clear that full cost recovery models can work. Working with its regulator, the city of Edmonton, EPCOR adopted a performance-based rate structure in 2001. The structure establishes performance targets the operator is required to meet for water quality, system reliability, customer service, safety, and the environment. Failure to meet these targets can result in financial penalties to the operator. Many of the standards exceed the province of Alberta's provincial drinking water standards, which themselves are more stringent than the National Guidelines for Canadian Drinking Water Quality recommended by Canada's Department of Health.

Rates are set annually, with cost increases set at a rate below inflation. This is a built-in incentive for the operator to achieve its targets efficiently, as the company is limited in the costs it could flow-through to customers. Nevertheless, the rate structure ensures that customers are paying the full cost for their current service, including the costs of infrastructure renewal. When major new investments in infrastructure are needed, such as a recent capacity addition at one of the water treatment plants, rate changes are announced in advance and phased-in over years so that customers enjoy stable, predictable rates.

The regulatory structure also ensures that the search for efficiencies is done in a way that protects system performance. For example, the regulator has set annual targets for the number of water main breaks, the time to repair, and the volume of water lost in the distribution system. These targets create an incentive for maintenance and re-investment in the existing infrastructure. Today, water main breaks in Edmonton are at their lowest level since the 1960s (even though the distribution system is much larger), and the distribution system's water loss rate is 70 percent less than the Canadian water utility average, due to ongoing investment to maintain and replace existing infrastructure.

These efforts, and a robust public education program, have helped the city achieve national and international recognition for its water conservation results. Since the initiation of the performance-based rate structure, water consumption has declined 14 percent. Today, Edmonton residents are using 50 percent less water per person than Canadian residents in cities without water meters and 15 percent less than those in other large metered cities in Canada. Conservation efforts have extended the life of existing water treatment facilities by 15 years.

Edmonton's experience has demonstrated that true-cost models create the funding base required for improved system performance and provide incentives for conservation that can be implemented with public support. Where true-cost models are accompanied by strong system management and/or performance-based regulation, communities can achieve further benefits.

11.4 Enforcing laws

Another aspect of water system management that needs significant reform is Canada's regulatory and enforcement regime. Regulators must begin enforcing existing laws to better manage upland watersheds, or put water quality in jeopardy for future generations.

Enforcement encourages good management, and provides a strong incentive for investment in the system. Owners and operators of water and wastewater systems will invest in their operations if they are held liable for poor performance.

Canadian governments have rarely held operators accountable for failing to meet essential regulatory, public health, and environmental standards. In a recent speech to the Greater Victoria Chamber of Commerce, Elizabeth Brubaker, executive director of Environment Probe, a Toronto-based environmental and public policy research institute, offered her assessment of enforcement at publicly managed water and wastewater systems in Canada:

> Many Canadians have embraced what I call 'the myth of public-sector accountability.' Many believe that there is something inherently accountable in the municipal operation of utilities. Their thinking is as follows: since municipalities aren't focused on earning a profit, they can devote themselves to good performance. They can be responsive to the public and to regulators, rather than to corporate shareholders. They can be transparent without endangering some competitive advantage. And, should something go wrong, the political bosses can be held accountable through elections.
>
> Regrettably, experience doesn't bear this out. Believe me, I wish it did. I would love to be able to say that municipal governments are doing a great job of treating water and sewage. I would love to be able to say that provincial governments are doing a great job of regulating them. And I would love to be able to say that voters are holding them all accountable at the polls. But it wouldn't be true.
>
> Across Canada, public owners, public operators, and public regulators are falling down on the job. On the water side, Walkerton was a publicly operated system. North Battleford was a publicly operated system. Kashechewan – another publicly operated system. On the sewage side, all of our most notorious polluters – Victoria, Halifax, St. John's – have publicly operated systems. There is nothing inherent in public operations that guarantee responsible performance.[20]

In fact, studies show that publicly managed water and wastewater operators are among the most frequent offenders. Why? In part, this is because many municipal governments are protected by liability limitations and, in part, it is because they have the capacity to pass on the costs of non-compliance to taxpayers. Without meaningful consequences for the operator, there is little incentive for accountability.

There is also a difficult and recurring conflict: since provincial governments often provide capital grants to municipalities for publicly run water facilities, they also understand that strict enforcement could require expensive upgrades.[21] In many cases, governments that carry a regulatory responsibility also understand that by prosecuting offenders they would actually be prosecuting themselves.

In that same speech, Brubaker cited the example of Victoria, which is currently in the process of designing and sourcing its first wastewater treatment system. Three times in the 1990s, environmental coalitions attempted to use private prosecutions to enforce the provisions of the federal Fisheries Act that forbids the deposit of deleterious substances into water frequented by fish. The prosecutions were taken over by the provincial attorney general's office, which then stayed the charges.

Elsewhere, the instances of non-compliant public systems are legion. In Ontario, for example, 101 sewage facilities were out of compliance with provincial government limits in 2002. These 101 instances were penalized by a total of three charges and one fine – a $10,000 penalty for failing to ensure the facility was run by a licensed operator.[22]

The situation occurs in many other jurisdictions. Of the 78 First Nations water operations in Alberta, only 14 were fully certified as recently as February 2006.[23] Numbers like this are not only indicative of enforcement shortfalls but also serve to show us that smaller communities are struggling to attract and keep qualified staff.

The safety and security of water supplies are critical to public and environmental health. It is hardly a rhetorical question, then, to ask: "What is the point of our laws if we are not going to enforce them?"

Over the long run, enforcement would create financial incentives and public pressure for operators to invest in infrastructure, training, and innovative water quality systems. It also will shine more light on the importance of expert management of water and wastewater systems – an issue that leads to the most controversial of the five changes raised by this chapter: the use of public-private partnerships.

11.5 Partnerships

To meet the challenge of providing safe, quality drinking water and reliable, environmentally responsible wastewater services, provinces and communities across Canada are entering into partnerships with expert providers who can design, build, and operate advanced water and wastewater infrastructure.

These partnerships are delivering results. They have allowed communities to keep local public ownership and regulation of infrastructure, while at the same time providing access to expert external managers and the latest innovations in design, construction and technology; risk sharing; and accountability. They also have lowered costs and improved service for customers. They have reduced demand on local watersheds by encouraging consumers to conserve water, and to act responsibly when it comes to caring for the environment.

Private-sector organizations can offer resources to communities that the public sector may not otherwise be able to effectively provide. Rural and remote communities in particular find it difficult to attract and retain qualified water operators, and lack the resources to retain a full range of experts in water and wastewater treatment, distribution, maintenance, and management.

Water is a life essential. Communities must have a safe and reliable supply not only to survive, but to sustain themselves and to allow for future growth and development.

Partnerships also allow the public sector to share costs and risk, while maintaining public ownership and regulation. This does not mean governments should necessarily divest themselves of assets and retreat to a purely regulatory role. Rather, using its interest or ownership in certain water system assets, governments can ensure that the contracted operator meets pre-determined performance levels.

An effective system must involve a strong and vigorous public sector – one that sets a clear, rule-based regulatory regime, working in tandem with municipal and private-sector players to offer a sustainable and reliable water supply open to alternative-delivery models. Neither the public nor private sector can deliver effective results alone; it is their ability to work collaboratively through strong and well-structured partnerships that makes them effective.

In a well-structured partnership, the risks of cost overruns, service demand and schedule delays are borne by the private sector, not the taxpayer. Competitive tendering can encourage innovative private-sector solutions to facility management, design, and construction. These partnerships also offer government greater flexibility to tailor projects to best meet local needs.[24]

Opponents of public-private partnerships often suggest these projects experience higher costs, since the private sector must borrow at higher interest rates than government because government is considered a less risky investment – governments can always return to the taxpayer in the event of cost overruns.

Yet despite higher borrowing costs, the evidence points to the contrary. In the United Kingdom, reports by the Treasury indicate that public-private partnerships experience overall cost savings of 20 percent, compared to publicly procured operations. The report also found that only 24 percent of these projects were delivered late, compared to 70 percent in the public sector. Cost overruns occurred only 22 percent of the time under these partnerships, compared to 73 percent in the public sector.[25]

EPCOR has delivered similarly positive results for many communities using public-private partnership models, bringing major construction projects in on-budget and on-time. On Vancouver Island, for example, EPCOR worked with the District of Sooke to build that community's first sewer system and wastewater treatment plant for 8,700 residents. The project was completed for $5 million less than budget, six months ahead of schedule. Even more importantly, it represents a step toward resolving a long-standing concern around the dumping of raw sewage into the ocean. These projects also create high-quality long-term employment opportunities in the region, including unionized positions that often deliver better compensation than that offered by local governments.

Partnerships have another advantage – they are an extremely effective way of ensuring that two of the changes discussed above are implemented: the use of true-cost pricing as an incentive for conservation and support infrastructure renewal, and the vigorous enforcement of laws protecting water supplies. Private sector operators have strong financial incentives to comply with legislation, as do its officers, directors and employees, and public bodies that enforce water laws are removed from the inherent conflict created by the dilemma of self-enforcement. Moreover, private operators have nowhere to hide costs, and no room for error when it comes to the timeliness or quality of their work – they cannot subsidize themselves from the tax base, and they must deliver on their performance targets or face penalties.

The most striking proof of the power of contracts is their use in the communities that have been victimized by drinking water contamination. Milwaukee residents have put their wastewater treatment plant under contract, and demanded that it meet higher standards than those required by the state – or face heavy fines. Walkerton has turned its water utility over to a private operator, as has the community of Kashechewan.

A report prepared for Ontario's SuperBuild Corporation sums up the situation well: "Private sector involvement in, and alternative forms of governance of, water and wastewater utilities, can enhance utilities' accountability to stakeholders and to public policy objectives in general. A key element of that accountability is the separation of operations and the regulation of operations, which can help ensure better enforcement, compared to self-regulation ... [A] better focus of inquiry lies in 'accountability' as opposed to 'control.'"[26]

11.6 Multi-stakeholder approach to the management of upland watersheds

Accountability, rather than control, is also a theme for the final change: the integration of watershed management strategies with larger land-use policies and planning. It has been proven that the most effective watershed management strategies are based on involvement from all levels of government and private-sector partners and users.

Public safety must be a first priority, and to provide quality water in sufficient quantity, water suppliers must identify the hazards/risks to water supplies, assess and manage those risks, support watershed management and planning implementation, and employ best management practices.

EPCOR's most significant water operation serves more than one million residents in 45 communities in the Edmonton metropolitan region. Those residents draw their water from the North Saskatchewan River watershed. Within Alberta alone the river flows over 1000 kilometers, draining an area of 80,000 km^2 as it passes through five natural regions and draws upon 18 sub-watersheds. Over its remaining course, the river joins with the South Saskatchewan as part of the Nelson River Basin and empties into Hudson Bay.

That source of protection is and will always be the first step in an effective multiple-barrier approach to drinking water treatment. To reinforce this belief, EPCOR produced a Source Water Protection Plan (SWPP) in December 2007 to protect communities by identifying potential hazards – such as land uses and contaminant sources – that have, or could have, an effect on the North Saskatchewan basin and/or water treatment plant process, and to evaluate the level of risk such hazards pose to drinking water.

The challenge lies in how to provide for source protection given the scope of the watershed and the range and volume of users within it. In Alberta, the answer has been to establish multi-stakeholder partnerships that bring together governments, water and wastewater operators, industrial users, agricultural producers, water researchers, non-government organizations, First Nations, and others who may impact the watershed.

There are now more than 90 stakeholder groups engaged with the North Saskatchewan Watershed Alliance. Together, the partners have conducted research into the sources of *Cryptosporidium* and *Giardia* contamination within the watershed and the potential risks to human health of using reclaimed water, established monitoring on the river basin (including tributaries, wastewater lagoons and storm sewer outfalls), and assessed the impact of spills on river water quality and treatment plant operation.

Their work includes the development of an Integrated Watershed Management Plan, which will provide a framework for protecting, maintaining and restoring a healthy, natural watershed system. The plan also will address the protection of the aquatic environment and its associated necessary flow needs, and guide decisions on future water licensing applications.

Further, the Alliance has completed a "State of the Basin" report, and an educational "Watershed Toolkit" for use by voluntary groups. Supplementing this work, there are partnerships that address water quality and public awareness of watershed protection within city boundaries, facilitate the adoption of beneficial management practices by farmers, ranchers and processors to reduce the impact of agriculture production on the environment, and provide watershed education programs within the province's school curriculum.

For example, EPCOR has joined with the Rocky Riparian Group (RRG) in Alberta – a community-based team promoting healthy watersheds – to mitigate the impact that livestock have on water quality in the upper watershed. Funding was provided for a solar-powered watering unit that the RRG uses to demonstrate to farmers that water can be brought to livestock year round, instead of taking the livestock to water.

When it was published in 2002, Alberta's "Water for Life" strategy concluded that "Protecting water quality proactively reduces risks and is more efficient than treating the water later."

The best way to protect water quality on large watersheds with multiple users is through partnerships that engage governments, the private sector, community organizations and researchers. No one level of government can accomplish the task alone.

Effective watershed protection also should engage major water users and wastewater treatment operators to coordinate opportunities for water recycling or "grey water." In many jurisdictions, particularly those with significant industrial water use, water recycling offers a way to reduce stress on the watershed.

11.7 Conclusion and policy implications

The challenges facing Canada's water systems can best be described as multi-dimensional and multi-faceted in origin, although certainly not unique. A proper solution requires a diverse stakeholder approach that first reconsiders the role of the public and private sectors and, then, appropriately defines them for the future.

Water supply and quality are issues that no longer exist in isolation. A key underlying theme is conservation, which eases the burden being placed on local watersheds, and allows individuals to take action to protect the environment.

As a company that also generates power, EPCOR actively engages in the climate change discussion, constantly seeking solutions for reducing greenhouse gas and other air emissions. Efforts to address the challenges facing Canada's water system must take both economic and environmental considerations into account.

The ability to consistently deliver a safe and reliable supply of water depends on two key considerations: securing a sustainable quantity and quality of raw water, and building and managing sustainable systems for its treatment, distribution, and effective demand management.

Based on experience and the available evidence, this chapter argues that both the supply of raw water and the sustainability of infrastructure are threatened by rising demand, declining infrastructure, and inadequate watershed protection practices.

Canadians should meet these challenges with five changes:

1   the acknowledgement that there are serious concerns about the security and safety of Canada's water supply;
2   the acceptance of the principle that consumers should pay the full cost of water supply and delivery;
3   the enforcement of existing laws;
4   the deployment of alternative service delivery models, including public-private partnerships, to help improve the performance of our water supply systems;
5   the integration of multi-stakeholder watershed management strategies into land-use policies and planning.

These changes will help secure the future delivery of safe and reliable water, and offer a model to other jurisdictions.

While Canada is endowed with remarkable supplies of natural resources, the population has not faced the challenges that stem from inter-state conflict over water. However, Canadians have made positive strides toward improving their water systems in the wake of recent water quality incidents, including making greater use of innovative technologies.

Governments also are tightening regulatory requirements and making better efforts to control and monitor water quality. In Alberta, for example, the province's "Water for Life" program is educating the public about water scarcity, and pointing to a new way of governing water in this province in the future.

Governments, industry and citizens must work together to agree on solutions to the challenges outlined in this chapter.

Well-structured partnerships have the ability to manage infrastructure and personnel challenges in pursuit of the long-term goals of building strong and reliable water systems. The process begins with proper upland watershed management. It is supported by broader public awareness of the importance of water to quality of life and the future. And it culminates in the sustainable delivery of clean, safe drinking water. Although global and climate change will add new dimensions to these challenges, continuing efforts in this arena will serve as an example that will help others in managing their water.

Notes

1 Environment Canada, *Quickfacts*. Available online at http://www.ec.gc.ca/WATER/en/e_quickfacts.htm (Accessed 9 August 2006).
2 Environment Canada, *Quickfacts*. Available online at http://www.ec.gc.ca/WATER/en/e_quickfacts.htm (Accessed 9 August 2006).
3 Environment Canada, *Quickfacts*. Available online at http://www.wsc.ec.gc.ca/hydrometric/main_e.cfm?cname=hydrometric_e.cfm (Accessed 9 August 2006).
4 Alberta Environment, *Allocation versus consumption*. Available online at http://www3.gov.ab.ca/env/water/GWSW/quantity/waterinalberta/allocation/AL4_all_vs_con.html (Accessed 12 December 2006).
5 Alberta Environment (2002) *Water for life: facts and information about water in Alberta.*
6 Eggertson L. (2008) *Investigative report: 1766 boil-water advisories now in place across Canada.* 2008 April 7 [Epub ahead of print]. Available online at http://www.cmaj.ca/cgi/rapidpdf/cmaj.080525.
7 City of Edmonton (June 2002) *Emergency Services Hazard Analysis Report.*
8 OECD Observer, *Water and farms: toward sustainable use.* Available online at http://www.oecdobserver.org/news/fullstory.php/aid/1801/Water_and_farms: Towards sustainable_use.html March 2006.
9 Swain, H., Lazar, F., and Pine, J. (2005) *Watertight: the case for change in Ontario's water and wastewater sector* (Toronto: Expert Panel on Water and Wastewater Strategy, Government of Ontario), 53.
10 Ibid.
11 Gaudreault, V. and Lemire, P. (2006) *The age of public infrastructure in Canada.* Ottawa: Statistics Canada.
12 Swain, H., Lazar, F., and Pine, J. (2005) *Watertight: the case for change in Ontario's water and wastewater sector* (Toronto: Expert Panel on Water and Wastewater Strategy, Government of Ontario), 53.
13 Alberta Environment (2006), *Backgrounder: water for life, investments for the future of Alberta's water.*
14 Environment Canada (2005) *2004 Municipal water use repor*, Ottawa: Environment Canada.

15 Weyerhaeuser *et al.*, *Forest sector presentation to HG LUP community forum*. Available online at http://ilmbwww.gov.bc.ca/ilmb/lup/lrmp/coast/gci/docs/Licensee_LUP_Presentation.pdf#search=%22%22Stumpage%20rates%20by%20province%22%22, April 2004.

16 Canadian Association of Petroleum Producers, *Alberta's oil and gas royalties*, Available online at http://www.capp.ca/raw.asp?x=1&dt=NTV&e=PDF&dn=100066#search=%22government%20royalties%20per%20barrel%20oil%22, September 2007.

17 Ministry of Energy, Province of Alberta, *Minerals royalty rates*. .energy.gov.ab.ca/minerals/699.asp, September 2007.

18 Alberta Environment, *Water legislation fact sheet*. Available online at http://www3.gov.ab.ca/env/water/Legislation/FactSheets/GeneralInfo.pdf, August 2006.

19 Puzic, S. Flush if water rates make you mad. *Windsor Star*, 2 August 2007.

20 Brubaker, E. *"The future of water and wastewater in British Columbia: the case for public-private partnerships."* Presentation to Greater Victoria Chamber of Commerce, 2 May 2007.

21 Brubaker, E. (2002) Liquid assets: privatizing and regulating Canada's water utilities. *Environment Probe*, Toronto, 131.

22 Brubaker, E. (2003) *Revisiting water and wastewater utility privatization*. Presentation to the Public Goals, Private Means Research Colloquium, Faculty of Law, University of Toronto, 3 October 2003.

23 CBC News Online. *The state of drinking water on Canada's reserves*. Available online at http://www.cbc.ca/slowboil/Alberta.html (Accessed 20 February 2006).

24 Burleton, D. (2006) *Creating the winning conditions for public-private partnerships in Canada*. Toronto: TD Economics, TD Bank Financial Group.

25 Ibid.

26 The Cadmus Group *et al.* (2002) *A Study of Best Practices in the Water and Wastewater Sector*. Toronto: Ontario SuperBuild Corporation.

12 A case study in the management of international waters

Dennis L. Schornack and John Nevin

Created by the Boundary Waters Treaty of 1909, the International Joint Commission (IJC) serves to prevent and resolve disputes relating to the use and quality of boundary waters and to advise the governments of Canada and the United States on related questions. The two governments have turned to the Commission on more than 100 occasions for assistance, on issues such as navigation and power generation in the St. Lawrence River, pollution in the Great Lakes, and the apportionment of water in the St. Mary and Milk River watersheds. It is asserted that the IJC has largely been successful in its dual roles as regulator of projects (e.g. dams) that affect water levels and flows on both sides of the boundary and as a nonbinding advisor to the governments on controversial issues relating to both transboundary water quantity and quality. Several examples of the IJC's work are cited, including recommendations that have resulted in new treaties or binational agreement, resolving longstanding issues over waters shared between the two countries. Reasons for the success of the IJC are categorized into two types: first, those that are contextual and cannot be affected by the Commission; and second, those that are procedural and within the Commission's control. Contextual reasons include the provisions made for equality in the Treaty; the vital importance of water; geography; the comparable affluence of the party countries; social, economic, and cultural ties; and the fact that only two countries are involved, thus making consensus easier to achieve. Procedural reasons include the IJC's commitment to decision by consensus; use of a binationally balanced joint fact-finding process based on science; the independence of commissioners and Commission-appointed study teams; a focus on public engagement; the ability to depoliticize issues; and the capacity to take the time needed to reach consensus without pressure from the party governments. Under the right conditions, the IJC model may have the potential to work in other international contexts.

12.1 Introduction

The first step in evaluating the success of the IJC is to define what is meant by "success." Without a definition, success cannot be measured, nor can the reasons for that success be identified. Sometimes, defining success is easy. For example, in the corporate world, success might be defined in terms of market share or profits.

To a politician, success might be defined as being re-elected or elected to higher office.

In sports, success can be measured by games won and championships claimed. For example, after just giving up a home run in the bottom of the ninth inning to lose a critical game against a key rival, a famous major league baseball pitcher put it very simply when he said: "Sometimes you're the windshield, and sometimes you're the bug." Measuring success cannot get any simpler than that.

But in the case of an international treaty organization charged with resolving disputes and managing shared waters, what is success, and how can it be measured? Is success the number of disputes avoided? But how do you measure something that never happened?

Is the absence of complaints from the party governments or their citizens a measure of success? Since neither country has ever advocated abolishing the IJC or revising the treaty under which it was formed, is this an indicator of success?

Does the fact that the United States and Canada have never engaged in armed conflict over shared waters – at least not since the IJC was created – reflect success?

Is success measured by popular perception? Some say that perception is reality. Certainly, positive popular references to the IJC are evidence of a widely held public belief that the IJC is a successful treaty organization.

But what is the reality? Is the IJC truly as successful as its reputation would have us believe and, if so, what are the reasons for that success? Moreover, is the IJC model one that can be transferred or translated to other international water management contexts?

12.2 Measuring the success of the IJC

The authors start with the premise that the IJC has indeed been successful in achieving its mandate under the Boundary Water Treaty "… to prevent disputes regarding the use of boundary waters and to settle all questions which are now pending between the United States and the Dominion of Canada involving the rights, obligations, or interests of either in relation to the other or to the inhabitants of the other, along their common frontier, and to make provision for the adjustment and settlement of all such questions as may hereafter arise …"[1]

One yardstick provided by the treaty to measure the success of a primary aspect of the Commission's work is applications. Article III of the Treaty provides that "… no further or other uses or obstructions or diversions, whether temporary or permanent of boundary waters on either side of the line, affecting the natural level or flow of boundary waters on the other side of the line shall be made except by authority of the United States or the Dominion of Canada within their respective jurisdictions and with the approval as hereinafter provided, of a joint commission, to be known as The International Joint Commission."[2] Perhaps the most concrete work done by the IJC is to approve and regulate dams located in boundary waters or in transboundary rivers for the benefit of people in both countries.

In this regard, the Commission has successfully approved 49 out of 61

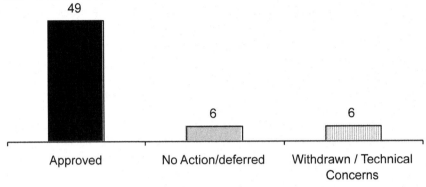

Figure 12.1 Status of applications.

applications. In six cases, no action was taken or a decision was deferred, usually at the request of the applying government. The remaining six applications were either withdrawn by the applicant, or dismissed for technical reasons. In 40 cases in which the IJC approved applications for structures, the IJC retained jurisdiction over the structures by creating expert international boards of control to manage or oversee the particular structure, or by assigning the work to an existing board. In the remaining nine cases of approved applications, the IJC determined that no control board was necessary.

IJC-approved projects range from a dam on the St. Mary River that is managed by its International Lake Superior Board of Control to the Grand Coulee Dam on the Columbia River, the third largest hydroelectric dam in the world.

The second major aspect of the IJC's work under the Treaty, and thus another yardstick by which to measure its success, is references. A reference is a "... question or matter of difference ..." between the United States and Canada that is referred "... from time to time ..." to the IJC "... for examination and report ..." The Commission investigates and reports upon the "... facts and circumstances of the particular questions and matters referred ..." and provides the governments with "... such conclusions and recommendations as may be appropriate ..." The Commission's conclusions and recommendations are not binding upon the governments, and "... shall not be regarded as decisions of the questions or matters so submitted either on the facts or the law, and shall in no way have the character of an arbitral award."[3]

Since 1909, there have been a total of 57 references made to the IJC by the governments. The topics for these references have ranged from questions concerning the pollution of the North American Great Lakes in 1912, to the impact of Alburg-Swanton Bridge and Causeway on water quality in Mississquoi Bay of Lake Champlain in 2005.

It is understandable, given the advanced stage of developed water use in the transboundary region, that the number of applications for structures that have an impact on water levels and flows on the other side of the boundary has declined steadily over the years. In fact, there has been only one such application since 1990, and few since the 1960s. On the other hand, the number of references appears to ebb and flow with the times, reaching a peak in the 1960s and 1970s when the environmental movement and concerns over water quality were growing, and when water levels on the North American Great Lakes were high.

The combination of both applications and references constitute an IJC "docket" of some 118 actionable items over its 100-year history. In taking action on these items, the Commission has rarely failed to reach agreement, that is, at least four of the six commissioners willing to sign their names to either a record of decision or final report to the governments. Indeed, over its century of existence, the Commission has divided along national lines and submitted separate reports in only two instances, and both relate to the same dispute – the apportionment of water in the St. Mary and Milk rivers and the associated watersheds of the Waterton and Belly Rivers.

Both the St. Mary and Milk rivers arise in the mountains in US Glacier National Park. Portions of the St. Mary River are diverted into the Milk River that flows north into Canada and then east for several hundred miles before again turning south back into the United State in eastern Montana. The waters of the Milk River, along with the addition of the St. Mary diversion, are heavily used for irrigation in Alberta, Canada. By the time the Milk River reaches eastern Montana where its water supports smaller, less advanced irrigation needs, its waters are greatly diminished. In dry years, farmers on both sides of the border demand more water than is available for use.

Article VI of the Boundary Waters Treaty is entirely devoted to the St. Mary and Milk rivers apportionment, but the vague Treaty language provides for conflicting claims in both countries. The IJC issued an apportionment order interpreting the Treaty language in 1921, and disputes have flared from time to time since then, usually associated with arid conditions and low water supplies. However, the Commission has not yet been given a reference agreed to by both governments to reopen and potentially revise the order.

Ironically, the dispute over the allocation of the St. Mary and Milk rivers was

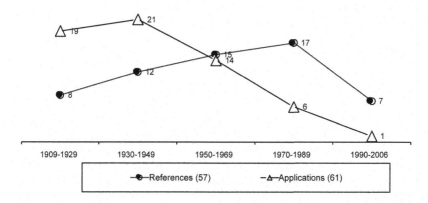

Figure 12.2 Trends in applications and references.

one of the original reasons that the United States and Canada signed the Boundary Waters Treaty. The original 1921 apportionment order withstood a request by the United States to reopen the order in 1927, when Canada did not concur, and in 1984, a reference to study the use and apportionment of water in the contiguous Waterton and Belly rivers watersheds divided along national lines. The controversy concerning the allocation of water in this arid area of the continent continues to this day, but at least the existing order provides some certainty for people who depend on these waters for irrigation, and they are able to plan accordingly. The advent of climate change and the shrinkage of the glaciers that supply this system are expected to lead to continued demands for the IJC to reopen and revise the 1921 order.

It is interesting to note that the adjudicatory function provided to the Commission in Article X of the Treaty – in which the two governments can refer questions to the IJC for a binding decision – has never been invoked. Apparently, this is one treaty tool that the two nations have not found useful. And on some occasions, the two governments have agreed to avoid the IJC altogether, signing treaties that create other arbitral bodies. However, with these minor exceptions, the United States and Canada have consistently turned to the IJC to address some of the thorniest water management issues that have arisen over the past century.

Everyone is familiar with the old adage regarding the three most important factors in valuing real estate – location, location, and location. When it comes to determining the success of the IJC, the three most important factors appear to be timing, timing, and timing. A perfect example of this IJC adage was a reference to the Commission in 1920 to study the potential for improving the St. Lawrence River between Lake Ontario and Montreal, Canada, for deep-water navigation and power generation.

In response to IJC recommendations, in 1932, the United States and Canada signed the Great Lakes-St. Lawrence Deep Waterway Treaty, also known as the Hoover-Bennett Treaty. However, in 1934, the treaty was defeated in the US Senate and, in 1941, an agreement for the development of navigation and power in the Great Lakes-St. Lawrence Basin was signed by the two countries but not approved by the US Senate as required by the US Constitution. Clearly, the timing was not right, but shortly after World War II, conditions changed and the project gained new life.

This time around, the issues were broken into three parts. First, the Niagara Treaty of 1950 set a minimum flow for waters cascading over Niagara Falls at specified times to protect both power and tourism interests. The IJC was given a reference to investigate and make recommendations concerning the nature and design of remedial works necessary to enhance the beauty of Niagara Falls, while at the same time, permitting the production of added hydropower. Second, in 1952, application was made by both governments to the IJC for approval of works to generate electric power in the international section of the St. Lawrence River. And third, governments enacted legislation and entered into an agreement to construct the St. Lawrence Seaway through an exchange of diplomatic notes. Construction of the massive Moses-Saunders Dam was completed in 1958 and the Seaway was completed in 1959. The projects combined employed 25,000 people at a cost of more than US$1 billion. The IJC retained jurisdiction over the management of the dam through a control order and the appointment of an international board of control.

12.3 Focus on results – examples

As the foregoing shows, the IJC has played a critical role in the development and continuing management of water resources in the transboundary region. The results of the Commission's work in evaluating and approving applications can be seen in dams built, rivers diverted, and reservoirs created. However, with respect to references – studies requested by the governments on sensitive issues – have IJC recommendations been implemented?

It must be remembered that the IJC does not have the mandate or authority to implement its own recommendations, and that these recommendations are not binding upon the national governments. With respect to references, the IJC is neither a program manager, nor a regulator; it is simply a recommender and advisor to the governments. The responsibility for implementation belongs to the governments of the United States and Canada, so it is somewhat unfair to judge the Commission, based on the action or inaction of the two governments alone. However, the extent to which they are actually implemented reflects the quality of the IJC's recommendations, how well they address the topic of the reference, and how they fit with governmental agendas.

A comprehensive assessment of the status of IJC recommendations has never been attempted, but perhaps that assessment should be part of an overall review of the work of the IJC as it approaches its hundredth anniversary in 2009. Lacking that detailed analysis, however, the anecdotal evidence seems to indicate a solid record of success. In addition, when implementation efforts have been assessed in specific cases, e.g. its recommendations regarding flooding and flood control on the Red River, the outcomes have generally been positive.

Other examples include the IJC's very first reference – on water levels in the Lake of the Woods – which resulted in a consensus report and recommendations in 1917. In response, the United States and Canada signed a treaty known as the 1925 Lake of the Woods Convention and Protocol that established elevation and discharge requirements for regulating Lake of the Woods, based on IJC recommendations. Likewise, in another dispute referred to the IJC in 1940 concerning the apportionment of the Souris River shared by North Dakota, Saskatchewan and Manitoba, IJC recommendations were implemented immediately after they were first issued in 1941, as were subsequent IJC recommended revisions in 1958, 1992, and 2000.

A capstone achievement of the IJC was its report to the governments in response to their reference in 1964 on "Pollution of the Lower Great Lakes." The Commission recommended urgent remedial action to arrest the degradation of Lakes Erie and Ontario and the international section of the St. Lawrence River. IJC also recommended that the governments work together to set specific and measurable water quality objectives, and to authorize the IJC to serve as an independent "watchdog" to monitor the effectiveness of governments' efforts to clean up the lakes. To implement these recommendations, President Nixon and Prime Minister Trudeau signed the Great Lakes Water Quality Agreement (GLWQA) in 1972. Again, the times were right and the GLWQA coincided with the enactment of a wide range of other environment laws and regulations in both countries, including the US Clean Water Act.

The success of the GLWQA makes it a landmark in transboundary water cooperation and management. For example, it has resulted in steps by the governments of the United States and Canada to eliminate direct point-source inputs of pollutants into the Great Lakes and has worked to stop and reverse eutrophication. The GLWQA created a framework for continued binational cooperation to protect and maintain the quality of the waters contained in the Great Lakes by establishing built-in mechanisms for periodic review and revision. The GLWQA is a "living document" that has been revised to meet contemporary needs in 1978, 1983, and 1987. The substantial and measurable gains in water quality made in the 1970s and 1980s have slowed, and new threats – such as invasive species – have emerged. To address these contemporary challenges, as of this writing, the IJC is in the process of completing its most recent review and is preparing recommendations to once again revise the GLWQA to meet extant challenges.

Similar to the previously cited example of the St. Lawrence Seaway, there is a notable example in which the timing for the IJC's involvement just wasn't right. In 1913–14, the IJC undertook what might be the largest water quality study in human history, or at least in North American history, sampling water quality in United States/Canada boundary waters from Montana to Maine and Saskatchewan to New Brunswick. Nearly 1500 sampling sites were identified and 17 laboratories were installed to analyze nearly 18 000 water samples. The study found that water supplies in the Detroit River, the Lower Niagara, and the St. John River, The Rainy River, and Lakes Erie and Ontario had very high levels of bacterial contamination, making the water unfit to drink or swim. The science was accurate and the recommendations to the national governments were visionary and far reaching, among them:

- disinfect vessel sewage;
- develop regulations for protecting water intakes;
- prohibit discharge of garbage and sawmill waste;
- restrict and regulate discharges of industrial and other waste;
- install collection and treatment facilities for human waste;
- treatment of sewage before discharge;
- tine screening or sedimentation plus disinfection.

In 1920, at the request of the two governments, the IJC submitted a draft treaty for implementing its recommendations. The treaty would have transformed the IJC from recommender to regulator and put the Commission in charge of implementing a new, regulatory wastewater treatment regime on both sides of the border. Perhaps because the recommendations threatened the sovereignty of the two nations, the recommended treaty was never signed. Then, as today, such a transfer of sovereign domestic regulatory authority to an independent international body is virtually unthinkable, and perhaps less far-reaching recommendations for cooperative international action might have been implemented sooner.

Some might consider another example of the IJC overreaching was the reference it received in 1971 to investigate and recommend measures to improve the lifestyle of residents in Point Roberts, Washington.

Residents of Point Roberts, Washington, must travel many miles from the United States mainland through Canada to reach their homes, creating issues with the application of customs laws and regulations, delivery of health services, law enforcement, and utilities. Instead of answering the specific questions of the reference, the binational board set up by the IJC to examine the matter recommended the creation of an international park and conservation and recreation area extending from Gabriola Island to Whidbey Island in the San Juan-Gulf Islands Archipelago, and from west to east from Vancouver Island to the mainland coast of Washington, including Point Roberts and its environs. The governments' reaction to these creative recommendations was so negative that any further opportunities for cooperation to resolve the original issues was foreclosed and, in 1977, the Commission halted work on the reference.

However, despite the few blemishes associated with overreaching recommendations, the IJC's record is dominated by successful resolution of dozens of issues that could have poisoned relations between the United States and Canada. Instead, the IJC has served as a vital link between the two countries, a vehicle for dispute prevention and resolution, the fostering of good relations, and the promotion of cooperation to the benefit of people in both countries consistent with its treaty mandate.

12.4 Reasons for success

Having established, at least anecdotally, the success of the Commission, let us examine some of the reasons for this success. The reasons divide into two basic camps: those that are contextual and beyond the control of the Commission, and those that are procedural or methodological and thus within Commission control.

12.4.1 Contextual reasons for IJC success

One reason for the IJC's success is the very nature of water itself. Water is essential for life. To some, water is a gift from God, as we see, for example in the Bible and the Torah. In Deuteronomy it says, "For the Lord thy God bringeth thee into a good land, and land of brooks of water, of fountains and depths that spring out of valleys and hills." And the Koran says, "We have created every living thing from water." Some speculate that it may even be that the fundamental human need for clean water compelled the creation of the first communities as people organized to use and share it for life-sustaining purposes. As a senior international water advisor to the US Army Corps of Engineers, Dr. Jerry Delli Priscoli, has noted, "Indeed, water may actually be one of humanity's great learning grounds for building community."[4]

Throughout the ages, people have learned to share water because there is simply no alternative. One might even say that when it comes to water, the imperative to consensus is virtually absolute. Indeed, the alternative to such cooperation is war. This realization leads the authors to agree with researchers who believe that water is not a source of conflict, but a source of comity. For example as Yoffe and Wolf conclude:

> Accounts of conflict related to water indicate that only seven minor skirmishes have occurred in this century, and that no war has yet been fought over water. In contrast, 145 water-related treaties were signed in the same period. War over water seems neither strategically rational, hydrographically effective, nor economically viable. Shared interests along a waterway seem to consistently outweigh water's conflict-inducing characteristics. Furthermore, once cooperative water regimes are established through treaties, they turn out to be impressively resilient over time, even between otherwise hostile riparians, and even as conflict is waged over other issues.[5]

So, in the case of the IJC, the success of the Commission can in part be attributed to the nature of water itself.

Related to this point is the massive volume and even geographic distribution of the waters shared between the United States and Canada – it is much easier to manage abundance than scarcity. For example, the volume of the Great Lakes alone is in excess of six quadrillion gallons. Yet, even with the seeming abundance of water, reaching final agreement on a management regime for using or diverting Great Lakes water has still proven elusive. For example, it has recently taken the eight Great Lakes state governors and two Canadian provincial premiers over five years to sign the Annex 2001 agreements concerning the diversion and consumptive use of Great Lakes' waters. It is expected to take at least that long again for state legislatures and congressional action to seal the deal on the United States side. Such difficulty may be attributed in part to the fact that only one percent of Great Lakes water is renewed each year, and the large number of governmental, private, individual, and organizational interests that must be balanced. On the other hand, in arid transboundary regions in which scarcity is the norm – such as the previously referenced watersheds of the St. Mary and Milk rivers – conflict and controversy have bubbled for more than a century, and continue to this day.

A third contextual reason for success is rooted in geography. Simply put, transboundary rivers run both north and south. Along the United States-Canada boundary, many rivers flow north from the United States into Canada, while others flow south, from Canada into the United States – creating both upstream and downstream interests in both countries. At the same time, from the Great Lakes east, the international boundary cuts right through the middle of the Great Lakes and part of the St. Lawrence River, making both countries equally concerned about upstream and downstream interests.

This geographical state of affairs is a great example of "what goes around comes around." Since both countries have up- and downstream interests, there is often an incentive to reach agreement; otherwise, an offending upstream party could face problems in another watershed in which they are the offended downstream party. Perhaps the guiding principle here is the hydrological equivalent of The Golden Rule: Do unto others, as you would have them do unto you. So when it comes to water, following The Golden Rule is great impetus for agreement.

Another contextual reason for IJC success in water management is success itself. That is, both Canada and the United States enjoy economic success so they can afford to invest in a wide range of measures to improve the management and conservation of the waters they share. Both countries are affluent, have advanced technologies, and thus have the capital and human expertise to keep the waters clean and useful, or to manage problems as they arise.

By illustration, the authors reference the familiar, if sometimes controversial "U" of the Kuznets Curve adapted to an environmental context. As wealth, standards of living, and economic development increase, so do associated pollution and health concerns. But above a certain threshold, once basic needs are met and resources become available, society seeks to enhance environmental quality, pollution declines, and public health improves. One might even argue that the inverted "U" is narrowed in free democratic societies such as the United States and Canada in which the public can effectively demand investment in environmental protection. On the other hand, the inverted "U" may be stretched for political systems in which public input is suppressed.

In more specific terms, more affluent people in more affluent nations can cook with electricity or natural gas rather than with wood or charcoal. Forests can be managed and replanted sustainably instead of simply cleared. Wealthy communities can recycle and reuse and afford to pay the costs of installing smokestack scrubbers and other pollution controls. But in the case of IJC management of transboundary water, the important point is that the United States and Canada are at the same state of advanced economic development and thereby have similar abilities to invest in environmental protection.

Yet another contextual reason for success relates to the social, cultural, and economic "ties that bind" the United States and Canada, and the fact that they share at least one common language. While some contend that United States values clash with Canadian values, on a very basic level, the countries are far more similar than different. Indeed with more than US$1 billion in goods traded across the border every day, the economic incentives for cooperation are obvious and continue to grow. Other ties include binational associations of state, provincial, and local governments, as well as nongovernmental organizations and industries. The entire United States-Canada transboundary economy is highly integrated.

A seventh contextual reason for success may make the authors sound like numerologists, but when looking at systems of governance, numbers make a significant difference and, in this case, there are only two countries involved. The

Figure 12.3 Maps of rivers flowing North and South.

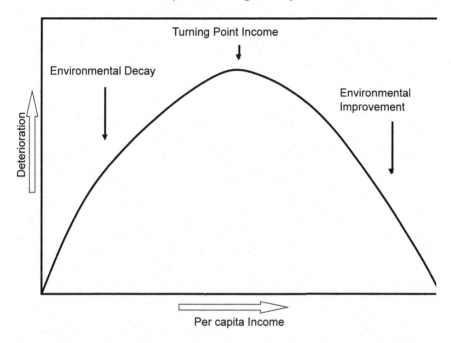

Figure 12.4 Environmental Kuznets curve.

number "2" inherently defines the notion of fairness and equality. Think of how we describe deals – fifty-fifty, even-handed, a marriage. When it comes to fairness, an equal division in half is the easiest way to get deals between two partners done.

The bottom line is that where the operating rule to resolve disputes is consensus, the bigger the number, the harder it is to reach agreement. At the IJC, with only two countries, everything is done in twos – binational balance is maintained on the Commission and on all IJC-appointed study boards, boards of control, and even in the budgeting for IJC operations. However, when there are three or more parties, reaching consensus is far more difficult. Larger numbers make fair decision-making more complicated and time consuming, and have the potential for diluting results.

The final contextual reason for IJC success is the Boundary Waters Treaty of 1909 that created the IJC. The IJC's success is rooted in the commonality of interests in shared waters that are explicitly stated in the Treaty. For example, the IJC's role in dam management (levels and flows) is done in accord with water-use priorities specified in the Treaty, in order of precedence: sanitation and drinking; navigation; and hydropower and irrigation.[6] Over the years, the value of such clear direction in the Treaty has proved critical to effective decision-making in that no decisions with respect to approvals for structures affecting water levels and flows have been successfully challenged in the courts of either country, or even through the legislative process.

Article VIII of the Treaty provides that each country "… shall have, each on its own side of the boundary, equal use and similar rights in the use ...”[7] of boundary waters, but while priority uses are enumerated, not all-possible uses of shared waters are addressed in the Treaty. For example, missing are uses of shared water for recreational swimming and boating, riparian enjoyment and protection from floods and, of course, conservation of the environment. Clear Treaty direction allows the IJC to benefit other uses only where enumerated uses are not significantly harmed. Indeed, Article VIII stipulates that “... no use shall be permitted which tends materially to conflict with or restrain any other use with is given preference over it ...”[8] In this case, the drafters of the Treaty intended that uses not listed would certainly fall below those that are specified. In addition, the Commission must require as a condition of its approval, provisions protecting and indemnifying all interests from damages that might result from changes in water levels and flows.

Most importantly, the Treaty created the Commission on the basis of complete equality, despite the differences in national populations and economies. At the same time, while providing for equality, the Treaty also protects national sovereignty and the ability of the respective governments to make decisions affecting their side of the boundary. For example, Article II guarantees each side “... exclusive jurisdiction and control over the use and diversion, whether temporary or permanent, of all waters on its own side of the line which in their natural channels would flow across the boundary or into boundary waters.” It is only when such use or diversion results in injury on the other side that rights arise on that side – rights equivalent to those if the injury were on the same side as the diversion. Setting this balance in the treaty has been a key to the effectiveness and success of the IJC.

12.4.2 Procedural reasons for IJC success

Turning from context that is not under IJC control to the factors that it does control, there are several operational and methodological reasons for IJC success in managing shared, international waters. First and foremost, IJC success lies in its operating imperative to reach consensus on all decisions. Great effort is made to avoid minority reports or “split decisions.” Indeed, the Commission rarely votes on questions before it; information is collected and discussed until consensus is reached. While this process may take a long time, the result is worth the effort due to the inherent strength of agreements made by consensus.

Second, the process by which consensus is achieved is vitally important. For example, in response to a reference from the governments, the IJC normally starts its investigation by appointing a binational board or task force to conduct joint fact-finding. This investigative body includes equal numbers from each country and also attempts to pull in officials from the various levels of government with interest in the topic of study. This same composition of members holds true for IJC boards of control that manage structures under continuing IJC jurisdiction and for specialized work such as monitoring the allocation of water in the St. Mary and Milk rivers. Also, both national section offices of the IJC establish liaisons to the boards and study groups that work together to facilitate progress and help build consensus.

Joint fact-finding based on scientific analysis is the core method employed by the IJC, giving its recommendations weight and credibility. As part of the process, study team members agree upon exactly what is to be measured, how it is to be measured, and for how long. Just as important is the ability to look over each other's shoulder, to review published literature and to benefit from experiences on both sides of the border. The result is one set of science-based facts, arrived at in an agreed-upon way, using identical instruments and methods for use by the Commission in its deliberations.

Most typically, the experts who serve on IJC boards work for the respective governments and academic institutions and are highly respected in their fields. Yet, they do not "represent" their governments or institutions. As a condition of their appointment by the IJC, they agree to serve in their "personal and professional capacity" as experts in a given field of study. This construct is sometimes hard to understand, and sometimes it is difficult for such individuals to take off their official hats in government or academia and put on their hats as independent experts, but the IJC milieu affords them the opportunity to set those potentially biased interests aside.

Another benefit of this arrangement is that government officials, even though they are not serving in that capacity, bring to the table knowledge and experience regarding the kinds of recommendations that will realistically be implemented by their respective governments. This "reality check" helps to ground the recommendations that the Commission itself ultimately submits to the governments and enhances the prospects for their implementation.

All along the boundary, IJC control boards installed to manage structures in boundary waters like dams create a mechanism by which issues can be addressed binationally at the local and regional level. Over time, and with a very small investment, much dispute prevention is accomplished through these bodies. When issues arise in one country, board counterparts are able to pick up the phone and call someone they know in the other country. The issues may not even be within the specific jurisdiction of the board, but the personal connection allows board members to act as "sentinels" to alert the Commission to incipient disputes so that action may be taken to address issues before concerns rise to the level of the national governments.

A third factor within IJC control is the IJC's commitment to engage the public. The Treaty affords "… all interested parties a convenient opportunity to be heard."[9] In this regard, once the Commission has received a report from a board or study team, the Commission holds hearings in order to hear from the public. Recently, the IJC held the first bilingual Web dialogue in which 250 Great Lakes residents were able to offer their views, ask questions and interact with various experts will full translation in near real-time.

Fourth, the status conferred upon commissioners themselves is critical to their success as a commission. Presidents and prime ministers appoint commissioners in whom they have high levels of confidence because commissioners are given great independence from the influence of their appointive governments. This independence does not mean that national interests are to be disregarded; it means that government officials make decisions free of pressure from government interests, and without direction from higher officials.

The fifth controllable factor sometimes conflicts with the previous two and that is the ability of the IJC to keep a low profile – to fly under the radar. All IJC work and the work of its study teams are conducted in drab conference rooms and workshops, not under the glare of the media. IJC work documents are not subject to freedom of information laws in either country. Commissioners do not shun publicity, but rather use their positions to raise public awareness about critical water quantity and quality issues. Commissioners are not elected, they are appointed, and they do not seek political gain from their positions. This approach that focuses on depoliticizing issues encourages the development of consensus, prevents positions from hardening, and gives the governments the opportunity to accept and implement IJC recommendations on their own terms.

The sixth factor is the ability of the Commission to take its time – the value of being deliberate and free to set its own timetable cannot be discounted. When asked to be expeditious, the IJC has been able to respond to the needs of governments, completing references within a specified time frame. For example, a recent reference to solicit public comment on the review of the Great Lakes Water Quality Agreement was completed in six months and included comments from more than 4100 people.

In the past, the process for completing study and reaching agreement has taken several years. Sometimes, conditions have changed and the question being addressed is no longer an issue of concern. But at other times, the passage of time has allowed for positions to soften, for science to advance and provide new evidence, and for political or other pressures to ease. As previously noted, timing is everything. Currently though, references are typically concluded within a year of being issued by the governments.

Finally, IJC is successful because it does not have to address every problem. Indeed, under the Treaty, governments retain the right to resolve disputes between themselves. This is a right they exercise on occasion simply with an exchange of diplomatic notes, with examples including the construction of the St. Lawrence Seaway and most recently, an agreement for a Canadian company to pay $20 million for a US Environmental Protection Agency study of heavy metal pollution in the Columbia River and Lake Roosevelt in Washington state. Such notes might even expand the role of the IJC, as did recent notes giving the IJC additional responsibilities in the Souris River watershed.

This is another example of the power of "two" because such deal-making is much easier between two countries than it is among three or more. Over the years, many issues have been settled this way without engaging the IJC, but at the same time, the very existence of the IJC facilitates such resolutions because the parties want to avoid elevating the issue to the Commission.

12.5 Conclusion

Is the IJC model transferable to other contexts – to the Middle East or to the African Great Lakes? Based on the preceding analysis, one can surmise that the IJC is not a model for everyone. Not every treaty can be born to be successful the way the Boundary Waters Treaty has been. In particular, consensus is much more difficult with three or more parties and the realities of geography and climate can trump the wisdom of this particular instrument. But given the right circumstances, the Treaty and the processes employed by the IJC can work elsewhere.

For example, the governments of Tanzania, Kenya, and Uganda recently signed a new agreement regarding the sustainable development of Lake Victoria in Africa. The new pact creates a Lake Victoria Basin Commission that has powers similar to the IJC, and the pact itself is similar in many respects to the Boundary Waters Treaty. This development holds great promise and the IJC is investigating ways to help the Lake Victoria Basin Commission find its own path to success.

Looking forward to the IJC's second century, how will it maintain its record of success? The authors believe the key is thinking small and local, watershed-by-watershed along the boundary, strengthening local capacity to address and resolve concerns. Success or failure in the future will depend upon how well the IJC pursues this agenda, because all disputes start small and local. If it can deploy its existing resources – its boards of control – and develop new ones where needed to facilitate solving problems at the local level, during early stages, before they become full blown international disputes, then the IJC will continue its record of success.

This "Watershed Initiative" is a new approach to dispute prevention currently being explored by the IJC. If it is successful, it will mean fewer references from the national governments, but it also will mean greater cooperation. Vigilance, active prevention, and the development of local capacity to resolve localized disputes are the keys to another century of IJC success.

Postscript to Chapter 12

In the preceding chapter, Dennis Schornack and John Nevin attribute the exemplary success of the International Joint Commission over the past century to a number of important factors, including the independence of the Commissioners and a commitment to joint fact-finding and consensual decision-making. Of these two primary factors, independence may be the most important. Independence means that, once appointed, boundary commissioners are removed from direct political influence and serve without government instruction. Independence frees commissioners to make fair and objective decisions in matters that might otherwise be compromised by narrow interests or by the political agendas of parent governments.

Less than a year after preparing this chapter, on July 10, 2007, Commissioner Schornack's appointment as Boundary Commisioner and as the US Chair of the International Joint Commission were terminated by President George W. Bush. The reason for the termination was Schornack's refusal to subordinate a Boundary Commission decision to the ideological and political interests of the

Bush Administration. The Boundary Commissioners, consisting of Schornack and a Canadian counterpart, decided by consensus to require removal of a newly built concrete wall located within the twenty foot (six meter) wide "clear vista" that defines the US-Canadian boundary. Protection of this "clear vista" is required by the relevant boundary treaty and is consistent with more than a century of Commission practice.

The Bush Administration asserted that the disposition of the wall was to be determined by the United States Department of Justice and not the International Boundary Commission. The Department of Justice refused to commit to the removal of the wall despite the decision already reached by the Commissioners.

Administration officials also threatened Schornack with the loss of his US Chairmanship of the International Joint Commission, a paid position, in an effort to pressure him to submit to their authority and their property rights agenda, even though the Joint Commission post and the Boundary Commissioner post were created by different treaties and had different duties. In this way, the Administration challenged the independence of both entities.

A legal challenge of the Administration's action is now before the US Court of Appeals in the Ninth Circuit. Central to the legal challenge is the international character and independence of the International Boundary Commission. The cavalier dismissal of the Chairman of the International Joint Commission because of a dispute related to his capacity as International Boundary Commissioner exposes both Commissions to interference and loss of independence. It is more than a little ironic that just when the history of the Commission permits the factors which explain its success to be identified, a parent government would seek to undermine that success.

Henry Vaux, Jr., Series Editor

Notes

1 Treaty Between the United States and Great Britain Relating to Boundary Waters, and Questions Arising Between the United States and Canada.
2 *Ibid.* Article III.
3 *Ibid.* Article IX.
4 Delli Priscoli, Jerome 1997, « Water and civilisation: reframing the debate on water and conflict, » a paper delivered at the Ninth World Water Congress, Montreal, Canada, September 1–6.
5 Yoffe, S. and Wolf, A. "Water, Conflict and Cooperation: Geographical Perspective." *Cambridge Review of International Affairs.* Vol. 12 #2, Spring/Summer 1999, pp. 197–213.
6 *Ibid.* See Article VIII.
7 *Ibid.* See Article VIII.
8 *Ibid.* See Article VIII.
9 *Ibid.* See Article XII.

13 An overview of the International Joint Commission of Canada and the United States

Jack P. Blaney

One hundred years ago, the United States and Canada sealed a treaty that, in some ways, was far ahead of its time.

At the turn of the last century there were two disputes over the use of shared waters: one for the allocation of the St. Mary's and Milk Rivers in the West, and one over the use of the Niagara River between Lake Erie and Lake Ontario. The Boundary Waters Treaty of 1909 dealt with these two issues but, perhaps more importantly, also created a comprehensive, rules-based regime with an effective dispute avoidance and settlement mechanism that has worked to prevent and resolve transboundary water disputes between Canada and the United States for almost 100 years. This regime has effectively dispelled the old adage that is often referred to in western North America that "whiskey is for drinking; but water is for fighting." Instead, transboundary water and (in some cases) air disputes between Canada and the United States have been dealt with peacefully and, for the most part, amicably by pursuing the common good of both countries.

The basic purpose of the Boundary Waters Treaty is to avoid or resolve disputes between Canada and the United States over waters that run along or across the international boundary. The treaty thus created a unique international institution – the International Joint Commission of Canada and United States (IJC) – to help the two national governments achieve the treaty's objectives.

The IJC has two principal responsibilities: a so-called "application" function and a "reference" function. Under the application function, the IJC is requested by the governments to approve certain projects (such as dams) in waters that flow along or across the boundary and to oversee their operation. Under the reference function, the IJC investigates and advises on matters that are assigned to it by the governments.

The Boundary Waters Treaty is worded and applied, and the Commission operates, on the basis of absolute equality between the two countries. This may be considered remarkable given the disparity in the size of their populations and economies – the United States is 10 times the size of Canada in both its population and its economy.

The Commission has six members – three appointed by the United States and three by Canada. All commissioners have equal authority and power. The Commission's Rules of Procedure (Rule 2) require that two chairs – one for the

Canadian section and one for the U.S. section – be appointed by the commissioners of each section. However, in practice, the governments have selected who will serve as chairs.

The U.S. commissioners are appointed at the highest level in the U.S. Federal Government, that is by the President with the concurrence of the Senate. Their Canadian counterparts likewise are appointed by the highest level in the Government of Canada, the Governor-in-Council (the cabinet).

The treaty allows decisions by a majority of commissioners, and the Commission's rules require that at least four commissioners concur in any decision to ensure that all decisions have the support of at least one commissioner from each country. In fact, in current practice, the commissioners usually reach decisions by consensus.

Unlike many other international organizations, commissioners do not formally represent their countries. Instead, on appointment, each commissioner signs a declaration, based on Article XII of the treaty, which states:

"Each commissioner … shall, … make and subscribe a solemn declaration in writing that he will faithfully and impartially perform the duties imposed upon him under this treaty." The everyday application of this declaration is that commissioners feel obliged to act in the best interests of both countries.

It is important to emphasize that the IJC was created, and operates, as a binational organization, not a bilateral one. That is, it operates without instructions from the governments; commissioners are not delegates of their countries; commissioners are expected to work in the spirit of the treaty.

The Commission has dealt with almost 100 matters since its inception in 1911. Over that time, it has divided formally along national lines on only two occasions. Both occasions involved the use and allocation of water in the arid western region.

As already noted, the Boundary Waters Treaty created a comprehensive rules-based regime for dealing with transboundary water issues between Canada and the United States.

Article I sets out rights to navigation of the ships and citizens of the two countries. Article II deals with jurisdiction and control over the use and diversion of waters that subsequently flow across the boundary or into boundary waters. Articles III and IV set out requirements for binational approval – either by the governments or the IJC – (1) for certain projects in boundary waters that would affect levels or flows in the other country, and (2) for certain projects in transboundary rivers or in waters flowing from boundary waters that would raise levels across the boundary in the upstream country. In cases in which the IJC is asked to provide approval, the Commission must follow certain principles that have been agreed upon by Canada and the United States as set out in Article VIII. These include that each country shall have equal and similar rights in the use of boundary waters on its own side of the border; that an order of precedence shall be observed among municipal, navigation, power, and irrigation uses; and that in cases in which obstructions in one country raise the natural level in the other country, the IJC "shall require, as a condition of its approval thereof, that suitable and adequate provision, approved by it, be made for the protection and indemnity of all interests on the other side of the line which may be injured thereby."

Article IV of the treaty also contains one of the most fundamental and far-reaching principles that govern water relations between Canada and the United States. In a clear, straight-forward, and unqualified sentence the two countries agree that boundary waters and waters flowing across the boundary must not be polluted in either country to the injury of health or property in the other country. The environmental consequences of this declaration are remarkably prescient, and it took international law some time to catch up with the intent and purpose of this article.

The treaty gives the IJC a number of responsibilities. First, as mentioned above, it must respond to "references" – formal requests from the two national governments to look into a specific matter or problem along the border and to make findings and recommendations for action by the two governments to resolve the problem. (Although these references have usually been related to transboundary water and air issues, they can, in fact, be directed to any matter or problem along the border. In one instance, the Commission was asked to look at social and economic issues concerning Point Roberts, a small community that is part of Washington State, but which can be reached by land only by going through British Columbia.)

Reports on references are not regarded as decisions, and do not have the status or character of arbitral awards. However IJC reports are also released to the public at the same time as they are submitted to the two governments, and the force of public opinion can often be brought to bear in support of the Commission's recommendations. Also, by custom, the direction to the IJC to undertake a reference comes from both governments in the same terms, and at the same time. There is therefore an implied obligation on both governments to provide the Commission with the resources that it needs to carry out the reference, and to deal with the Commission's report in a responsive way. A high percentage of IJC recommendations have been acted upon by the two governments.

In addition to being asked to address specific problems, the Commission also receives long-term, permanent references from the two governments. These include requests to assist and oversee the way in which the governments carry out certain other international agreements between themselves. This is done in the Great Lakes Water Quality Agreement and in the International Air Quality Agreement which will be discussed below.

The treaty does provide, in Article X, for the governments to refer matters to the Commission for a binding arbitral award. Such references, however, require the concurrence of the U.S. Senate and the Canadian Governor General in Council. No references under Article X have ever been given to the Commission.

As also noted earlier, the Commission makes decisions on applications for approval to build certain structures in boundary waters, in waters flowing from boundary waters, and in transboundary rivers. Such applications for structures are submitted to the Commission through the government of the country in whose territory the project will be built. That government makes an initial determination whether binational approval is required under the treaty, and, if so, whether the

IJC will be asked to approve the project or whether the project should be approved by a special agreement between the two governments. The apportionment of water under these IJC control orders (Orders of Approval) has obvious economic, environmental, and social impacts. In these cases, the Commission can decide to allow the application, to deny it, or to allow it with conditions – the latter is usually what has happened. If an Order of Approval with conditions is made, the IJC then sets up an international control body (Board of Control) to oversee its implementation.

As a matter of practice, and consistent with the spirit of the treaty, the Commission requires that all its boards and other advisory bodies be made up of an equal number of members from Canada and the United States. Further, these members serve the Commission in their personal and professional capacities and not as representatives of their governments, employers or other institutions. Most members are drawn from various levels of government or from universities. There are obvious benefits to be gained from having officials from both countries work out solutions to binational issues in the impartial atmosphere of an IJC board. The Commission, in turn, makes recommendations to governments, and, if the governments decide to act on them, the governments may call on the same officials to implement those recommendations. The boards play a vital role in joint fact-finding which serves as a basis for building consensus at all levels.

The IJC has 15 such control bodies along the entire U.S.-Canada boundary. They govern the operation of dams on the Columbia, Okanogan, and Kootenay Rivers in Washington State and British Columbia, and on the St. Croix and St. John Rivers in New Brunswick and Maine. They also are responsible for overseeing the operation of structures on the St. Mary's River at Sault Ste. Marie that control the outflows from Lake Superior into Lakes Michigan, Huron, and Erie, and the operation of works in the international section of the St. Lawrence River – near Cornwall and Massena – that control the outflows from Lake Ontario. (The IJC also has a control board that oversees flows in the Niagara River, but it does so under a reference under Article IX, rather than pursuant to an Order of Approval under Articles III and VIII.)

In a few cases, the governments have concluded special agreements like the 1950 Niagara River Diversion Treaty and the 1964 Columbia River Treaty which, in effect, establish special regimes for those rivers that supersede the general provisions of the Boundary Waters Treaty. Even in these cases, however, the governments have often turned to the IJC for advice in developing and implementing these special agreements.

There is no appeal from the Commission's decisions on Orders of Approval. However, the IJC may review and amend its own orders, either on its own initiative or in response to an outside request. In 1997, the Commission informed the governments that because many of its Orders of Approval have been in place for a very long time, the IJC intends to review all its orders systematically as circumstances permit.

A special IJC study board has undertaken a five-year examination of Lake Ontario and the St. Lawrence River system to determine whether the Commission's existing control order should be modified to take into account factors, such as the environment and recreational boating, that were either not considered or have changed since the Commission's Order of Approval was last amended in 1956. The Commission is now consulting governments and seeking comments from interested members of the public before deciding whether to amend its existing Order of Approval. (Under Article XII of the Boundary Waters Treaty, the Commission is required to give all parties interested in a matter before it a "convenient opportunity to be heard," and the Commission must adopt rules of procedure that are "in accordance with justice and equity," as that phrase is understood in the two countries.)

The IJC has just begun a review of its control order at Sault Ste. Marie for the Upper Great Lakes – Lakes Superior, Michigan, Huron, and Erie.

The waters of the Great Lakes are one of the world's most precious natural assets. The quality of these waters is critical to the Great Lakes' ecosystem and to the nearly 40 million people on both sides of the border who rely on it for drinking water, food, work, and recreation.

In 1972, the Great Lakes Water Quality Agreement was signed by Canada and the United States in response to the growing concerns of the millions of people living around the lakes about the lakes' deterioration and, more specifically, in response to IJC reports about their poor condition.

The 1972 agreement was replaced six years later by the current 1978 Great Lakes Water Quality Agreement in which the two governments committed themselves "to restore and maintain the chemical, physical, and biological integrity of the waters of the Great Lakes Basin Ecosystem."

The Great Lakes Water Quality Agreement requires the IJC to assist the two governments in implementing the agreement. This includes making a major report at least every two years to the governments and to the public assessing progress and providing advice and recommendations on how to achieve the agreement's objectives. Special reports on particular issues related to water quality may be issued at any time.

Significant progress has been made in restoring the lakes since the first Great Lakes Water Quality Agreement was signed in 1972. However, serious problems remain, and new threats continue to emerge, such as new chemicals and pharmaceuticals, invasive species, and the effects of intensive agriculture and ongoing urbanization.

The agreement provides that every six years – after every third biennial report from the Commission – the two national governments must carry out a review of the agreement. The Commission's last biennial report, issued in September 2004, triggered the need for a new review by the governments, which is now under way. At the request of the governments, the Commission held an extensive round of public meetings in the Great Lakes Basin to obtain the views of the public, and it passed these views on to the governments. The Commission also prepared its own advice to governments.

The Commission has focused in recent years on the highly contentious issue of bulk removals of water from the Great Lakes Basin, including diversions through means such as canals, pipelines, or modified channels. In 1998, the IJC was called upon in a reference to report on whether the waters of the Great Lakes could sustain bulk removals of water to locations beyond their basin, particularly to the United States.

This reference followed an application to Ontario by the Nova Corporation in 1998 to export water by tanker from the Ontario side of Lake Superior. Although the Ontario license for this export was later rescinded, the Nova application caused a great deal of public concern about other possible bulk water removals from the lakes.

The IJC issued an interim report in 1999, and a final report in 2000, titled, "The Protection of the Waters of the Great Lakes." The IJC found that the Great Lakes are not a renewable resource and do not offer a vast reservoir for an increasingly thirsty world. The report noted that although the Great Lakes contain about 20 percent of the fresh water on the earth's surface, only 1 percent of this water is renewed each year from snowmelt and rain. If all interests in the basin are considered, there is never a "surplus" of water in the Great Lakes system. The Commission concluded in its 2000 report that existing international trade law obligations do not prevent Canada and the United States from taking measures to protect their water resources and preserve the integrity of the Great Lakes Basin ecosystem. The Commission also concluded that removals of water from the basin reduce the resilience of the system and its capacity to cope with unpredictable stresses, such as climate change. The Commission therefore recommended that governments take a number of specific measures to ensure that removals of water from the basin and consumptive uses in the basin will not endanger the integrity of the Great Lakes Basin ecosystem. The Commission confirmed these recommendations in a follow-up report in 2004.

The U.S. Congress had earlier passed the Water Resources Development Act of 1986, which stated that no diversion is allowed from the lakes if the governor of any Great Lakes state objects, even if the project does not involve their state.

In 1999, Ontario enacted a water-taking and transfer regulation, which generally prohibits transfers out of Ontario's part of the Great Lakes and the St. Lawrence basin. Quebec also generally prohibits transfers of water outside that province. In December 2002, the Canadian government proclaimed amendments to the International Boundary Waters Treaty Act (Bill C-6) and issued International Boundary Waters Regulations which prohibit new bulk removals from Canadian boundary waters, including the Great Lakes-St. Lawrence Basin.

On 18 June 2001, the eight U.S. Great Lakes states and the Canadian provinces of Ontario and Quebec concluded Annex 2001 to the 1985 Great Lakes Charter, a non-binding, good-faith arrangement among the Great Lakes states and provinces designed to protect the lakes. After lengthy negotiations, the Great Lakes governors and premiers signed agreements on 13 December 2005 to implement the annex and, with limited exceptions, to ban new diversions outside the Great Lakes–St. Lawrence River Basin. The water resources agreement among the Great Lakes states and Ontario and Quebec will again be a non-binding, good-faith arrangement (because the states and provinces do not have the authority to conclude international treaties between themselves). However, a water resources compact or agreement among the U.S. Great Lakes states alone will be binding under U.S. law. These agreements must still be implemented through state and provincial legislation, and, under the U.S. Constitution, the compact will also have to be approved by the U.S. Congress.

Although not expressly stated in the Boundary Waters Treaty, it has been recognized for some time that the Commission's inherent responsibility for preventing and resolving transboundary disputes requires it to alert governments to situations along the border that have the potential for transboundary conflict so that early action can be taken to avoid or resolve that conflict. This can be one of the Commission's most valuable roles.

The duty to alert is explicit with respect to transboundary air issues. In 1966, the governments gave the IJC a reference that requested the Commission "to take note of air pollution problems in boundary areas ... which may come to its attention from any source. If at any time the Commission considers it appropriate to do so, the Commission is invited to draw such problems to the attention of both Governments."

The Commission also has been given a number of other ongoing references that require it to look at air issues. These include a 1975 reference on the state of air quality in the Detroit-Windsor and Port Huron-Sarnia areas; a reference in the 1978 Great Lakes Water Quality Agreement with respect to reducing atmospheric deposition of toxic substances to the Great Lakes Basin Ecosystem (Annex 15); and a reference in the 1991 Air Quality Agreement to invite public comments on progress reports and provide the governments with a synthesis of the public's views.

Looking to the future, the Commission has come to recognize that local people, given appropriate assistance, are best positioned to resolve local transboundary issues. The Commission also believes that effective trust-building and problem-solving capabilities at the local watershed level will substantially prevent, reduce, and perhaps, in some cases, eliminate the need to directly involve the two national governments or the IJC in a full formal reference to resolve specific international watershed issues. In the Commission's view, creating such local solution-building capabilities will represent a significant investment in the management of the precious water resources that Canada and the United States share.

To move this idea forward, the Commission advised the governments in June 2005, in a discussion paper on the International Watersheds Initiative, that the IJC's first priority under this initiative is to strengthen the watershed capabilities of its boards in the St. Croix, Rainy, and Red River watersheds. The Commission expects that these watershed initiatives will be successful and that others will follow. This initiative is a high priority for the Commission, and provides an opportunity to manage amicably the United States' and Canada's precious and shared water resources.

The mission statement which captures succinctly the Commission's responsibilities, states:

The International Joint Commission prevents and resolves disputes between the United States of America and Canada under the 1909 Boundary Waters Treaty and pursues the common good of both countries as an independent and objective adviser to the two governments.

In particular, the Commission rules upon applications for approval of projects affecting boundary or transboundary waters and may regulate the operation of these projects; it assists the two countries in the protection of the transboundary environment, including the implementation of the Great Lakes Water Quality Agreement and the improvement of transboundary air quality; and it alerts the governments to emerging issues along the boundary that may give rise to bilateral disputes.

In the words of one close observer: "An uncommonly good treaty."

Acknowledgement

I want to recognize the substantial contributions of Michael Vechsler to this chapter.

14 Water management in mountain regions

The impact of large dams

Pedro Arrojo-Agudo

During the twentieth century, the dominant approach with respect to water management has been based on supplying side strategies and massive public subsidies. This approach has induced the development of large dams, mainly in mountain areas, flooding inhabited valleys, affecting the livelihood of riparian communities, and degrading aquatic biodiversity. During the last few decades, this approach has fallen into crisis and new ecosystem approaches have emerged, based on the principles of sustainability, inter-territorial equity and participative governance. A new and better perspective has transpired with respect to water and river management in mountain regions.

14.1 Introduction

One of the factors that has impacted mountain regions the most during the twentieth century has been, without any doubt, the construction of big dams, flooding inhabited valleys, and seriously degrading the biodiversity and the livelihood of riparian communities. The dominant water management approach during the twentieth century has induced supplying side strategies based on developing large-scale hydraulic infrastructures, and relying upon massive public subsidies. A brief historic analysis of these strategies will allow us to understand better the role mountain regions played in water management during this century.

14.1.1 Hydraulic structuralism in the twentieth century

A comparison of Spanish and American hydraulic history may seem imbalanced, given the vast size difference between the two countries. Nevertheless, it is quite interesting to observe that, despite different cultural and historical realities, parallel processes exhibiting profound similarities have emerged since the end of the nineteenth century. Therefore, we will use the experience of both countries as a reference for a water management model, which has dominated the entire world over the course of the twentieth century (Arrojo and Naredo. 1997).

The fascinating history of the colonization of the American west showed water to be one of the main protagonists in how the colonization process was organized. The first colonies introduced by Spanish missionaries along the California coast, between Los Angeles and San Francisco, benefited from the introduction of Arab irrigation methods with their refined drainage techniques.

Later, in the American Midwest, Mormons used their legends and beliefs to make the introduction of irrigation a centerpiece of their colonization strategy. Their vocation as "God's chosen people" was to transform the desert between the Green River and the Snake River into a new American Promised Land. By the end of the nineteenth century, they controlled approximately 2,500 hectares of irrigated lands in the middle of the desert. (Reisner 1993). After successfully irrigating alluvial areas (with good natural drainage), they met with failure in the steppe regions in which salinity and drainage problems sorely tested their scarce knowledge of irrigation. But they were soon applying the Arab drainage techniques used in the irrigation systems of the Spanish missions in California.

The repeated failure of private initiative to construct the great water works made possible by civil engineering led to the application of John Wesley Powell's thesis to the effect that the projects should be implemented using the financial and management capacity that a modern, well organized state could offer. In 1902, the United States government launched the first public program of great irrigation works through the newly formed Bureau of Reclamation. In less than a half century, thousands of great dams were built, generally in mountainous regions, along with tens of thousands of kilometers of large canals through the most rugged topography and inhospitable deserts. This resulted in millions of hectares of irrigated land on behalf of "public interest" through public financing.

Another use that would justify the construction of large dams in the general interest was hydroelectric power. Beyond its economic value, hydroelectric power production became a military priority, due to the aeronautical industry's need for aluminum. In fact, American military supremacy during World War II was largely attributable to its capacity to produce hydroelectric energy in order to satisfy the voracious aeronautical industry's appetite for aluminum to build combat aircraft.

In Spain, hydraulic engineering traditions have their historical roots in the ancient Roman Empire, although it is in Medieval Muslim Spain that cultural developments in Al-Andalus would foster the most advanced engineering, drainage, and irrigation techniques of the era.

By the eighteenth century, the French "Enlightenment" would lead to more advances in civil engineering in the area of grand navigation canals which, in Spain, would stimulate progress with regard to irrigation-related objectives. Important projects, such as the Imperial Canal of Aragon, the Castilla Canal, the Murcia Canal and the construction of important dams permitted the implantation of irrigation systems over tens of thousands of hectares. But it is during the nineteenth century that the development of hydraulic engineering establishes the foundation for modern hydraulic structuralism. A range of laws encouraged the private sector to take the initiative with regard to irrigation and regulation works (Pinilla 1997). Nevertheless, the few attempts that were made failed in Spain as they had in the United States. These projects required large investments and long-term amortizations, which rendered the private finance model untenable.

Costa's Regenerationist Movement, except for multiple contextual differences, would generate theories, approaches, and projects similar to those proposed over the same time period by Powell in the United States. In similar fashion, Costa defended the introduction of public initiative as a key to promoting large-scale irrigation and water control works. In 1902, the same year in which the first public, large-scale irrigation plan was drawn up in the United States, the National Plan for Hydraulic Development ("Plan Nacional de Aprovechamientos Hidráulicos") was approved in Spain. Soon, water management was organized by catchment basin, and the Hydrographical Confederation of the Ebro River became the first Catchment Basin Agency in the world.

However, in 1936, the civil war and the victory of fascism marked a hiatus in Spanish social, cultural and political life, preventing the implementation of regenerationist hydraulic plans for almost two decades. In the 1950s, these plans would be reintroduced, thus giving rise to a sort of "hydro populism" in the service of the regime, which became quite popular.

After the death of Franco, cultural inertia combined with existing interests would prolong both the existence of a hydraulic bureaucracy and its attendant power structures, as well as that of old ideas, conceptions, and structuralist strategies (Diaz Marta 1993).

As a result of having made the development of large hydraulic works a priority irrespective of the political ideology of the government in power, Spain is currently one of the countries with the most hydraulic infrastructure per inhabitant and per square kilometer in the world, with 53 000 hm3 of reservoir capacity, the same as that of California, which is similar in size (Arrojo and Naredo 1997).

With this approach, mountain regions became the best spaces for building the large dams that could regulate water flows in the main rivers with two main goals: large-scale irrigation schemes and hydropower production.

14.1.2 The crisis of the structuralist model and of supply-side strategies

By the 1960s in the United States, the congressional representatives of the Eastern states (who contributed the major part of public funds) began to protest against the large investments in hydraulic mega projects in the Western states. As a result, cost-benefit analyses and the refilling of government coffers depleted by these investments within reasonable time periods became requirements. Nevertheless, repeated failures to comply with these commitments called into question a management model that had held sway for half a century.

Throughout this period, the Bureau of Reclamation (a civil institution) along with the U.S. Army Corps of Engineers (a military institution that promoted civil works projects) became powerful lobbying and pressure groups. The large-scale and frequently shady dealings involving construction, and hydroelectric power, along with agricultural and urban land speculation in connection with large-scale hydroelectric projects led to the invention of the term "pork barrel" (Reisner 1993) to refer to the system of public financing of large-scale hydraulic works in the United States.

The disappearance of salmon in the great rivers along the Pacific coast and the flooding of emblematic natural areas began to weigh on the public conscience. Public pressure, for example, blocked the construction of the Echo Dam on the upper Colorado River, but did not, on the other hand, prevent the construction of the Glen Canyon Dam. In 1963, millions of Americans reacted with consternation to images of the flooding of 320 kilometers of the emblematic Grand Canyon of the Colorado River and its tributaries in order to produce electricity.

Tenacious criticism of the financial accounts and increasing ecological sensitivity would make the system totter on its foundations. In 1978, President Carter, confronting powerful lobbies dominating the Capitol, vetoed the projects on the so-called "hit list," which was essentially a long list of large-scale hydraulic projects that were to be definitively abandoned. Thus, the heralded change in the approach to water management strategy was made explicit. Dozens of large dam projects intended to supply Los Angeles, such as the Klamath River or Columbia project with its 2,000 kilometers of canals and 450 kilometers of tunnels, were set aside (Reisner 1993).

In Spain, while Franco was in power, the regime's ruling families, along with large electric and construction companies, turned large-scale hydraulic projects into private business opportunities, based on the use of public funds. In an authoritarian regime in which criticism was impossible, bureaucratization and corruption profoundly degraded the model.

Unlike in the United States, where major urban areas above a certain size were never flooded (with the exception of Hispanic and Indian settlements), in Spain, the construction of more than 1300 large dams resulted in the flooding of numerous inhabited valleys, affecting hundreds of towns, especially in mountainous regions (Arrojo and Naredo 1997).

In addition, a large number of fluvial ecosystems experienced serious ecological degradation, resulting in the extinction of species as emblematic as the sturgeon, salmon or eel. Furthermore, water quality and the regenerative capacity of fluvial ecosystems was seriously compromised as a result of which the consequences of a clearly unsustainable water management model became manifest.

In the 1990s, the announcement of a national hydrological plan (NHP) that would involve the flooding of 200 valleys gave rise to a public protest movement against the construction of new dams, mainly in mountain areas affected by these dams. This movement gained momentum as a result of the proposal to construct a huge inter-basin water transfer from the Ebro River. Beyond those directly impacted, this movement mobilized more than a million citizens against the NHP and in favor of a new water culture (Nueva Cultura del Agua) between 2001 and 2002. This massive mobilization resulted in the blockage of European funds intended to make the execution of these proposed large-scale works possible. After the elections, under the new government, and within the legal framework of the new EU Water Framework Directive, the decision to abandon the Ebro Transfer Project and to revise most of the projected big dams closed the process in a way similar to the "hit list" veto in the United States (Arrojo 2003).

14.2 Values at stake in mountain regions

During the twentieth century, the principle of the domination of nature led to productive water management approaches. The predominant supply-side strategies, based on large hydraulic works paid for by public subsidies (and consequently with a weak economic outlook), introduced an approach entirely based on the exploitation of resources (water and territory). This had dramatic social and environmental consequences, mainly in mountain areas.

In headwaters regions, which usually coincide with mountain areas, the most important values at stake are:

* The regional value of the valleys for population settlement.
* Environmental values tied to landscapes and mountain ecosystems.
* The hydroelectric potential of high-elevation waters.
* Values and uses tied to high water quality.
* The opportunity costs inherent in the orographic potential for constructing hydraulic works.
* Recreational and emotional values frequently connected to the development of services.
* The value of controlling upstream water for downstream irrigation.
* Environmental values and services downstream, along with their economic benefits.
* The relationship between ethical values and the maintenance of an equitable distribution of socioeconomic resources at the inter-regional level.

Unfortunately most of these values have not been taken into account under the water management model, which dominated the twentieth century. The only questions considered to be of importance were water as a resource, the power capacity of water, and the potential of valleys as water reservoirs.

14.2.1 The value of valleys for population settlement in mountain regions

In its final report published in London at the end of 2000, the World Commission on Dams (WCD), recognized that, although they had precisely calculated the millions of cubic meters that could be stored in more than 45,000 large dams constructed in the world over the course of the twentieth century, they had been unable to calculate how many people had been forced out of their homes and towns when regions were flooded by these dams. The overall global level of physical displacement could range from 40 to 80 million (WCD 2000).

From my perspective, what is most impressive about these figures is not so much their magnitude, but rather the lack of knowledge and the level of imprecision surrounding them. Declaring "from 40 to 80 million" involves the recognition that it is simply not known – a tragedy carried out stealthily and silently.

The major part of these displacements occurred in mountain regions in which the affected populations are usually considered marginal. The WCD report itself underscores that such calculations refer only to those people directly affected by flooding of their homes, while it is noted that the number of people forced out of their homes as an indirect consequence of dam construction is much higher than the number forced out as a direct consequence.

The greatest affliction borne by the mountain regions as a result of the impact of large dams is, without a doubt, the loss of social networks, both in the flooded valleys themselves and in other areas connected to and dependent on the flooded regions. Frequently, the flooded valleys integrated entire regions as a result of having constituted central cores with their attendant health services, schools, and commerce. Although we are discussing water management in mountain regions, the most precious and scarce resource is usually the habitable lands themselves; in other words, the valley bottoms rather than the water.

Mountain populations often consist of socially and politically vulnerable minority groups. Difficult communications and hard living conditions have created distinct and relatively closed ways of life which have favored the conservation of identity markers and cultural values whose preservation is extremely important not only for the communities themselves but for society as a whole. Nevertheless, these elements of social and cultural identity are as fragile as they are valuable. The breaking up of regional valley settlements usually results in a diaspora and in the destruction of the community as such and, therefore, in the irreversible disappearance of those values. For this reason, economic compensation and resettlement in other areas (which are not even guaranteed in many cases) do not assure the continuing cohesion and survival of these communities.

In many cases, as we shall see below, the ecological impact of hydraulic policy on rivers located in headwaters regions has had the most severe socioeconomic consequences on riverbank communities downstream.

Recently, the progressive recognition of social values involved when a big dam is projected to flood inhabited valleys in Spain has led to proposed Territorial Compensation Plans that are used to imply similar costs to the investment budgeted for the construction of the dam itself.

14.2.2 Environmental values connected to mountain landscapes and ecosystems

Mountain regions have historically been poor. Severe environmental conditions have hindered both agricultural, economic and other development (for example in industry, and commerce) while keeping populations low. For thousands of years, nature set limits to growth, and the land's inhabitants respected and wisely managed these limits in a sustainable way. This permitted the conservation of ecosystems in their unspoiled state, while in other regions, such as in grassland areas, human settlement was characterized by a harmonious and sustainable relationship with the natural environment.

With industrial and urban development, migrants leaving for the cities abandoned these lands. Mountain regions came to be considered as inhospitable areas with little value to society as a whole. Nevertheless, some decades later, the accelerated environmental and social degradation experienced in urban areas, and even in a large number of rural areas, has generated a growing appreciation for the role of mountain areas in conserving environmental quality and promoting health. In summary, the contradictions inherent in the unsustainability of our development model have led to the emergence of an appreciation for ecological and aesthetic values related to mountain landscapes in regions that until recently were marginalized and abused.

In many countries, mountain areas constitute a priceless repository of pristine natural heritage. As a result, nature and national parks, biosphere reserves and other entities set up to protect the integrity of this heritage from the encroachments of our destructive consumer society abound. A large number of these threats are connected to water management. The wholesale construction of large dams to regulate water flows, the proliferation of hydroelectric miniplants, or the construction of ski resorts with artificial snow are examples of these.

In this general context of relatively well-preserved natural environments, rivers, lakes, and wetlands in the headwaters of catchment basins tend to be the best-preserved aquatic ecosystems. The obvious dependence of middle and lower elevation river sections on high elevation river flows means that the conservation of headwater regions has ramifications that extend far beyond the importance of conserving the ecosystems that they host.

When we discuss the importance of conserving headwaters, we are referring not only to water quality or to aquatic ecosystems in their unspoiled state, but also to other environmental values connected to the conservation of regions; for instance, forests and vegetative cover, taking into account their interconnectedness with rivers, lagoons, and aquifers. The extent to which these regions are conserved will influence erosion intensity, run-off and the rate of percolation, which feeds aquifers in their role as natural river regulators.

Lastly, it is necessary to underscore that ecological dependence is not one directional, from the headwaters down to the middle and lower elevation river courses; in fact, the way in which these lower courses are managed also has an important impact on higher regions, especially with regard to the conservation of migratory fish species, such as salmon and eel.

14.2.3 The hydroelectric potentiality of water in up-land regions

Above and beyond their ecosystem and environmental functions, river flows in headwater regions store high levels of potential energy (with respect to sea level) and, in addition, add high value due to their low contamination levels and low concentrations of dissolved salts. We will analyze the ramifications of these characteristics in the next section. This potential energy can be exploited as hydropower, offering a renewable energy source with high opportunity value. In fact, it can be characterized as high-quality energy for three fundamental reasons:

1   greenhouse gases are not produced;

2   it is renewable;
3   it is a controlled source whose production can be concentrated during peak hours.

Nevertheless, although this energy source is characterized as clean, the infra-structures required to produce it create environmental impacts that cannot be seen in this positive light. In many cases, at issue are large reservoirs whose societal and environmental impact is well known; in other cases, what is at issue are the miniplants which frequently result in the drying up of long stretches of riverbeds in mountainous regions or, at least, in their ecological degradation and the loss of many recreational uses, such as white-water rafting, fishing, and bathing.

14.2.4 Resource values and uses connected to high water quality in mountain regions

In the upper reaches of fluvial basins, water quality tends to be high, because it has not yet received contaminating spills or saline drainage. In arid regions, such as the Mediterranean, the saline content of river flows is particularly important. Declining water quality related to salinity, resulting from both human intervention and natural processes such as salt leaching in the drainage from salty areas, negatively affects the use-value of this resource. This progressive decline in river-flow quality from its essentially pure state in headwaters regions down to its final mixing with seawater in estuaries can be measured in energy units through the energy required to restore the water quality using reverse osmosis.

The productivity problems engendered by saltiness in irrigation waters are well known. In addition, the range of possible uses presented by such water is drastically reduced (urban water in EU requires less than 1000 µS/cm). Without a doubt, the extent to which water quality is an important resource value reaches its maximum expression in the willingness of consumers to pay for bottled drinking water. The high-market value attached to mineral waters, reflects the increasing importance of health as a value. As is well known, these high-quality waters generally originate in fluvial headwater areas. The tendency of multinationals to appropriate springs is indicative of a business approach that revolves around marketing these high-quality waters.

14.2.5 The opportunity cost of orographic potential for setting up big dams (flow control)

The rugged relief found in mountainous regions has constituted a value that has played an extremely important role in hydraulic policy as practised over the course of the twentieth century. As one would expect, it is in these territories where we can find the highest ratio of dam regulatory capacity to unit price invested. Along with these factors, the fluvial regime itself and the intended uses of the river flows constitute key determinants of control efficiency. In sum, what is involved is an opportunity value derived from the minimization of regulatory costs.

As one would expect, the construction of more than 45 000 large dams over the course of the twentieth century in the most suitable closed valleys has resulted in the imposition of the law of diminishing marginal returns and marginal costs increase. The study on the evolution of the control efficiency of dams in the United States, published in 1984 by the United States Geological Survey, is highly significant. After undertaking a detailed study of the 100 largest dams in the United States constructed between 1920 and 1960, the report concluded that the volume of flow regulated as a function of the physical capacity of these reservoirs decreased by a factor of 35.

In this sense, the opportunity value of mountain regions as areas favorable for this type of regulation projects has been decreasing as new project costs have increased and control efficiency continues to decrease.

14.2.6 Recreational and emotional values frequently connected to the development of tourist amenities

The increasing appreciation of environmental and scenic values in mountain regions centers particularly on rivers, which have become key areas for offering recreational services. Activities such as canoeing and white-water rafting, along with others such as canyoning or sport fishing have changed socioeconomic realities and perspectives for many mountain regions. In many cases, beyond these types of activities, rivers are coming to define regional identity while becoming key tourist attractions.

Often, these values are intangible and difficult to measure in monetary terms in a consistent way. Nevertheless, the activities and services promoted around mountain rivers permit the painting of an accurate economic portrait through an analysis of the profits generated by these activities, or through a calculation of the consumer surplus achieved using methods such as "travel cost" The scientific-technical articles quantifying these environmental intangibles related to recreational and emotional values published over the last two decades reflect an increasing appreciation of their importance as society has become more aware of these values. In many cases involving large dams, the monetary quantification of this type of impact has resulted in costs that are nearly the same as the budget for construction of the dam itself. For instance, in the case of Biscarrués Dam, in Spain, the consumer surplus derived from the sacrificed rafting services was assessed on 6 billion pesetas (US$45 million at 1993 rates)at the beginning of the 1990s, when the budget for building the dam was 9.5 billion pesetas (US$57 million at 2000 rates) (Arrojo and Fernández 2000).

14.2.7 The resource value of irrigation downstream

Especially in arid and semi-arid basins, irrigation has encouraged economic and social development. As was explained before, since the beginning of the twentieth century the technical capacity to control massive river flows by means of large dams has made possible the cultivation of approximately 300 million hectares, according to the FAO (McCully 2004), and another 130 million hectares using underground water (Llamas and Martínez-Santos 2005).

Irrigation in these regions and climates not only doubles crop production, but also guarantees harvests (freeing them from the effects of variations in rainfall) and permits crop diversification.

However, the introduction of new irrigation works, which until a few decades ago was considered an engine for development, is now being questioned for a variety of reasons:

- The law of diminishing marginal returns and increasing marginal costs calls the profitability of this type of projects into question.
- The steep decline in the profitability of agriculture, caused by the negative inflationary differential in the sector (surpassing the growth in productivity), is currently accelerated by market liberalization (Arrojo 1998).
- The sustainability crisis affecting aquatic ecosystems and the grave social consequences as a result of the construction of large dams in mountain regions.
- The degradation and salinization of the soil in irrigable regions which now affects 20 percent of the world's irrigable land area, according to calculations published by the World Commission on Dams in its final report (WCD 2000).

In addition, the supply-side strategies characterized by massive public subsidies upon which has depended the development of large-scale irrigation has promoted inefficient use of water with the result of lack of economic rationality.

The WCD final report concludes: "… irrigation dam projects in the WCD Knowledge Base have all too often failed to deliver on promised financial and economic profitability …" "A sectorial review of technical, financial and economic performance suggests that of the dams in the Knowledge Base, those designed to deliver irrigation services have typically fallen short of physical targets, did not recover their costs and have been less profitable in economic terms than expected" (WCD 2000).

Even the World Bank recognized, in post-evaluation studies of irrigation projects funded by the Bank, that half the projects were unprofitable and more than three-quarters returned less than expected at appraisal.

In Spain, the assessment of the main large-scale irrigation projects under construction, linked to conflictive big dams (as Itoiz, Biscarrués, Castrovido, Yesa), present clear negative cost-benefit balances, with costs around €0.19 /m³ for developing extensive crops with a net margin around €0.12 /m³ (including subsidies) (Arrojo 2004).

Lastly, in each case it is necessary to carefully analyze the social values at stake. In some cases, these new irrigations have involved land redistribution, thus generating profound changes in social and economic structures. In other cases, under the guise of the common good, the interests of rich and influential corporate sectors have been favored. This is illustrated in the case of the Dez dam (McCully 2004), the largest dam built in Iran during the 60s. The project aimed to irrigate

80,000 hectares and benefit thousands of small-scale growers. However, the Shah decided that foreign agriculture and livestock companies (Chase Manhattan Bank, Bank of America, Shell, John Deere & Co, Transworld Agricultural Development) would achieve more efficient production for export. More than 17 000 peasants were driven from their lands.

14.2.8 Values and social-environmental services at stake downstream

Due to the reign of Hydraulic Structuralism throughout the twentieth century, there has been a tendency to disregard the social and environmental impact produced downstream by large hydraulic infrastructures. Rivers have been viewed as simple H_2O canals instead of as living ecosystems. What was overlooked from this perspective is that rivers not only direct vast quantities of water draining out of basins, but also direct large solid and nutrient flows. In addition, there has been a tendency to ignore the importance of the biodiversity harbored by riparian environments. And lastly, there has been a tendency to underestimate the grave socio-economic impact produced all over the world downstream by these hydraulic works, especially on poor communities whose way of life is strongly connected to ecosystems and fluvial cycles.

The direct and indirect impact of the unsustainable exploitation of rivers, lakes, and wetlands on natural production of food worldwide has been and continues to be serious, especially with regard to the natural productivity of protein-rich foods. It should be noted that fish is one of the principal sources of protein in the majority of underdeveloped or developing countries. It is often said that fish is the "poor man's protein." In Africa, this source accounts for more than 20 percent of animal proteins, on average; in Asia it accounts for almost 30 percent (ICLARM 1995). For many poor, inland communities around the world lacking access to coastal fisheries, the availability of fresh water fisheries is a key to their survival.

Throughout the twentieth century, the construction of large dams has been one of the key factors contributing to the drastic reduction of river fishing grounds with the resultant extinction of many species of fish and molluscs essential to the diets of riverbank communities. Some well-documented cases, among many others worth mentioning, are the Urra river in Columbia (WCD 2000), the Singkarak project in Sumatra, Lingjintan in China, Theun Hinboun in Laos, or Pak Mun in Thailand (Hubbel 1994). In all of these cases, large reservoirs upstream created serious obstacles to nutritional subsistence for thousands of persons in poor riverbank communities downstream.

We find another example of this in Southeast Asia where Thailand's accelerated industrial growth is motivating the construction of a system of large dams and inter-basin diversions from the Upper Mekong in order to provide cheap electricity and water resources. This group of mega projects threatens to cause serious ecological breakdowns with disastrous impacts on riverbank communities. It is estimated that 52 million people depend on the sustainability of the Mekong, from which they derive both agricultural products and fish for their nutritional sustenance (Moreth 1995).

But it is not only river fisheries that have been seriously affected; coastal fisheries, whose dependence on rivers has been definitively established, have suffered as well. The case of Aswan dam, on the Nile River, is paradigmatic. A year after having closed the dam, the sardine and anchovy harvest fell by more than 90 percent in the eastern Mediterranean. Today it is known that these species, among others, spawn in the estuaries of large rivers, taking advantage of the high concentration of continental nutrients which result from the sharp rise in water level in springtime. These nutrients fertilize marine life, especially in enclosed or semi-enclosed seas, which are generally poor in plankton. A similar breakdown occurred in the Sea of Cortes (in Baja California) as a result of the diversion of the Colorado River to irrigate the Imperial Valley and buttress urban development in the Los Angeles-San Diego corridor in the United States (Postel 1996).

Serious modifications in the natural cycle of many of the world's great rivers due to the construction of headwaters dams have eliminated traditional forms of agricultural production tied to fluvial flooding cycles. This has seriously compromised basic food production for many people. Such impacts have been particularly significant in African countries such as Niger, Chad, Nigeria, Sudan, Senegal or Mali, among others. In the north of Nigeria, the construction of the Bakalori dam over the Sokoto river led to the disappearance of 53 percent of traditional crops linked to the cycles of river flooding in the plains of the middle and lower basins, destroyed the grazing lands that served as a base for livestock in the zone and seriously affected the aquifers, depleting vital water reserves during periods of drought (Adams 1992). Similar cases have occurred, as indicated in reports published by the World Commission on Dams, along the Senegal River, as a result of which nearly 800 000 people experienced difficulty with traditional crop cultivation; near the Sobradinho reservoir in Brazil, with negative consequences for 11 000 peasant families; and near the Tarbela and Kotri dams in Pakistan, with the resultant loss of traditional grazing lands along nearby floodplains (WCD 2000).

As a large number of studies have shown (Abramovitz 1998), traditional food production systems (where fishing, livestock, forestry and agriculture are wisely combined) are not only more sustainable but also produce more (or give a better production) than methods depending on large dams in high basins.

In spite of its seriousness, much of the socioeconomic impact does not emerge in official statistics. The reason for this is that the harvests derived from these food sources, wisely managed in a sustainable relationship between rural communities and their surroundings, traditionally goes to local markets and self sustenance. From the point of view of market rationality, it is usually claimed that such modes of production suffer from low levels of economic efficiency. Nevertheless, if the social and environmental values at stake are taken into account, and if we adopt objectives that include sustainability and fairness, that so-called "inefficiency" becomes a high level of ecological-social efficiency. It is necessary, in short, to discern objectives when it comes time to define parameters of efficiency. When the objective is to resolve social and environmental problems rather than to produce more market value, it is necessary to define indicators of ecological-social efficiency. In this respect, the preservation of social structures and traditional methods of production in rural areas, in general offers communities the opportunity of development without losing their identity and cohesion. This is finally highly efficient (Arrojo 2005).

14.2.9 Ethical values promoting inter-regional equity in relation to socio-economic development

As previously indicated, mountain regions have been considered poor areas with scarce potential for economic development and demographic growth. From this perspective, the decision has often been made to sacrifice entire valleys, even when still inhabited, in order to exploit these regions as simple storage areas for regulating volumes of water destined to promote the development of regions and cities downstream.

Hydroelectric production has rarely been used to generate development in mountain regions themselves. The establishment of unified tariff models has prevented energy transport costs, leading to costs in remote industrial and urban zones lower than in the vicinity of turbine locations. As a result, primacy has been given to the concentration of industrial development in urban areas downstream.

With regard to agrarian development, it is evident that rugged relief offers few opportunities while the plains located in middle- and low-elevation basins have traditionally offered favorable areas for implementing large-scale irrigation works.

Lastly, the need for vast quantities of water for urban uses has turned mountainous regions into high-quality water storage areas for this urban development.

For decades, all of these demands have guided water management strategies and planning models favoring large regional imbalances. Mountain regions have ended up being sacrificed for the benefit of others in the name of the omnipresent "general interest."Currently, these management models and approaches have entered into crisis, not only for ethical reasons related to inter-regional inequity, but also because of social, environmental, and economic arguments. The very concept of sustainability of the continental aquatic ecosystems is currently under debate and still being designed, from both a scientific perspective and also a social one (social construction of the concept and its corresponding commitments). However, it seems evident that from this dynamic process, the tendency points towards diagnosing the present degradation of our rivers, lakes, wetlands, and aquifers as being unacceptable, owing to the dumping of pollutants and excessive water extractions. If we add the serious effects on the health and basic resources of many communities, and the serious effects on the human rights of entire settlements affected by large dams, we can see a clearer picture of the eco-social complexity of these problems of unsustainability.

14.3 The need for a new ethical approach

It is evident that the values at stake, related to water management, are quite diverse. Because of this, when the value of water is spoken of in generic terms, we run the risk of opening an obscure and confusing debate in which, assuredly, fertile ground for demagoguery will be created. Although water is a well-defined chemical compound, H_2O, what is important is to distinguish its diverse roles, clarifying the values that come into play and the diverse ethical categories to which such values give rise (Arrojo 2005).

14.3.1 Functions, values and rights involved

If we think about other natural renewable resources, such as wood, we do not encounter as many problems. Beyond clarifying under what circumstances we should extract it from nature so as not to destroy the health of the forest, the management of the lumber obtained does not cause controversy. Once we have determined the restrictions imposed by the need to manage a forest in a sustainable way, it seems reasonable to manage the lumber extracted in accordance with the exigencies of the market. The key to this relative simplicity lies in that the value of the wood is consistently exchangeable for money, whether it is used to build ships, manufacture chairs, tables or closets.

However, in the case of water, the roles and values involved are more complex and affect ethical categories at a different level. The European Declaration for a New Water Culture, signed in Madrid by 100 scientists from different European Union countries at the beginning of 2005, proposes the establishment of four ethical categories (FNCA 2005):

Water-life: water for life, related to basic survival functions of both human beings and animals in their natural habitat, which should be recognized and prioritized in such a way that ecosystem sustainability is guaranteed, with universal access to adequate amounts of quality water constituting a right.

Water-citizenry: water for the common good, as an instrument for safeguarding health and social cohesion, related, for example, to water supply and sanitation services in connection with the social rights of citizens.

Water-business: water for economic growth, for legitimate economic activities, connected to productive work, in connection with the right of every individual to improve his or her standard of living. This water use must be granted at a third level of priority, given that it would be unethical to allow such uses to interfere with water rights and uses pertaining to previous categories.

Water-crime: water for illegitimate business activity with consequent destructive withdrawal practices, toxic spills and other socially unacceptable practices; such uses should be avoided and prosecuted to the full extent of the law.

If we reflect on the diverse set of values and rights at stake, which stem from each of these categories, we will understand that they correspond to different spheres from an ethical point of view.

14.3.2 Deficiencies and errors associated with the current neoliberal approach

In our opinion, Herman E. Daly is right when he argues:

Some claim that human-created capital and natural-resource capital can be exchanged, and that, consequently, the idea of a limiting factor (for production) is not applicable. Nevertheless, I think it is quite obvious that human-produced capital and natural capital are essentially complementary and only marginally exchangeable.

Using less technical language, the Spanish saying that "only fools confuse value and price" encapsulates the same judgement using different words. In summary, unlike wood, water engenders uses and values that are not manageable by way of simple economic exchange relations because these uses and values cannot be consistently replaced by capital goods. In this sense, it is essential to differentiate these uses and to distinguish the diverse ethical categories with respect to value and right that are connected to them, in order to set priorities and establish suitable management criteria.

Nevertheless, based on the neoliberal principles that substantiate the reigning model of globalization, different water uses tend to be seen as economic utilities that can be replaced by capital goods and, therefore, expressed in monetary values to be managed within the context of market dynamics. Despite the fact that this is the reasoning applied in general by the World Bank (BM) and the World Trade Organization (OMC), their water policies are, in fact, filled with serious contradictions. On the one hand, in the name of economic rationality, developing countries are subjected to intense pressure to privatize their water supply and sanitation services, thus giving rise to serious social and political conflicts. On the other hand, the World Bank maintains the basic components and scripts associated with its old supply-side strategies in the area of general water management (related to agriculture, industry, and energy). Without a doubt, vested interests behind hydraulic mega projects around the world are still very influential, both at the level of large multinational construction and hydroelectric companies, and at the level of domestic political and business networks. For this reason, the World Bank itself, despite the contradictions entailed, is still willing to finance supply-side strategies, based on the subsidized promotion of large-scale hydraulic projects, thus flying in the face of economic rationality and burdening the public debt of impoverished countries.

14.3.3 The need for a new water culture, based on new ethical principles

The surmounting of the "domination of nature" paradigm by way of the "sustainability" paradigm will require profound cultural changes. It requires that we accept the challenge of managing the biosphere, based on ethical principles of equity for the sake of posterity. This means recovering the holistic perspective embodied in the Aristotelian concept of "economy," and going beyond the narrow mercantile approaches that dominate the reigning model of globalization.

But, above all, it means recognizing the diversity of values and different ethical levels that come into play. Within the range of values identified, those such as the right of a community to its traditional living areas, or society's right to conserve the ecological integrity of its aquatic ecosystems that are connected to fundamental ethical principles, should be given priority. In fact, the third generation of human rights currently being debated includes communities' rights to peace and healthy ecosystems. In its final report, the WCD acknowledged that many of the community evictions carried out to construct large dams have amounted to transgressions of human rights, with special consequences on communities living in mountain regions.

Beyond respecting these basic ethical principles, another goal is to recover emotional values connected to the landscape, the territory, and the identity of communities; and to recover environmental services, along with values related to enjoyment and quality of life which are offered to us by rivers, lakes and wetlands when they are in an good ecological state.

14.4 Conclusions and policy implications

The most advanced water laws, such as the EU Water Framework Directive, incorporate the challenge of implementing new models of ecosystem management, thus advancing beyond traditional approaches to water management in which water is seen as simply a resource. Going back to the comparison with wood, in the same way that we have progressed from the simple exploitation of forests to new policies of sustainable forest management, we can extend this sustainable management approach to rivers, lakes, and wetlands as live ecosystems. The restoration and conservation of the ecological health of our river courses becomes a paramount objective. This involves the imposition of severe restrictions on traditional hydraulic policies, especially upstream with regard to the conservation of fluvial biodiversity and the maintenance of consistent river flow cycles.

In addition, an ethical commitment to respecting mountain peoples' right to live in their valleys correlates strongly with notions of democratic governance. This commitment is buttressed by our moral obligation to redress a long history of injustices and imbalances that mountain regions have suffered as a result of our historical hydraulic policies.

Beyond the restrictions imposed by the need to respect the aforementioned ethical principles, the old supply-side strategies associated with enormous public subsidies are now tending to give way to demand management strategies in keeping with the New Water Culture. Under these new approaches based on economic rationality principles (as "full cost recovery") the construction of large-scale hydraulic infrastructures is very often non-viable. In fact, the majority of new projects demonstrate viability only when they count on enormous public subsidies, because a cost benefit analysis always produces a negative balance sheet.

The aforementioned arguments in favor of sustainability, economic rationality and democratic governance tend to close a loop and open another one, based on new objectives and strategies. Mountain regions have come to be perceived as natural areas of great value in which conservation policy plays a growing economic role in the form of a developing tertiary sector. Fluvial headwaters' regions have been acknowledged as highly valuable parts of our natural heritage with the result that specific laws such as the American Wild and Scenic River Act now protect them. Even from a strictly economic point of view, rivers whose headwater basins are well conserved become much more valuable as rivers than as water, in the same way that a tourist beach is more valuable as a beach than as a sand quarry for construction.

The value of water quality in headwater basins is increasing the value of springs as strategic resources for drinking water. Private appropriation of these sources needs to be carefully evaluated.

Adopting a perspective based on new management models, the availability of scarce water resources for economic uses should be seen as an unavoidable property to be managed rather than as a tragedy to be avoided by way of public subsidies and ecosystem degradation. In the water-business category, criteria with regard to economic rationality should be imposed, based on the principle of full cost recovery. The opportunity cost (when the resource is scarce), together with financial and environmental costs, should be included among the costs to be borne by the user.

References

Abramovitz, J. N. (1998) *Aguas amenazadas, futuro empobrecido: el declive de los ecosistemas de agua dulce.* Cuadernos Worldwatch. Bakeaz (Edt.). Bilbao.

Adams, W.M. (1992) *Wasting the rain: rivers, people and planning in Africa.* London: Earthscan.

Arrojo, P. (1998) Perspectivas socioeconómicas del uso del agua en el regadío en España. *Tecnología del Agua,* n° 179, pp. 66–78.

Arrojo, P. (2003) Spanish National Hydrological Plan: reasons for its failure and arguments for the future. *Water International,* Volume 28. No.3. Official Journal of the International Water Resources Association (IWRA), pp. 295–303.

Arrojo, P. (2004) Un nuevo enfoque de racionalidad económica en la gestión de aguas. In Arrojo, P. and Aguilera, F. (coords.) *El agua en España: propuestas de futuro.* Madrid:. Fund. Alternativas (edt), pp. 155–80.

Arrojo, P. (2005) *El reto ético de la nueva cultura del agua: funciones, valores y derechos en juego.* Barcelona: Edt. Paidós. Barcelona.

Arrojo, P. and Fernández, J. (2000) *Biscarrués-Mallos de Riglos: inundación o modernización.* Zaragoza: Egido Editorial. Saragossa, Spain.

Arrojo, P. and Naredo, J. M. (1997) La gestión del agua en España y California. Bilbao. Bakeaz, number 3 of the *Nueva Cultura del Agua,* collection.

Díaz Marta, M. (1993). *Antecedentes de la planificación hidrológica en España y propuestas actuales.* 'Revista de Obras Públicas' May 1993, pp. 29–38.

FNCA (2005) *European Declaration for a new water culture.* Zaragoza, Spain: Fundación Nueva Cultura del Agua. Saragossa, Spain.

Hubbel, D. (1994) Thailand's Pak Mun Dam: a case study. *World Rivers Review,* 4th trimester, 1994.

ICLARM (1995) *From hunting to farming fish.* Consultative Group on International Agricultural Research (CGIAR). Washington D.C.: World Bank.

Llamas, R. and Martínez-Santos, P. (2005) Intensive groundwater use: silent revolution and potential source of conflicts, editorial in *Journal on Water Resources Planning and Management*, American Society of Civil Engineers, September–October, 337–441.

McCully, P. (2004) *Silenced rivers: the ecology and politics of large dams.* Proteger Ediciones – Argentina.

Moreth, M. (1995) *Environmental concerns facing Cambodia.* paper presented in the seminar: Mekong: *International Seminar for Sustainable Development through Cooperation;* held in Washington DC, Nov–Dec 1995.

Pinilla V. (1997). *Evolución histórica del regadío en Aragón en el siglo XX.* Working Paper in the Department of Applied Economy. University of Saragossa.

Postel, S. (1996) *Reparto del agua: seguridad alimentaria, salud de los ecosistemas y nueva política de la escasez.* Bakeaz (Edt); Bilbao: Cuadernos Worldwatch.

Reisner M. (1993) *Cadillac desert: the American West and its disappearing water.* (Penguin Books – editado por Penguin Group).

WCD (2000) *Dams and development a new framework for decision making: the report of the World Commission on Dams.* London: Earthscan Publications Ltd.

Conclusion

15 Overcoming the constraints for a more integrated and adaptive water management

A new agenda for upland waters

Alberto Garrido and Ariel Dinar

The management of upland waters has profound implications for entire watershed areas in high and low latitudes, in wet as well as arid climates, in developed and developing countries. About half of the world's population depends on rivers originating in alpine and mountainous regions. The impacts of global climate change in upland regions are complex and subject to large uncertainties. This chapter summarizes the most salient conclusions of the volume's contributions. Among these stand the opportunities for using models to inform policies, identify interdependencies of hitherto unrelated phenomena and generate easily interpretable images, maps, and experimental data of alternative scenarios. The role of transdisciplinary work, and the possibilities of upscaling and downscaling the analysis of local and global phenomena enable better and science-based governance within and across jurisdictions. Finally, a new research agenda is identified in light of the volume's main findings, that includes developing conceptual and practical notions of integrative and adaptive management to accommodate projected global change effects; promoting institutional frameworks that enable proactive management and equity along upland and lowland tracts, across countries sharing watersheds and generations.

15.1 Introduction

In 1989, Ives and Messerli published a book that was meant to disprove the hypothesis that Nepali peasants should be held responsible for floods in heavily populated plains of the Ganges, Brahmaputra, Indus, and other major rivers (Ives and Messerli 1989). In a major effort to attack the Theory of Himalayan Environmental Degradation, Ives and Messerli criticised the validity of data, theoretical models and applications of numerous studies that in their view did not prove the alleged connection with mountain people and flood plains disasters. Theirs was an effort that illustrates the relevance of the studies compiled in this volume, and attests to the progress made in understanding the ongoing processes in many world rivers. While Ives and Messerli "[tried] to separate out the several linkages between its components and [subjected] them to critical examination" (p. xvii), most of this book's chapters take advantage of the opportunities that more comprehensive and encompassing approaches now permit.

The world's most valuable water resources originate in mountainous areas. However, the most valuable water uses are in the flood plains, deltas, and transition zones in the coastal areas. With very few exceptions, human life and economic development in mountain regions lag behind those of the lowlands (Messerli *et al.*, Chapter 2; Arrojo-Agudo, Chapter 14). For centuries, rivers have been channeled, harnessed, and controlled in order to tame their capricious forces, enclose their territory, and ensure a stable supply to consumers and businesses. Colosal human works have been erected for these purposes, creating massive sources of energy, providing protection to settlements and people, generating continous access to water resources, and becoming the sink for the wastewater of billions of people. The livelihood of the human race is dependent on the entire water cycle, but the river component is perhaps the most critical one because of its permanent presence in the land and its connection to human life.

Because most rivers originate in mountain areas, the processes and phenomena occuring there have dramatic consequences for the lower reaches and the rivers' dynamics. Small climatic variations in upland regions change the entire flow patterns of river systems. Industrial, urban, or agricultural pollution deteriorates ecological quality for water courses for hundreds or thousands of kilometers before reaching deltaic zones. Because well-known mountain systems, like the Alps or the Rocky Mountains, give birth to widely known rivers like the Rhône, or the Columbia, we tend to disregard the importance of less-known upland regions that are equally critical to most world rivers. In many arid and semi-arid environments, more than 90 percent of the rivers' total discharge originates in mountain areas.

This volume seeks to enhance this common theme, describing the general context (Messerli *et al.*, Chapter 2) and highlighting specific case studies that focus on the Rocky Mountains (Sauchyn *et al.*, Chapter 3), the Rhône (Bravard, Chapter 5; Pahl-Wostl *et al.*, Chapter 6), the Jordan (Ayadi, Chapter 9; Hoff, Chapter 10) and Lake Kinneret (Rimmer, Chapter 4), the upland areas in Spain (Arrojo-Agudo, Chapter 14) and Tunisia (Benabdallah, Chapter 8). Some of the underlying processes, like climate change and drought risks are analyzed from the perspective of Mexico, and the Western United States (Adams and Peck, Chapter 7), or the connection between green and blue waters in the Jordan, and the Tana in Kenya (Hoff, Chapter 10).

The chapters that comprise this volume have provided different views on some of the most critical factors affecting upland water management. Using different lenses and standpoints helps us understand the multifaceted policy dimensions that should be included in the core of our decision-making process. Partial approaches will most likely fail, because we now have the means to establish causal connections between distant variables both in time and space. The effects of an upland hydropower reservoir can be connected to the recession of deltaic zones and the disturbance of fisheries in the transition zones (the case of the Ebro in Spain, Arrojo-Agudo, Chapter 14). Modeling developments, intense data collection systems, and continous monitoring enable us to refocus our policies and to look at the big picture of entire river systems, without losing sight of the microscopic changes occuring in specific sites. Upscaling and lowscaling calibration methods permit multiple views of rivers that can be used to predict the effects of climate change on the river runoff, the temperature of a single lake, and the disappearance of a fish species (Bravard 2008, Chapter 5).

This volume teaches us about the interdependencies of some of these ongoing processes and reflects on alternative management approaches that encompass future sustainability. It contains theoretical as well as quite practical lessons that should influence the actions of researchers and decision makers. The main messages that can be drawn from the volume are elaborated in the following sections.

15.2 Key elements

15.2.1 The contexts are becoming increasingly more complex

Some of the chapters in this volume provide the background for these complexities. First, Messerli *et al.* (Chapter 2), setting the stage for subsequent chapters, show that large uncertainties still blur the connection between climate change and upland river dynamics. If 40 percent of the planet's people depend on water supplies originating from snowpack and glaciers' discharge, what kind of projections can we make to plan ahead to face future challenges of global warming? As some of the volume's chapters show, we are still surrounded by numerous uncertainties in well-studied watersheds and in almost total ignorance about most others. Second, Rimmer in Chapter 4, Ayadi in Chapter 9, Bravard in Chapter 5, and Sauchyn *et al.* in Chapter 3, respectively, show that the Jordan-Kinneret, the Rhône and some of the Canadian Rockies' rivers are experiencing irreversible changes. In the cases of the Rhône and the Rhine, two watersheds analyzed for decades, uncertainties compound because 30 to 50 percent of their total discharge originates in Alpine reaches (Messerli *et al.*, Chapter 2), where climatic models are more difficult to calibrate. Consider now the predictions that can be made for watersheds in the Andes, the Himalayas, and major mountain ranges of the world. Hoff (Chapter 10) reviews literature that predicts the following outcome for major Indo-Gangetic plains: a 30 to 40 percent increase of runoff in the Ganges resulting from glaciers' recession up to 2040, followed by a reduction of 50 percent of runoff beginning in four decades. Third, in arid and semi-arid regions, quantitative and qualitative parameters are closely related by non-linear relationships (Rimmer, Chapter 4). In the case of the Jordan and the Dead Sea, the Jordan Valley Authority must meet the needs of a very unpredictable flow of inmigrants, multiplying the already stressful conditions of the Jordan (Ayadi, Chapter 9). Fourth, new findings have been made on the connection between land uses and vegetation cover in the upland regions and the discharge to lower regions (Hoff, Chapter 10). Thus, water management must consider the combined effects of land use, uptake, flow controls, and precipitation regimes. Tunisia is one of the best examples of arid countries in which water policies and land-use policies have been more closely integrated (Benabdallah, Chapter 8; Iglesias and Moneo 2005).

Lastly, the context clearly trascends the evolution of man-made impacts and pressures and the underlying natural processes. It also involves political processes and governance structures. In identifying the reasons for success of the United

States-Canada International Joint Commission, created by the Boundary Waters Treaty, Schornack and Nevin (Chapter 12) mention the *contextual* reasons and those of procedure and control. Contextual reasons include conditions for equality in the Treaty; and the importance of water, and other socioeconomic factors common to both countries. Looking from West to East, the Canada-United States border can't be considered a simple context to solve water problems.

15.2.2 Modeling approaches are necessary in finding answers and designing tools for the management of upland waters

Sauchyn *et al.* (Chapter 3), Adams and Peck (Chapter 7), and Rimmer (Chapter 4) provide us with examples showing how models can inform policy decisions. There is nothing new in seeking science-based decision making. Models provide answers to policy questions and, in turn, feed modelers' minds with new questions. Hoff (Chapter 10) shows that green-blue waters should in some cases be jointly managed, a conclusion that surely has a lot of support from modeling efforts. By connecting green and blue waters, a need arises to connect hitherto unrelated policy areas: rain-fed agriculture and land use in the uplands, and water management in the lowlands. Very recently, the scientific community began to evaluate the consequences of afforestation in upland regions on downstream discharge (Hoff, Chapter 10). With the help of models, policies can be designed in such a way that more efficient and equitable outcomes arise from associating previously disjointed management areas.

Models also are becoming communication devices, displaying the outcomes in detailed cartographic representations (Pahl-Wostl *et al.*, Chapter 6). We are now beginning to see the potential benefits of intercallibrated systems of conflicting transboundary rivers. In the future, many discussions among countries sharing watersheds will be framed and convened around complex maps detailing flooding areas, drought indices, flow peaks, or any other contentious parameter.

15.2.3 Transdisciplinarity and upscale/downscaling issues

The fact that this book comprises contributions in which trandisciplinarity seems most convincing is attested by numerous examples. We can't sufficiently stress the policy implications of fertile collaboration across disciplines. Let's review some of the most illustrative examples contained in the volume. Hoff (Chapter 10) stresses the potential to increase runoff in the lower Jordan by changing land use in the upper reaches and capturing part of the 80 to 90 percent of rainfall that never becomes blue water. Similar implications are found in the Tana River in Kenya. Adams and Peck (Chapter 7) evaluate adaptation strategies to increasing drought risks and water scarcity using economic models that take into account water supply risks and the El Niño-Southern Oscillation (ENSO) projections.

Furthermore, in the area of global change, there always is a pressing need to delve into upscaling and downscaling processes. Entire watersheds cannot be analyzed in the absence of a global context, just as no system can be enclosed and isolated. Climate change is clearly an example, but migration, global food and energy prices, and globalization do also have profound effects and impacts on entire river systems. However, the opposite is also true: microscopic or small-scale processes occurring at specific sites or river stretches provide clues for major phenomena. Benabdallah (Chapter 8), Bravard (Chapter 5) and Rimmer (Chapter 4) make a few key points in their chapters on upscaling and downscaling effects.

15.2.4 Pro-adaptation versus pro-certainty approaches

In his encompassing review of the Rhône, Bravard (Chapter 5) does not find explanations for some of the most visible changes occuring in this Alpine and Mediterranean river. Evidence is clear about the changes and the direction of changes: the Rhône is becoming warmer, glaciers are shrinking and wildlife is changing. However, causal connections about some of these processes have not been established. Sauchyn *et al.* (Chapter 3) show compelling evidence that global warming may affect the flows of the Canadian Rockies' rivers, suggesting the need to adapt their management criteria.

Pahl-Wostl *et al.* (Chapter 6) argue that adaptation to uncertain outcomes is sometimes more efficient than attempting to diminish the effects of uncertainty. They look at the hydromorphological transformations of the Rhône during the twentieth century, focusing mostly on the part that flows in Switzerland, and conclude that the river should be given more space. For countries in which land is so valuable, this entails great obstacles, as it requires consensus among numerous jurisdictions, stakeholders and managers. Pahl-Wostl *et al.* (Chapter 6) take on the task of framing the learning and negotiation processes in a very detailed and thoughtful way.

The pro-adaptation approach has a major shortcoming that Pahl-Wostl *et al.* (Chapter 6) bring to the forefront – people have cognitive difficulties in imagining what living in an uncertain world means. In this case, models can offer a visual representation of an area such as the Rhône, and can include maps, graphs, and images that convey meaningful information about future uncertainties and what can be done to adapt. A science-based modeling approach that feeds more simplified descriptions of various scenario simulations is, we are taught by Pahl-Wost *et al.* (Chapter 6), one powerful means to guide the discussions among adversarial views. Perhaps it is the only way to ensure that non-experts can partipate in the decision-making processes, without losing focus and relevancy due to cognitive problems.

In an entirely different context, Blaney (Chapter 13), and Schornack and Nevin (Chapter 12) teach us how institutions succeed in adapting and using science-based arguments. The International Joint Commission of Canada and the United States (created by the Boundary Waters Treaty) is one example of institutional adaptation that has very few parallels in the world. In 97 years of history, 100 decisions (with only two exceptions) were approved unanimously by the 3+3 members of the Commission. Both exceptions concerned the arid west with the commissioners siding along nationalities.

15.2.5 *The role of mountain dwellers and businesses*

Arrojo-Agudo (Chapter 14) offers a narrative of the rationale behind the large mountain water schemes, showing the similarities between Spanish and Western U.S. water policies in the early twentieth century. The dichotomy between mountain and flood plains has always been tilted towards the city dwellers in the low lands. Harsh living conditions in upland regions have never given rise to thriving economies. On the contrary, per-capita incomes and household revenues are lower in upland regions than in lowland regions, both in developed and developing countries. As Messerli *et al.* (Chapter 2) argue, mountain regions have been seen through the lens of the lowland dwellers. Instead of seeking a better appreciation of mountain culture, mountain people have been seen as the people living in the headwater areas and in a frontier of inhospitable conditions. In the new post-structuralist paradigm, Arrojo-Agudo (Chapter 14) contend that mountain areas, sceneries, pristine waters, environment, and culture are to be seen as a wholesome entity – one of whose parts cannot be evaluated by standard cost-benefit analyses in the absence of the others. While in the past this was the usual strategy, the World Commission on Dams turned on the red light by demanding that projects should be reviewed along much broader criteria (The World Commission on Dams 2006).

In addition to the multifaceted mountain environment that only recently we are learning to appreciate in its fullest sense, there is also a business economy that depends on upland waters and resources. Mining industries, hydropower schemes, gas extraction schemes, and ski resorts thrive in mountain areas. Even for regions and catchments in which water has been perceived as limitless, like in the Canadian Rockies and the the Rhône, signs are now plentiful to think otherwise. Lowry's chapter reveals the fact that water resources in Western Canada are becoming increasingly scarce. He demands that users pay the full cost of water services and be taught about the necessity to restrain their consumption in response to growing scarcity signs. Also, as conflicts related to water pollution and scarcity become more frequent, there is a further need to invest more heavily in technology and water systems. This task can be undertaken by the private sector, if political agreements are reached at community and regional levels that enable a stable and transparent regulatory framework.

Lowry's view of pure public and private water operators is not very positive. His experience as a businessman and his analysis, based on casual observations across Canada, provide him rationale to argue for the formation of true partnerships between public agencies and private companies. One would surmise that Lowry's emphasis on the idea of partnerships is justified by the increasing antagonism between the civil society and the private business about the management and use of natural resources. This is a controversy that, far from being exclusive to Canada, is not bound to an easy settlement, unless common interests are identified for a wide and overarching coalition of the public and private worlds.

At first glance, it is easy to perceive some opposition between the views of Arrojo-Agudo (Chapter 14), and Lowry (Chapter 11). And yet, contentious as they may seem, other chapters of the book, especially those of Bravard (Chapter 5), and Pahl-Wost *et al.* (Chapter 6), help us identify a common ground. The rationale would go as follows: (1) mountain water resources will be subject to more uncertainty and climate sensitivity; (2) traditional hydrological modeling supporting hydropower schemes, river dams, and channeling gave rationale to projects that had at best dubious socioeconomic benefits, but were often endorsed by the public agencies; (3) uncertainties of river dynamics, pollution processes, and environmental disruption has put the "engineers-solve-everything" way of thinking under severe scrunity; (4) new toolboxes and thinking, while finding it difficult to penetrate the crust of well-established layers of scientific paradigms, provide more fertile and adaptative means for facing uncertainty instead of reducing it; and (5) the private sector should be ready to team up with public agencies to ensure a better adaptation to global change, enabling the former to focus on creating wealth and jobs by offering water services to society in public-private partnerships.

15.3 What lies ahead in the future?

The chapters of this volume look at widely divergent contexts and problems. A global view offered by Messerli *et al.* (Chapter 2) sets the stage for reviewing issues in North America, Europe, Africa, and the Middle East. While the problems reviewed are different in scope, context, and sensitivity to global change, there are a number of common themes cross-cutting through all of them. In a way, they synthesize what this volume is about and the lessons that can be drawn from it.

15.3.1 Interdependencies

In the past, dissociating the components of a whole system was a prerequisite to improving the scienfitic understanding of the phenomena of large time and space scopes. Upland regions were characterized by climatologists, geologists, hydrologists, and even anthropologists. Even in the narrower field of hydrology, the usual practice of dissociating surface flows from groundwater was forced by the lack of encompassing models that permitted a unitary treatment of both. In the last decade, however, models can now characterize the connections between the climate, the soils, the vegetation cover, and the water flows of an entire river system with striking precision. The whole system can now be represented and viewed at various scales, from the pixel in geographic information (GIS) systems to the entire basin, including the transitional waters in deltaic regions. The benefits of these encompassing modeling efforts are cumulative and can be applied to basins in developed countries. Using technology similar to that of cellular phones in the communication realm they also can be applied in the developing world. Hoff (Chapter 10) provides examples of Green Water Credits and Payments for Environmental Services as applied in upstate New York, South Africa, and the Tana in Kenya, which have equivalent problems, the same modeling and scientific bases, and the same policy solutions.

Perhaps its most significant implication for analysts, agencies, and practitioners is that interdependencies can now be understood and, as such, they should form the center of our thinking. This represents a real challenge for those who wish to move their specific knowledge frontiers or are moved by the sense of duty towards their community or constituency, as nobody can claim to have an encompassing knowledge of how interdependencies actually work in a specific context. Teamwork, opened minds, and critical thinking are required to live up to the expectations raised by our systems' encompassing models.

Another consequence of knowing more about the interdependencies embedded in complex systems is that countries must cooperate more closely with each other to ensure more equitable, sustainable, and efficient management of their shared rivers and water bodies. It is telling, in this sense, to observe the common practice of the IJC to appoint United States-Canada binational teams to address issues related to their shared rivers. Scientific knowledge is the main prerequisite for understanding a common problem and providing the basis for a negotiated agreement. However, as we learn more about interdependencies across national boundaries, we will start seeing green and blue water connections that perhaps form the basis of the claim of one country to another. Another example may be the effect of temperature increases caused by cooling plants, or the effect of escaped salmon from fish farms upstream. Recall that the motivation of Ives and Messerli (1989) was to clarify the alleged connection between the upland peoples in the Himalayas and the floods in Bangladesh.

15.3.2 Adaptive and integrated management

Following Pahl-Wostl *et al.* (Chapter 6), adaptative management is a way to cope with uncertainties as much as it is a learning process. In upland waters, uncertainties stem from numerous non-linear causal relationships with an origin of climatic processes. To a greater or lesser extent, all world watersheds have inspired long-term plans and projections, providing rationale to the construction of dams, chanelling corridors and points of abstraction and devolution. The benefits of planning and major works are uncertain. However, as we move on to future planning stages, as we amass growing evidence of climate change effects, and as we have more powerful tools to analyze entire watersheds' whole and their parts, we have a better understanding of our knowledge gaps and of the impossibility of having everything under control.

Adaptive management requires building very difficult consensus across jurisdictions, boundaries, disciplines, and all societal components. Opening the minds and going beyond each toolbox's scope are essential requirements. How do we react when we learn that temperature changes in, say Lake Kinneret in the Jordan or Lake Geneva in the Rhône, have a profound impact on the chemical and biological parameters of downstream waters? Cooling waters artificially is certainly beyond the imaginable, so adaptation to warmer waters may entail changes in other areas of management. Warmer water is becoming a serious hazard in many rivers around the world, including the Rhône (Bravard, Chapter 5), and in the western United States, western Canada, and Alaska (Adams and Peck, Chapter 7). In some cases, water temperature cannot be lowered to the minimum required to ensure adequate fisheries habitats, under any management regime.

Another area of recent concern relates to the geomorphological characteristics of highly regulated and channelized rivers. This issue is highlighted by Pahl-Wostl *et al.* (Chapter 6), in the Rhône, and by Adams and Peck (Chapter 7) in western Oregon rivers. Riparian restoration, river bed augmentation and flows enhancement may be cost-effective means to improve some of the most critical parameters. But this is proving extremely difficult to achieve in the Rhône because of the rigidities imposed by plant cooling needs and the existence of construction elements along the river banks.

Consider two further issues raised in this volume. How do semi-arid countries like Mexico or Spain adapt to the most severe climate change effects on their hydrological systems? For one thing, water demand in agriculture will grow because plants' evapotranspiration also will increase (between 10 to 15 percent, as projected in Spain). The complexity of the problem grows because both wildlife and rain-fed crops will absorb more soil moisture, reducing deep infiltration and run-off. The green and blue water connection described by Hoff (Chapter 10), will likely become a contentious issue for regions and jurisdictions. Eventually, the connection between land and water uses will impose new issues hitherto managed by non-overlapping agencies.

Another underlying theme in this volume is the effect of climate change on upland regions. Irrigators in Oregon can adapt better to more frequent but moderate droughts than to less frequent but intense drought (Adams and Peck, Chapter 7). The same authors show how farmers in southwestern Mexico can change their crop mixes in anticipation of ENSO, using risk-management models. Reduction of economic losses caused by El Niño can be achieved if forecast accuracy goes above 70 percent. Sauchyn *et al.* (Chapter 3) conclude their study of the effects of climate change in the runoff of western Canada rivers by stressing the needs to adapt the management criteria of reservoirs and uses. The kind of alteration of the drought regimes in all world watersheds resulting from global warming represents a major challenge, no matter how arid or water-abundant the prevailing conditions may be.

15.3.3 Governance and policy

No matter how dire the projections are, no adaptive management can succeed without good governance and policy. This is attested by the chapter by Ayadi (Chapter 9) about the Jordan Valley. No engineering dream, however sophisticated and detailed, can provide benefits in the absence of a governance model. This includes sound economics, law enforcement, demand management, water rights and tariffs, and quite a lot of outreach and education.

Good governance is in part dependent on generating scientific knowledge that is presented in ways that most people can understand. We cannot sufficiently stress the importance of communicating the consequences of alternative courses of actions in a concise and understandable fashion (Pahl-Wostl *et al.*, Chapter 6). This is a prerequisite for a successful negotiation among competing parties defending mutually exclusive positions on a given issue.

However, there is something missing in the chapter by Pahl-Wostl *et al.*, and that is leadership. Several book chapters tangentially touch on this issue. Schornack, Nevin, and Blaney, claim (modestly perhaps, being IJC commissioners themselves) some kind of leadership in framing tough transboundary problems between the United States and Canada, and enabling a solution. Consider for the moment what would have happened if the IJC had not reached unanimous agreements in the applications and references filed for consultation since 1911. All kinds of conjectures about commissioners breaking ranks from fellow commissioners might have surely ensued and, as a consequence, the IJC's credibility might have vanished. Leadership is important in appointing binational scientific teams to generate scientific knowledge about complex issues. Another crucial aspect of the IJC's potential for better governance of the shared watersheds between the United States and Canada is the fact that the non-binding recommendations issued by the IJC are made public at the same time they are submitted to the two governments. Consider for a minute the outstanding moral authority and credibility of 98 out of 100 decisions taken unanimously, made public, and officially communicated simultaneously, since 1911, on identified boundary problems. How could this be achieved without the basis of respectable, balanced, and rigorous binational scientific teams appointed by IJC's leadership?

Ayadi (Chapter 9) makes a compelling case for dealing with water scarcity problems in one of the most stressed watersheds in the world, the Jordan. If what he writes about the Jordan Valley Authority is implemented, we may see in the future a great vision turned into actions and strategies pointing in the right direction. Without leadership, most likely Ayadi's visionary account will become wet paper. Finally, leadership is also sketched indirectly by Messerli *et al.* (Chapter 2) by no other means than conveying the importance of mountains as water towers, the most valuable factories of fresh, pure, and completely recycled water resources.

15.4 Final remarks

This volume has probably raised more questions than it has provided answers. There is no need to convince anyone to think seriously about integrated and adaptive management when dealing with complex water problems. A revolution, for many years silent and of low profile, is now becoming vociferous in the political arena. Science-based decision making is now on top of the agenda, an unavoidable means to suppress emotional discussion and the source of narratives that flow from academia and make it to the popular media. This book provides numerous examples of processes occurring on regional, national, and global scales that illustrate what Beck (2006) identifies as one of the three key interdependencies that define the new cosmopolitism – namely, environmental interdependencies. The new world "risk society" of Beck, fully aware of the massive scale of the global environmental risks, has penetrated the political realm, both at national and global levels. We surmise from the chapters of this volume that a similar process is occurring in virtually all world regions and watersheds, including the Rhône and the western Canadian rivers, which were thought inmune to global change until very recently.

At the risk of oversimplifying, we would include the following for the research agenda in the upcoming decade:

- Developing new conceptual and practical principles for integrated management of upland waters;
- Developing more accurate models that include physical, chemical, and biological models to analyze the effects of global warming for entire watersheds;
- Evaluating resilience of ecological systems;
- Developing practical notions of pro-active governance of upland-lowland-floodplain water resources;
- Determining the institutional underpinnings that can bring developing countries and regions to sustainable modes of water use and management.

References

Beck, U. (2006) *The Cosmopolitan Vision.* Polity Press: Cambridge.

Iglesias, A. and Moneo. M. (eds) (2005). Drought preparedness and mitigation: analysis of the organizations and institutions. *Options Mediterranéennes,* 51. Zaragoza. Spain.

Ives, J. D. and Messerli, B. (1989) *The Himalayan dilemma. Reconciling development and conservation.* New York: The United Nations University and Routledge.

The World Dams Commission. (2006) *Dams and development: the report of the world commission on dams – a new framework for decision-making.* Available online at http:// www.dams.org/docs/report/wcdintro.pdf Accessed 15 February 2008.

Index

References in **bold** denote figures or tables.

Printed in the United States
by Baker & Taylor Publisher Services